WALL STREET'S PICKS 2001

WALL STREET'S PICKS 2001

A LITERARY PRODUCTIONS BOOK

DEARBORN™
TRADE
A Kaplan Professional Company

Associate Publisher: Cynthia A. Zigmund
Senior Managing Editor: Jack Kiburz
Interior Design: the dotted i
Cover Design: Design Alliance, Inc.
Typesetting: the dotted i
For Literary Productions: Series Creator/Executive Editor, Kirk Kazanjian

Published by Dearborn Trade, a Kaplan Professional Company

Printed in the United States of America

01 10 9 8 7 6 5 4 3 2 1

ISBN 0-7931-4105-2

CONTENTS

PREFACE

It's not easy gaining access to Wall Street's top minds. After all, most manage multi-billion-dollar portfolios and won't even consider taking you on as a private client unless you have $1 million or more to invest. It's even harder to convince these folks to let you pick their brains for a while, maybe over lunch or dinner, to learn their investment secrets and favorite stock or fund ideas for the coming months. Fortunately, with this book, you get instant access to many of the investment world's biggest stars. They'll let you in on their investment insights and strategies for the new year on every page of *Wall Street's Picks 2001.*

This is by far one of the most timely and user-friendly investment guides on the market today. Instead of focusing on a bunch of abstract theories or listing hundreds of possible investment choices (like many other publications), *Wall Street's Picks 2001* cuts through the financial jargon to bring you specific and current recommendations from the very best minds in the business.

In Part 1 of this new edition, you will learn the number-one favorite stock ideas for the year ahead, according to such gurus as Louis Navellier, Elizabeth Bramwell, Michael Murphy, Seth Glickenhaus, Elizabeth Dater, Martin Whitman, Art Bonnel, L. Roy Papp, Joseph Battipaglia, Ronald Muhlenkamp, James Collins, and many more. These are all successful investment managers who are at the top of their profession and consistently generate outstanding returns for their clients.

In essence, each panelist was asked to name the single stock he or she would own in 2001 if only one could be chosen. The answers are revealed in the form of in-depth reports on each selection—written in the experts' own words—including background information on the company, reasons for the recommendation, financial figures and charts, and a discussion of what kind of performance to expect as the year unfolds.

Because many readers are more interested in mutual funds, we have interviewed some of the country's leading fund analysts for Part 2. Following a general discussion about how funds work and why they are such great investment vehicles, you will find promising recommendations in various categories from such renowned fund authorities as Sheldon Jacobs, Harold Evensky, Thurman Smith, Michael Stolper, Janet Brown, and Bob Markman.

As previously mentioned, the idea behind this book is to bring together an investment dream team to help you develop a first-rate portfolio. It's the kind of inside information that used to be reserved exclusively for Wall Street's heavy hitters. This collective knowledge can't be found in any other book or magazine on the market today.

Of course, no pick is guaranteed to go up, and some may fall dramatically in price, despite the panel's optimistic expectations. That's all part of the risk you take when you become part-owner of a company through purchasing stock.

As usual, Part 3 features a complete biography of each advisor, describing his or her background, investment philosophy, and market outlook, along with other bits of advice you can use to make more money in the market.

Nationally syndicated personal finance columnist Humberto Cruz has called *Wall Street's Picks* one of only three investment books available today that survives the marketing hype. Humberto noted that Part 3 is perhaps the most valuable part of the book, because the insights these living investment legends share can help make you richer for many years to come.

In addition, even though this book is written in reader-friendly language, if you're ever confused by financial verbiage that seems like gobbledygook, simply turn to the back where you'll find a glossary that provides definitions of some of the more commonly used investment terms and phrases you will encounter in the pages that follow.

By the way, if you want to know how last year's contributors feel about the prospects for their investment ideas going into 2001, their latest buy, sell, and hold ratings can be found at the end of Part 3.

For now, sit back, relax, and enjoy what will hopefully be a very prosperous journey into the world of Wall Street's best advice on how to invest your money over the next 12 months.

part 1

THE TOP STOCKS FOR 2001

STOCK PICKS—
AN INTRODUCTION

Before we discuss this year's stock selections, it makes sense to review some of the important principles that should guide all of your investment decisions. To begin with, as all smart investors know, basing portfolio decisions solely on the economy, specific news items, or the direction of the Dow is a recipe for disaster. In fact, the richest and most successful investors understand the key to great profits is finding individual companies with stories and valuations so compelling that their share prices are bound to go up, regardless of what happens in the overall economy or underlying indexes.

Those who try to time the market usually end up making the least amount of money. That's because no one has created a foolproof system for predicting where stocks are headed. Though some look back and boast about how accurate they were at calling certain tops, bottoms, and crashes, they rarely mention the number of times their advice was wrong.

Investors versus Traders

It has often been said that *investors,* those who buy quality companies and stay in the market regardless of outside influences, drive Cadillacs, while *traders,* people who jump in and out on a regular basis, ride around in Chevys. History suggests this is true. Statistics show that the majority of all market gains are made on only a handful of trading sessions each year. Therefore, if you are out on those days, you can expect nothing more than mediocre returns or even losses.

An often-cited study shows that during the 1980s, the Standard & Poor's 500 index produced an average annual return of 17.6 percent. However, if you were in cash on the top-ten trading days during that period, the figure dropped to 12.6 percent. Had you been on the sidelines for the 20 best days, you would have earned a mere 9.3 percent. And if you missed the 30 biggest advancing sessions, your return could have plummeted to just 6.5 percent, less than the amount you would have earned in a money market fund. Clearly, not being fully invested is costly because stocks tend to move in "lumps." They rise or fall, and then remain stagnant for a while, before rallying up or sliding down again. This is further proof that market timing rarely makes sense.

Sure, it would be great to avoid every correction and bear market. But that's impossible to do. Those who make the right calls often owe their success to luck more than anything else. It's a point driven home by the great investor Sir John Templeton. When asked for his market outlook a few years ago, he replied, "In the 52 years I was in the investment industry, I was never able to answer that question. I just searched for those stocks whose prices were lowest in relation to earnings." In other words, he had a strategy and stuck with it, regardless of what was happening with the market.

Take it from Sir John: The secret to investment riches is finding the right stocks to be in at any given time. After all, though the major indexes may fall or go nowhere, some individual issues always manage to skyrocket. For example, back in 1994 the S&P 500 and Nasdaq each squeezed out a mere 1 percent gain, including dividends. Yet Microtouch Systems soared 555 percent, Cooper Companies leaped 227 percent, LSI Logic rose 154 percent, and Rock Bottom Restaurants jumped a full 128 percent for the year, proving that even though the overall market may be stagnant, it's possible to make a lot of money through superior stock selection. More recently, we've seen that the huge gains in both the S&P 500 and Nasdaq were primarily due to the stellar performance of just a handful of stocks. The majority of stocks have actually suffered huge losses or simply tread water during this time.

Uncle Sam Likes Investors, Too

Another reason to avoid running in and out of stocks is that you'll save on the profits you have to share with the government. As part of the Taxpayers Relief Act of 1997, Congress decided to cap all long-term capital gains for positions held more than 12 months at a maximum rate of 20 percent. This contrasts with the 30 percent-plus rate you could be forced to pay for short-term trades.

Building Wealth with Equities

By now you've figured out that growing rich from stocks requires you to construct a stable of spectacular companies with bright future prospects. But how can you, as an individual investor far removed from the inner workings of Wall Street, find these jewels for yourself? That's what Part 1 of this book is all about.

Over the past several months, dozens of the world's top investment experts were asked, "If you could choose only one stock to hold in the year 2001, what would it be and why?" The panelists represent leading portfolio managers, investment advisors, newsletter editors, and market strategists, all of whom have a slightly different style or area of expertise, giving you a truly diversified list of potential holdings. Plus, this year, for the first time ever, each panelist was then asked for a bonus pick, a second choice stock, if you will.

All of their responses were then put together in the form of easy-to-read research reports, written in their own words. There are a total of 25 primary companies, which are listed in alphabetical order. At the end of each main profile, you will find every panelist's bonus pick. Keep in mind this isn't a beauty contest to see who can pick the best performer, nor are these stocks you should buy in January and sell in December. Instead, they are quality companies that each expert considers to have great prospects for the new year ahead.

Dissecting the Information

Each discussion starts off with a table showing the primary company's ticker symbol, trading exchange, and industry, along with such data as current price, price-earnings ratio (PE), book value, and earnings per share. Next is a profile of the company that includes specific reasons why it was selected. You'll also find Tradeline graphs showing the stock's daily price patterns for the past 12 months, total return versus the S&P 500, and performance compared with its peer index. There's even a box containing important balance sheet numbers (like current assets, liabilities, and shareholders' equity) going back two years. You should also pay attention to each stock's estimated beta factor, which is included in the statistical box at the bottom of every profile. Beta measures a stock's price volatility compared to the S&P 500, which has a beta of 1. Simply put, a stock with a beta of 0.8 is 20 percent less volatile than the market overall, while a stock with a beta of 1.3 is 30 percent riskier. Within each profile, you'll find the mailing address, phone number, and Web site address you can use to request more information from the company. In addition, at the bottom of every report, you will find the panelist's bonus pick for the year, giving you a total of 50 stock investment ideas in all.

Please understand that these reports present predominately positive comments about the various companies, although each panelist also discusses possible risks. This stands to reason, because the recommending advisors are very upbeat about these stocks and their future prospects. However, there are always negatives to every story, so make sure you evaluate the potential downfalls of each idea before investing. Remember, not every optimistic expectation by these experts will come to fruition.

When choosing equities, it usually makes sense to stick with companies that report steady annual earnings growth, a characteristic shared by most of the stocks in this book. Sizable ownership by inside management is another bullish sign. It indicates that those in the know have enough faith in the firm to put their own money on the line. You'll learn much more about many different successful stock-picking strategies by reading the biographies in Part 3. In many respects, this is one of the most important sections of the book because the insights and advice these market masters provide are invaluable.

Stock Selection

Each stock has been chosen for a different reason, from low valuation to high future earnings potential, based on the advisor's particular style. In fact, every panelist has a unique process for selecting stocks. This information is spelled out for you in every discussion and should be an important consideration as you decide which ideas make the most sense for you, given your risk tolerance and overall objectives.

You'll notice the recommendations cover the gamut in terms of market capitalizations, industry groups, and geographic locations. There are some very big blue chips, namely General Electric and Sara Lee, smaller high-tech outfits with more risk, such as Siliconix and Littelfuse; and international concerns, among them ICICI Limited and Startec Global Communications.

Asset Allocation

As you peruse these pages, keep in mind the principles of asset allocation. You need to consider whether you even belong in stocks in the first place and, if so, to what extent.

Let's first make it clear that only investment capital should be put into the market. In essence, this is money above and beyond what you need to live on. Think of it as funds you could afford to lose without dramatically altering your lifestyle. Granted, no one invests to lose. But because the stock market is inherently risky, knowing you can afford to lose your investment capital won't scare you out just when you should be jumping in.

After you've identified your investment capital, you must outline your goals. If you're saving for retirement or a similar long-term objective that's at least five to ten years away, stocks should make up a significant amount of your portfolio. They are the only investment class to consistently stay ahead of inflation while providing the highest rates of return throughout history. (We'll delve deeper into the subject of asset allocation in Parts 2 and 3.)

Once you determine what percentage to devote to stocks, you should understand that smaller and international issues generally carry more risk than those that are larger and better known. Remember this as you evaluate which companies to purchase. If you consider yourself to be conservative, you might want to stick with only blue chips. If you're more moderate, perhaps several large companies sprinkled with a few small-caps and an international issue or two make sense. The brave, those shooting for huge gains and willing to take a potential roller-coaster ride, could concentrate almost entirely on smaller names with big prospects.

How many stocks do you need in your portfolio? Ask ten different people and you'll get ten different answers. An important rule of thumb is you should never put more than 5 percent of your total assets into any single investment. Therefore, to really reduce your downside exposure, you need at least 20 different issues. Some say you need upwards of 40 companies in your portfolio for proper diversification. Then there's Warren Buffett, who is among the greatest investors ever. He only holds a handful of stocks and has racked up enormous gains by concentrating on a select group of companies he knows well.

Just make sure you don't buy too many stocks in the same sector. If you simply own 30 high-technology stocks, your diversification is virtually nil. Spread your choices over many different sectors, so when one is out of favor, you can profit from another. Fortunately, the selections in this book are highly diversified in terms of size, industry, and even geographic location.

A good technique for developing a nice mix involves constructing your portfolio around a core. In other words, you choose a handful of great, mostly blue chip, companies that you plan to hold for the long haul and build some speculative names around them.

Remember, you will have to pay a commission for each stock you buy or sell. These charges can add up quickly and eat into your profits. You can save money by using a quality discount broker. Some brokers now execute trades on the Internet for as little as $5, so be certain to shop around. You'll no doubt agree there's no use paying those high full-service brokerage fees when you're acting on your own investment advice.

Limit or Market Orders?

Another decision you will face is whether to place market or limit orders for your stock selections. When you place a market order, you agree to pay whatever the prevailing price is at the time your order is executed, which may be more or less than the amount quoted by your broker.

On the other hand, limit orders allow you to set the terms. In today's crazy markets, limit orders make a lot of sense, even though some of the low-cost Internet brokers charge a bit more (usually $5) to execute them. Here's why: All stocks trade at a spread, which is the difference between the bid price and offer price. If a stock is trading at a bid of $15 and offered at $15.50, the spread is 50¢. With a limit order, you can specify that you will buy the stock only at $15. Otherwise, it would likely clear at market, or $15.50. It could be much higher, especially for a volatile Internet stock. Be advised, however, that while limit orders can save you money, they may take longer to execute, especially for thinly traded issues.

Limit orders are also used to set much lower price targets. For example, if you like a stock today that trades at $20 but only want to get in if it drops to $16, you can place a good-till-canceled (GTC) limit order for $16, which means the trade won't clear unless the issue hits your price point of $16. This may not ever happen, so be realistic if you place such an order.

Conversely, you can set stop loss limit orders once you've purchased a stock on the New York or American Stock Exchange to cushion your potential loss. Let's say you buy a stock for $20 and want to sell if it falls more than 10 percent. You can place a stop loss order for $18, which means the stock will automatically be sold if it reaches that level. This technique should be used with caution, given that the market has never been more volatile and many stocks today tend to bounce around several points during each trading session. If you're not careful, you could be sold out of a position even though the stock closes the day at a much higher price.

When You Should Buy or Sell

Unfortunately, when writing about the stock market, whether for a book such as this or for a daily Internet site, information and valuations can change dramatically in a matter of seconds. That's why we have included each analyst's price target for 2001 when available. If a stock has already reached this target by the time you read about it, you may want to determine whether this enthusiasm is sustainable or simply move on to another pick that appears to be a better bargain. If the company has just introduced a new product or acquisition that will make a significant contribution to earnings, it may merit the higher valuation. (As mentioned earlier, it's wise to favor companies with rapidly growing earnings.) If nothing has changed, however, perhaps the price has moved ahead of itself or reached full value. On the other hand, if a stock is trading well below its target price, it may be an even more compelling buy, assuming nothing catastrophic or scandalous has happened to change the fundamentals in the interim.

The question of when to sell is more difficult. Some feel you should never get rid of a quality company. Others suggest you let go when the price appreciates or depreciates to some arbitrary level, such as 20 or 30 percent above or below cost. You'll find plenty of advice on this subject in Part 3.

Needless to say, if something happens to cloud both the company's future prospects and your reasons for buying in the first place, this too may be a good reason to get out.

Before You Begin

A few final notes: Please don't invest in any stock just because a person you admire in this book likes it. Simply use that validation as a starting point. Then call or write the company (the location, phone numbers, and addresses are provided for each stock); request an annual report and form 10-K or view it on the company's Internet site; check out available research reports at your library, on the Web, or in your broker's office; talk with an investor relations representative; visit the company online; and ultimately make a decision as to whether the recommendation makes sense for you. Just because it's right for Louis Navellier, Elizabeth Dater, Martin Whitman, or anyone else doesn't necessarily mean it belongs in your portfolio. Use these suggestions as a launching pad, but do a little legwork to confirm everything in your own mind and, for heaven's sake, make sure you understand what you're buying. If a company is engaged in some exotic technology and you have no clue what it does, stay away. Keep an eye on how your ultimate stock selections perform, and remain informed about any new positive and negative developments surrounding them.

Be sure to read quarterly and annual reports, and keep good records. This will make your life easier when it comes time to pay Uncle Sam for capital gains and dividend interest. It's also smart to periodically examine and calculate your total return figures to see how you're doing, especially compared with the S&P 500, which is the industry's standard benchmark. In essence, you should run your investment portfolio like a business. Once you make a purchase, you become a part-owner in the company and have a duty to run your affairs accordingly.

Finally, always remember: There are no guarantees. Although the following stocks truly represent the best ideas of some wonderful investors, the market never goes straight up. All equities carry a significant amount of risk. Also, be aware that the various experts may own positions in the equities they recommend, either in personal and/or managed accounts. This is not necessarily a bad thing, but it's just something you should know. With that in mind, let's begin naming names of companies that could make you rich as we enter the second year of the new millennium.

AMERICAN POWER CONVERSION

Art Bonnel

Bonnel Growth Fund

Company Background

American Power Conversion (APC) is the leading producer of uninterruptible power supply (sometimes referred to as UPS) products. The most popular products are surge protectors. These products are designed for use with any electronic device, although most are used with computers. If you have a power surge or outage, many of these products have battery backups and can keep your computer running for an extra 5 to 12 minutes.

APC sells its products in various price ranges, from $25 on the low end to close to $200,000 on the high end. They are sold mainly through computer distributors, both in the U.S. and abroad. When you buy a computer, the sales person will often recommend that you buy one of these products to protect your computer from power surges. Foreign sales accounted for around 43 percent of the total pie in the most recent period. European and Asian sales should start to surge because these countries are coming out of a recession and people need APC's products.

Reason for Recommendation

I believe APC is well positioned going into 2001. The company has benefited from efforts to control manufacturing costs. For instance, it increased capacity utilization in 1999 by transferring production to lower-cost plants in the Philippines, which allowed the company to close one plant in the U.S. APC has also introduced a new symmetric power rate product in the U.S. to enhance and broaden its marketability. This will help to widen margins. Also, during 1999, in preparation for Y2K, companies spent about $1 billion fixing all of the problems that might happen to their computers in 2000. But many held back on making additional computer purchases to see what would actually happen. I think these same folks will start buying new computers over the coming year, and they'll likely want some APC products to go with these purchases.

Biggest Risks

There are other competitors in this area, but they're so small, I can't even remember their names. APC has 80 to 90 percent of the market. The biggest risk with the stock is that if there is a slowdown in the economy, or the market takes a big dive, consumers will pull in their horns and not buy as many computers. APC protectors are like insurance that you purchase for your computer. When you spend less money, you skimp on things like insurance.

Bottom Line

The stock trades for a fair PE multiple. I think it can move up to at least $60 per share in the next year, especially because earnings are clicking along at around 40 percent a quarter.

Contact Information: American Power Conversion
132 Fairgrounds Road
West Kingston, RI 02892
401-789-5735
<www.apcc.com>

BONUS PICK FOR 2001

BANK OF AMERICA

Symbol: BAC
Exchange: NYSE

Bank of America was formed by the merger of NationsBank with BankAmerica in late 1998. It is now the second-largest bank holding company with offices in 22 states and Washington, D.C. Bank of America has a well-diversified loan portfolio and a very low foreclosure rate. It's a very large company, with 155,000 full-time employees. But the main reason I like it right now is that once the Federal Reserve starts lowering rates again, which I believe it will, this stock has the potential to really move up. While you wait, you'll earn a small dividend and rest assured knowing you own a solid company in a sector that I expect to do well in the years to come.

American Pwr Conversion Corp

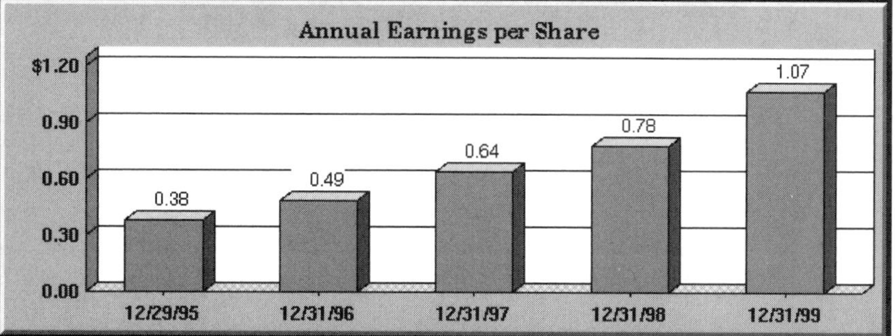

American Pwr Conversion Corp

Symbol: APCC Market/Exchange: Nasdaq NMS

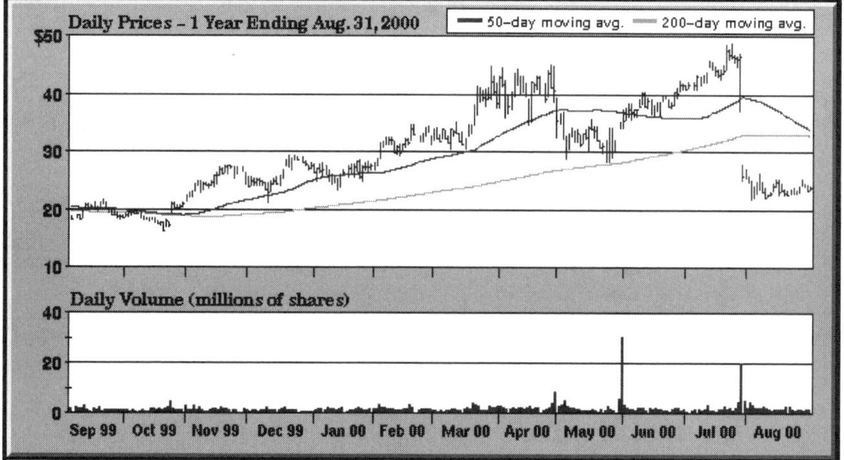

Latest Pricing Data (as of Aug. 31, 2000)		
Close (net change):	$23 13/16	(+7/16)
Day High & Low:	$24 1/8	$23 3/8
Volume & Avg. Volume:	1,792,000	1,927,106
52-Week High:	$48 27/32	July 24, 2000
52-Week Low:	$16	Oct. 19, 1999
Latest Dividend:	$0.00	
Ind. Ann. Div. & Yield:	$0.00	N.A.
12 Month EPS:	$1.08	June 30, 2000
P/E Ratio & Beta Factor:	22.05	1.249
Shares Outstanding:	193.840 million	
Market Value:	$4.616 billion	
Institutional Holdings:	55.05%	
Number of Institutions:	637	
Primary Market:	Nasdaq NMS	
Component of:	S&P 500	

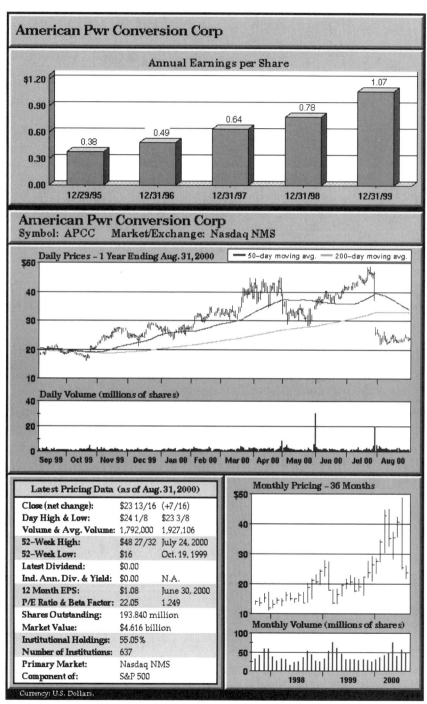

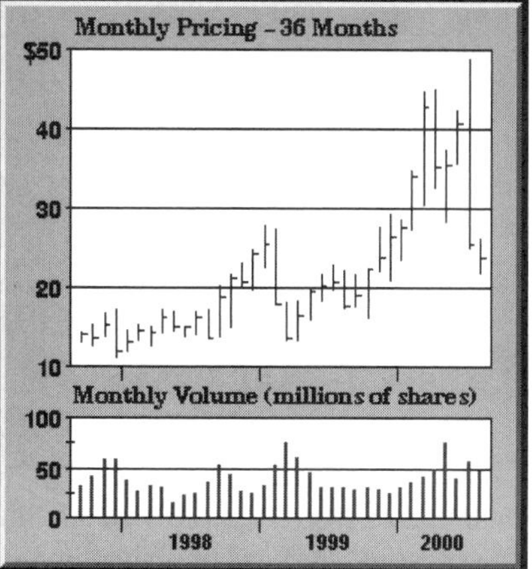

Currency: U.S. Dollars.

Source: Tradeline.Com, a Platinum Equity Holdings Company

American Pwr Conversion Corp

Symbol : APCC Market/Exchange : Nasdaq NMS

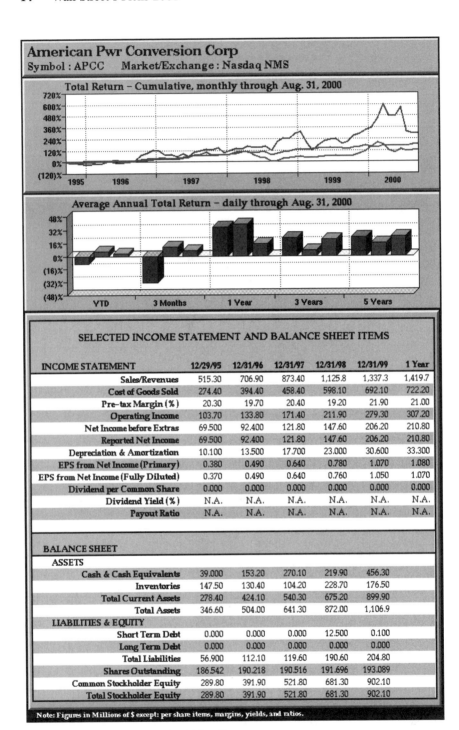

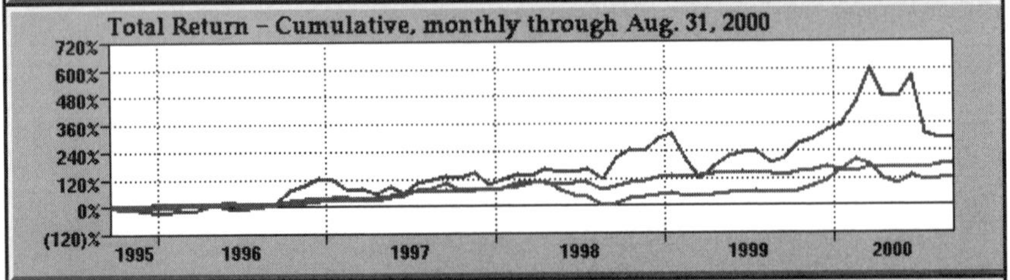

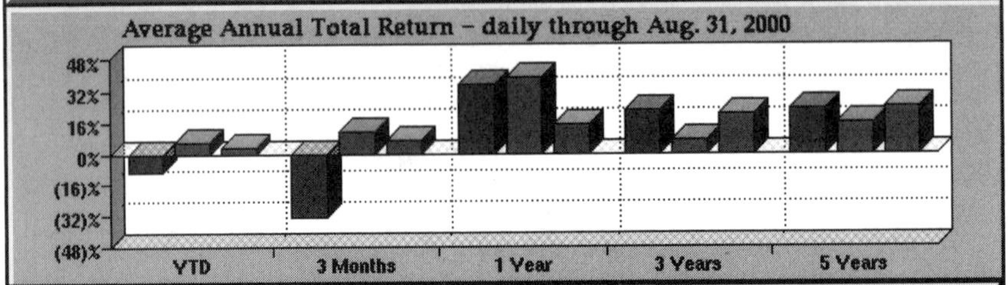

SELECTED INCOME STATEMENT AND BALANCE SHEET ITEMS

INCOME STATEMENT	12/29/95	12/31/96	12/31/97	12/31/98	12/31/99	1 Year
Sales/Revenues	515.30	706.90	873.40	1,125.8	1,337.3	1,419.7
Cost of Goods Sold	274.40	394.40	458.40	598.10	692.10	722.20
Pre-tax Margin (%)	20.30	19.70	20.40	19.20	21.90	21.00
Operating Income	103.70	133.80	171.40	211.90	279.30	307.20
Net Income before Extras	69.500	92.400	121.80	147.60	206.20	210.80
Reported Net Income	69.500	92.400	121.80	147.60	206.20	210.80
Depreciation & Amortization	10.100	13.500	17.700	23.000	30.600	33.300
EPS from Net Income (Primary)	0.380	0.490	0.640	0.780	1.070	1.080
EPS from Net Income (Fully Diluted)	0.370	0.490	0.640	0.760	1.050	1.070
Dividend per Common Share	0.000	0.000	0.000	0.000	0.000	0.000
Dividend Yield (%)	N.A.	N.A.	N.A.	N.A.	N.A.	N.A.
Payout Ratio	N.A.	N.A.	N.A.	N.A.	N.A.	N.A.

BALANCE SHEET					
ASSETS					
Cash & Cash Equivalents	39.000	153.20	270.10	219.90	456.30
Inventories	147.50	130.40	104.20	228.70	176.50
Total Current Assets	278.40	424.10	540.30	675.20	899.90
Total Assets	346.60	504.00	641.30	872.00	1,106.9
LIABILITIES & EQUITY					
Short Term Debt	0.000	0.000	0.000	12.500	0.100
Long Term Debt	0.000	0.000	0.000	0.000	0.000
Total Liabilities	56.900	112.10	119.60	190.60	204.80
Shares Outstanding	186.542	190.218	190.516	191.696	193.089
Common Stockholder Equity	289.80	391.90	521.80	681.30	902.10
Total Stockholder Equity	289.80	391.90	521.80	681.30	902.10

Note: Figures in Millions of $ except: per share items, margins, yields, and ratios.

Source: Tradeline.Com, a Platinum Equity Holdings Company

ANADIGICS

Sally Anderson
Kopp Investment Advisors

Company Background

Anadigics is a communications semiconductor company. It's a leveraged way to play on the high growth in the communications area. The company's significant areas of interest are components for wireless handsets, cable TV, and fiber optics. It has a one-of-a-kind six-inch gallium arsenide fab, which I believe gives Anadigics a fairly significant cost advantage in this process. Gallium arsenide is a specialty-based material used in the making of semiconductors, instead of silicon, which is the most popular material. The advantage of gallium arsenide is you get higher speeds and lower power. That makes it well-suited for many types of communications needs. Anadigics has increasingly moved to broaden its technology platform and now offers other "flavors" of gallium arsenide, primarily one known as HBT.

Reason for Recommendation

I think this company can grow in the 30 to 35 percent range for some time to come. Communications is an area that continues to expand rapidly, both in the U.S. and abroad. The mass use of cell phones is one reason for this. Cell phone penetration in the U.S. is estimated to be 30 percent now, with some estimates taking it to 60 to 80 percent within the next decade. I think the whole wireless handset market, which is the largest market for Anadigics, will continue to grow nicely, especially as the wireless Internet emerges. In addition, as broadband takes hold and cable gets a significant piece of that, Anadigics will be a beneficiary.

Biggest Risks

In the near-term, valuation is probably the biggest risk for this stock. It's not cheap, but I don't think it should be. Not with the kind of prospects it has. It sells at roughly two times its growth rate. That's not troubling to me, assuming the company is able to continue to execute on the game plan it has laid out in front of it. There's also plenty of competition in this space.

Bottom Line

Revenue for the latest fiscal year is expected to come in around $200 million. The company has a relatively new management team that I believe has reinvigorated it with these new platform technologies. This should significantly increase the company's potential addressable markets. Anadigics has also been spending a lot on research and development. The new products they are rolling out are the fruits of this above-average spending, which amounts to around 20 percent of revenues.

Contact Information: Anadigics, Inc.
35 Technology Drive
Warren, NJ 07059
909-668-5000
<www.anadigics.com>

BONUS PICK FOR 2001

TECHNE CORPORATION

Symbol: TECH
Exchange: Nasdaq

Techne is the world's leading supplier of research and diagnostic cytokines. Cytokines are basically proteins involved in cell-to-cell communication. These human cells are a key building block. Techne sells cytokines for use in the research process. When it comes to investing in telecommunications equipment, I have always preferred those companies that provide the picks and shovels, rather than trying to decide who is going to hit the homerun. That's the same case with this company. You're not making a bet on any particular drug. You're investing in the research process, which is definitely happening. Think of all the noise we're hearing about the mapping of the human genome. Plus, some $26 billion worth of drugs are coming off patent over the next five years, and it's important for drug and biotech companies to refill that pipeline. Techne will be a major beneficiary of this research. The company has grown by around 22 percent compounded over the past five years, and the consensus is it will probably be closer to 25 or 30 percent going forward. I wouldn't even be surprised if this company, which is nicely profitable, ultimately gets bought out. It has the kind of superb gross and pretax margins that many companies would kill for.

Anadigics Inc

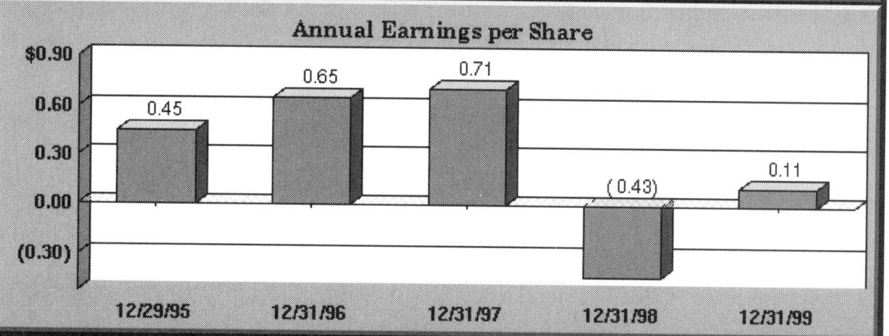

Anadigics Inc

Symbol: ANAD   Market/Exchange: Nasdaq NMS

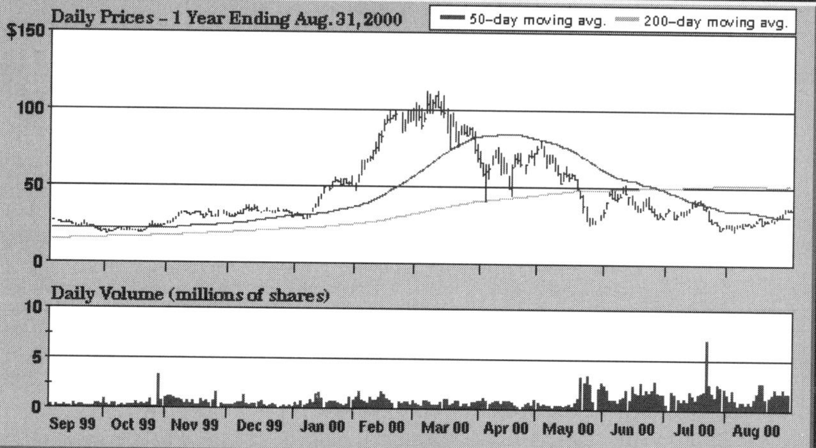

Latest Pricing Data (as of Aug. 31, 2000)		
Close (net change):	$36	(+1/8)
Day High & Low:	$37 1/2	$35 7/8
Volume & Avg. Volume:	1,656,000	920,173
52-Week High:	$112 1/8	Mar. 6, 2000
52-Week Low:	$17 7/8	Sep. 30, 1999
Latest Dividend:	$0.00	
Ind. Ann. Div. & Yield:	$0.00	N.A.
12 Month EPS:	$0.72	June 30, 2000
P/E Ratio & Beta Factor:	50.00	2.278
Shares Outstanding:	29.866 million	
Market Value:	$1.075 billion	
Institutional Holdings:	82.17%	
Number of Institutions:	253	
Primary Market:	Nasdaq NMS	

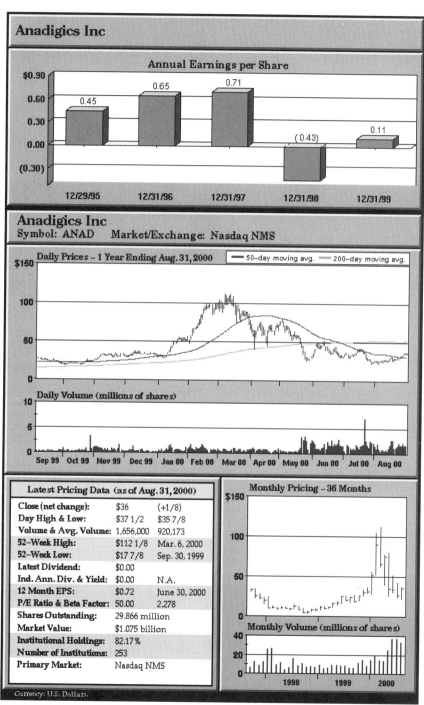

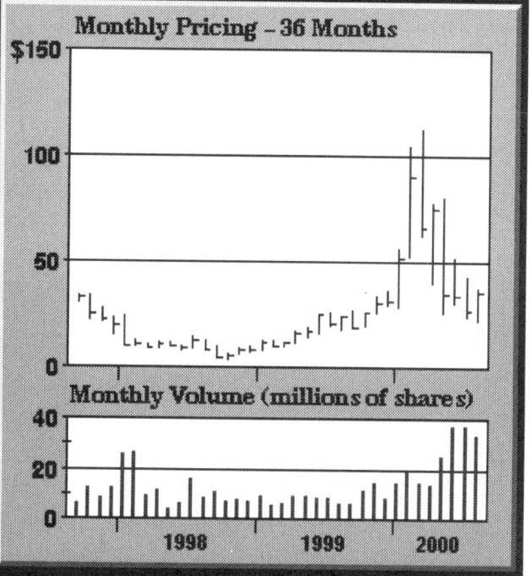

Currency: U.S. Dollars.

Source: Tradeline.Com, a Platinum Equity Holdings Company

Anadigics Inc
Symbol : ANAD Market/Exchange : Nasdaq NMS

Total Return – Cumulative, monthly through Aug. 31, 2000

Average Annual Total Return – daily through Aug. 31, 2000

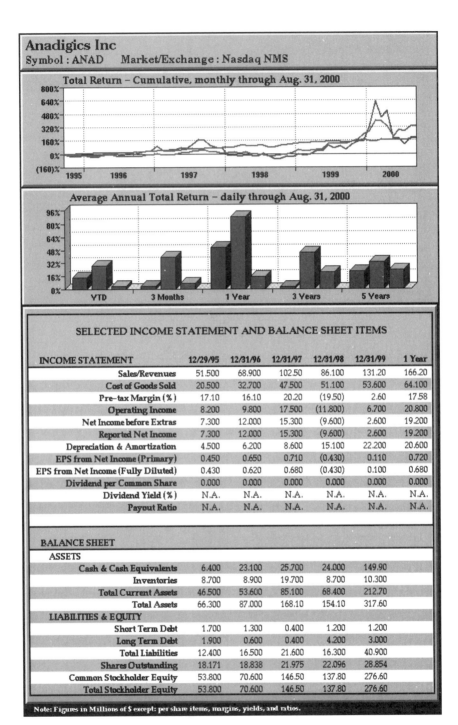

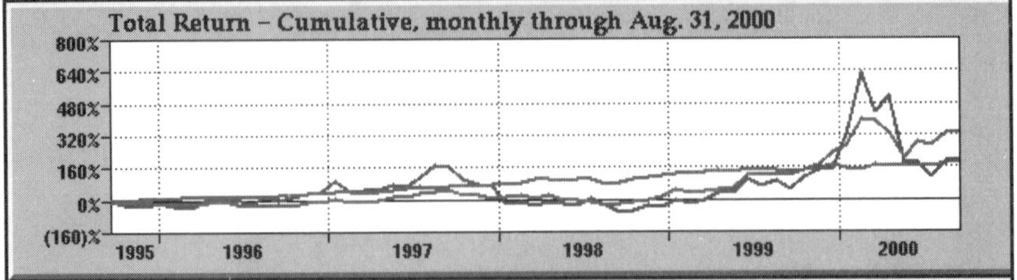

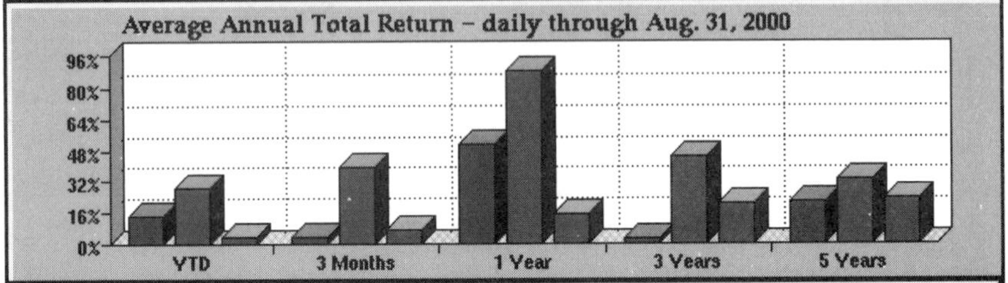

SELECTED INCOME STATEMENT AND BALANCE SHEET ITEMS

INCOME STATEMENT	12/29/95	12/31/96	12/31/97	12/31/98	12/31/99	1 Year
Sales/Revenues	51.500	68.900	102.50	86.100	131.20	166.20
Cost of Goods Sold	20.500	32.700	47.500	51.100	53.600	64.100
Pre–tax Margin (%)	17.10	16.10	20.20	(19.50)	2.60	17.58
Operating Income	8.200	9.800	17.500	(11.800)	6.700	20.800
Net Income before Extras	7.300	12.000	15.300	(9.600)	2.600	19.200
Reported Net Income	7.300	12.000	15.300	(9.600)	2.600	19.200
Depreciation & Amortization	4.500	6.200	8.600	15.100	22.200	20.600
EPS from Net Income (Primary)	0.450	0.650	0.710	(0.430)	0.110	0.720
EPS from Net Income (Fully Diluted)	0.430	0.620	0.680	(0.430)	0.100	0.680
Dividend per Common Share	0.000	0.000	0.000	0.000	0.000	0.000
Dividend Yield (%)	N.A.	N.A.	N.A.	N.A.	N.A.	N.A.
Payout Ratio	N.A.	N.A.	N.A.	N.A.	N.A.	N.A.

BALANCE SHEET						
ASSETS						
Cash & Cash Equivalents	6.400	23.100	25.700	24.000	149.90	
Inventories	8.700	8.900	19.700	8.700	10.300	
Total Current Assets	46.500	53.600	85.100	68.400	212.70	
Total Assets	66.300	87.000	168.10	154.10	317.60	
LIABILITIES & EQUITY						
Short Term Debt	1.700	1.300	0.400	1.200	1.200	
Long Term Debt	1.900	0.600	0.400	4.200	3.000	
Total Liabilities	12.400	16.500	21.600	16.300	40.900	
Shares Outstanding	18.171	18.838	21.975	22.096	28.854	
Common Stockholder Equity	53.800	70.600	146.50	137.80	276.60	
Total Stockholder Equity	53.800	70.600	146.50	137.80	276.60	

Note: Figures in Millions of $ except: per share items, margins, yields, and ratios.

Source: Tradeline.Com, a Platinum Equity Holdings Company

ANDRX

Joseph Battipaglia
Gruntal & Co.

Company Background

Andrx is a leader in the specialty generic drug business. It has a number of significant products, both filed at the FDA and tentatively approved, including the generic version of Prilosec (gastrointestinal disorders), which is the largest selling drug in both the U.S. and abroad. Other drugs that have recently come off patent that Andrx manufactures include generic versions of Cardizem CD (hypertension) and Dilacor XR (hypertension).

If you've had a prescription filled lately, you've probably noticed that your insurance company requires you to get the generic equivalent whenever one is available, or else you have to pay more out of pocket. This bodes well for Andrx.

Reason for Recommendation

You're going to see a dramatic surge in the revenues and earnings of this company as it establishes itself as one of the fastest-growing specialty drug and drug delivery companies. There are several significant drugs coming off patent and Andrx is in a position to get the approvals to produce them. It has a bigger pipeline coming in, and is poised to be first with the formulation and approval from the FDA. I look for revenues of this company to increase by 63 percent in 2001 over 2000, and 53 percent in 2002 over 2001. This is rapid and expansive growth. Plus, the company has a relatively small share base, with 65.8 million shares outstanding, and a float of 26.4 million.

Biggest Risks

We must watch to make sure Andrx gets these approvals in a timely manner from the FDA, and that other competitors aren't as savvy, in terms of legal battles and marketing their product offerings. Andrx also has to stay close to schedule on new product releases. This is a relatively young company, founded in 1992, but it has done very well thus far. I attribute that to a solid management team with long experience in the pharmaceutical and generic drug industries. The company really does have the capacity to produce the product, get it approved, and on the market rather fast.

Bottom Line

I believe that the specialty pharmaceutical industry represents one of the most attractive areas in health care due to its high growth potential. Andrx's growth is among the highest in the sector, driven by its pipeline of both speciality generic drugs and higher-margin proprietary drugs.

Contact Information: Andrx Corporation
4001 Southwest 47th Avenue
Ft. Lauderdale, FL 33314
954-584-0300
<www.andrx.com>

BONUS PICK FOR 2001

INTERNATIONAL RECTIFIER

Symbol: IRF
Exchange: NYSE

International Rectifier manufactures power semiconductors, which are essential building blocks in producing laptops, cellular phones, and other portable electronic devices. International Rectifier makes metal oxide semiconductor transistors. This isn't a technology that everyone has, but it is a very important product. These transistors basically manage the power within a PC or laptop to help minimize heat. Technically speaking, they are electronic components that refine electricity coming from a wall outlet or battery, enabling electronics to operate more efficiently. The power semiconductor is extremely important because as high-speed applications move into the market, regulating the power consumption is critical. The company has been around for some time, and boasts such customers as Compaq, Ford, IBM, Lucent Technologies, and Sony. I look for revenues in 2001 to reach $912 million, and I expect this stock to reach at least $80 per share by the end of the year.

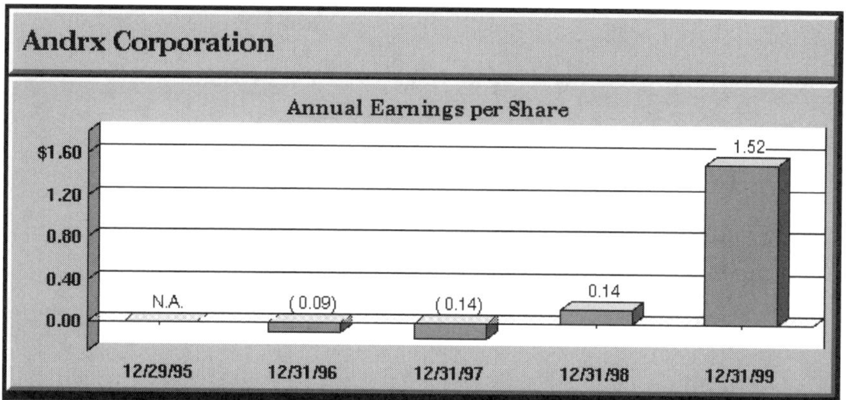

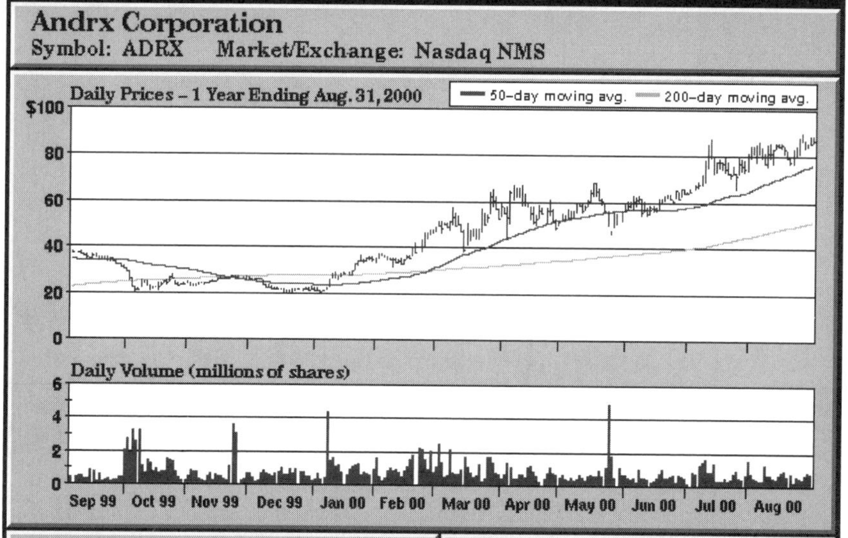

Latest Pricing Data (as of Aug. 31, 2000)

Close (net change):	$87	(+15/16)
Day High & Low:	$88 3/4	$85 1/2
Volume & Avg. Volume:	797,000	840,167
52-Week High:	$90	Aug. 25, 2000
52-Week Low:	$19 1/4	Dec. 20, 1999
Latest Dividend:	$0.00	
Ind. Ann. Div. & Yield:	$0.00	N.A.
12 Month EPS:	$1.13	June 30, 2000
P/E Ratio & Beta Factor:	76.99	0.749
Shares Outstanding:	69.028 million	
Market Value:	$6.005 billion	
Institutional Holdings:	48.99%	
Number of Institutions:	269	
Primary Market:	Nasdaq NMS	

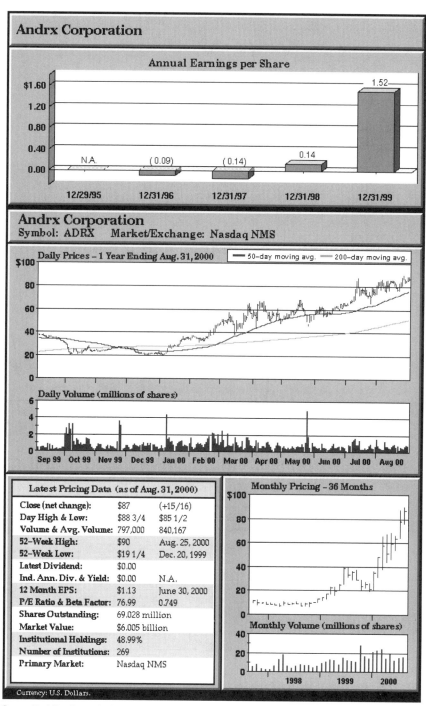

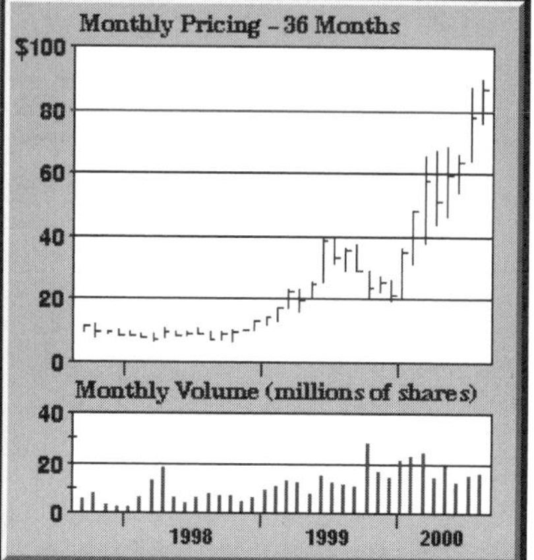

Currency: U.S. Dollars.

Source: Tradeline.Com, a Platinum Equity Holdings Company

Andrx Corporation

Symbol : ADRX Market/Exchange : Nasdaq NMS

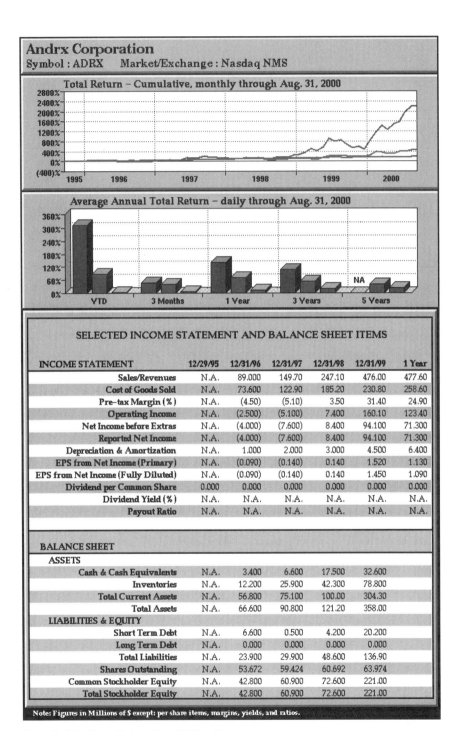

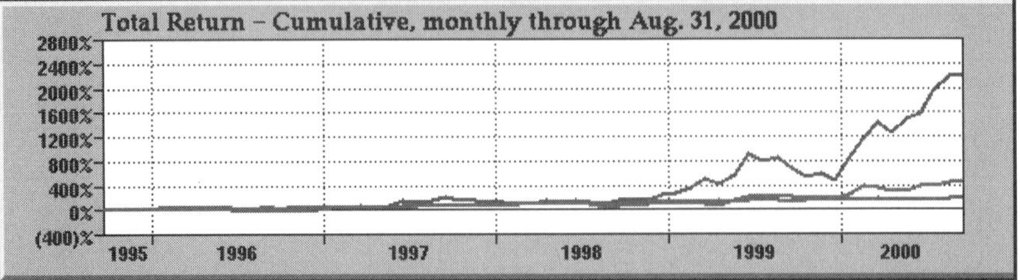

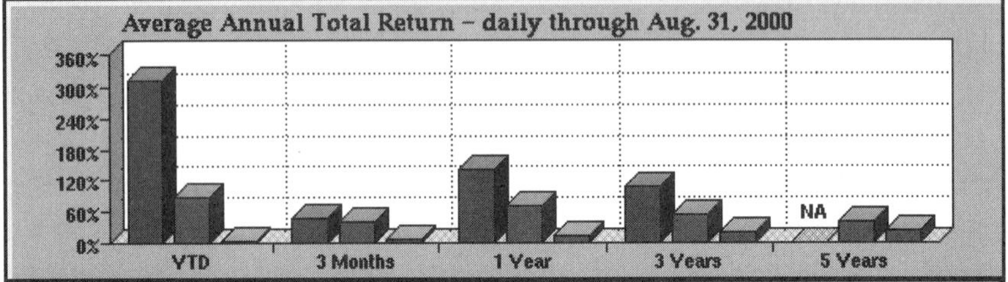

SELECTED INCOME STATEMENT AND BALANCE SHEET ITEMS

INCOME STATEMENT	12/29/95	12/31/96	12/31/97	12/31/98	12/31/99	1 Year
Sales/Revenues	N.A.	89.000	149.70	247.10	476.00	477.60
Cost of Goods Sold	N.A.	73.600	122.90	185.20	230.80	258.60
Pre-tax Margin (%)	N.A.	(4.50)	(5.10)	3.50	31.40	24.90
Operating Income	N.A.	(2.500)	(5.100)	7.400	160.10	123.40
Net Income before Extras	N.A.	(4.000)	(7.600)	8.400	94.100	71.300
Reported Net Income	N.A.	(4.000)	(7.600)	8.400	94.100	71.300
Depreciation & Amortization	N.A.	1.000	2.000	3.000	4.500	6.400
EPS from Net Income (Primary)	N.A.	(0.090)	(0.140)	0.140	1.520	1.130
EPS from Net Income (Fully Diluted)	N.A.	(0.090)	(0.140)	0.140	1.450	1.090
Dividend per Common Share	0.000	0.000	0.000	0.000	0.000	0.000
Dividend Yield (%)	N.A.	N.A.	N.A.	N.A.	N.A.	N.A.
Payout Ratio	N.A.	N.A.	N.A.	N.A.	N.A.	N.A.

BALANCE SHEET					
ASSETS					
Cash & Cash Equivalents	N.A.	3.400	6.600	17.500	32.600
Inventories	N.A.	12.200	25.900	42.300	78.800
Total Current Assets	N.A.	56.800	75.100	100.00	304.30
Total Assets	N.A.	66.600	90.800	121.20	358.00
LIABILITIES & EQUITY					
Short Term Debt	N.A.	6.600	0.500	4.200	20.200
Long Term Debt	N.A.	0.000	0.000	0.000	0.000
Total Liabilities	N.A.	23.900	29.900	48.600	136.90
Shares Outstanding	N.A.	53.672	59.424	60.692	63.974
Common Stockholder Equity	N.A.	42.800	60.900	72.600	221.00
Total Stockholder Equity	N.A.	42.800	60.900	72.600	221.00

Note: Figures in Millions of $ except: per share items, margins, yields, and ratios.

Source: Tradeline.Com, a Platinum Equity Holdings Company

APPLIED MICRO CIRCUITS

Louis Navellier
Navellier & Associates

Company Background

Applied Micro Circuits makes the chips that go into high-definition televisions (HDTVs). During the next decade, we will all have to upgrade to HDTV. I'm sure you all know that it's our God-given right as Americans to have a big screen TV, a Lazy Boy, and a satellite dish. You'll find that satellite dishes now sprout two receptors—one of which is used for HDTV. HBO is already broadcasting in HDTV, and the next Super Bowl will be telecast in HDTV. Before long, all of the cable and over-the-air channels must offer it.

HDTV gives you double the normal resolution, so it's a much better picture. The big manufacturers are currently making HDTV sets, but they will really get into gear as more people embrace the technology. (I already have several HDTV sets, and as prices come down, they will become increasingly popular.) I don't know whether Sony, Mitsubishi, Panasonic, or RCA will ultimately win the HDTV wars and have the most popular set. All I know is that Applied Micro Circuits will win because it makes the chip that goes into all these TVs.

Reason for Recommendation

Because I believe virtually everyone will upgrade to an HDTV over the next ten years, Applied Micro Circuits should enjoy a steady stream of business. While I'm sure some other competitors will come along and develop a knock-off chip, it will be hard for anyone to surpass Applied Micro Circuits. The company also makes high-performance, high-bandwidth integrated circuits for use in controlling the high-speed flow of transmissions through fiber-optic telephone networks around the world.

Biggest Risks

The stock isn't cheap, but earnings keep growing, so that doesn't worry me a lot. And while I'm not concerned about competition at this point, that's always something one must pay attention to.

Bottom Line

This is a stock that squares very well on all of my screens. Sales and revenues are skyrocketing. It's really running on all cylinders right now.

Contact Information: Applied Micro Circuits Corporation
6270 Sequence Drive
San Diego, CA 92121
858-450-9333
<www.amcc.com>

BONUS PICK FOR 2001

TRIQUINT SEMICONDUCTOR

Symbol: TQNT
Exchange: Nasdaq

TriQuint Semiconductor is a similar story, only this company makes the chips that go into navigation systems. When you buy a new Mercedes, for example, you can opt to get a computerized map on the dash that you can program to tell you where to go. Even if you're on the freeway in an unfamiliar area, it can show you how to bypass a traffic jam. Honda also has these systems available, and I would expect all of the automakers to use them over the next decade. We may not know we need HDTV or navigation systems, but one day they'll be common, and I want to own the companies making the chips that allow these devices to operate. TriQuent's sales have been growing at 76 percent annually. Earnings and margins are expanding nicely. The company is a baby monopoly, just like Applied Micro Circuits. Again, it doesn't matter which navigation system or automaker is most popular; all of them will need the chips made by TriQuint to run properly.

Applied Microcircuits Corp

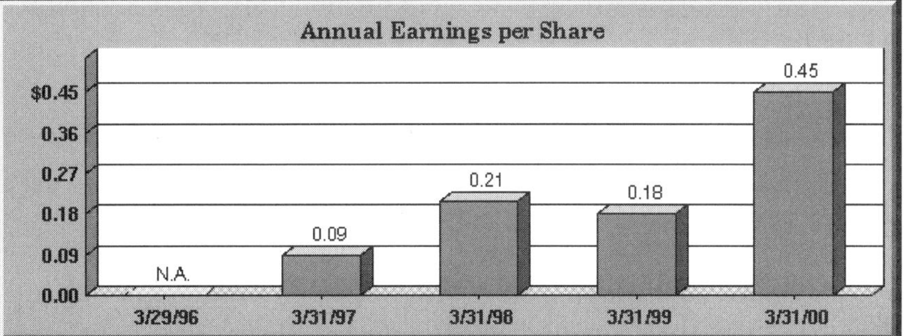

Applied Microcircuits Corp

Symbol: AMCC Market/Exchange: Nasdaq NMS

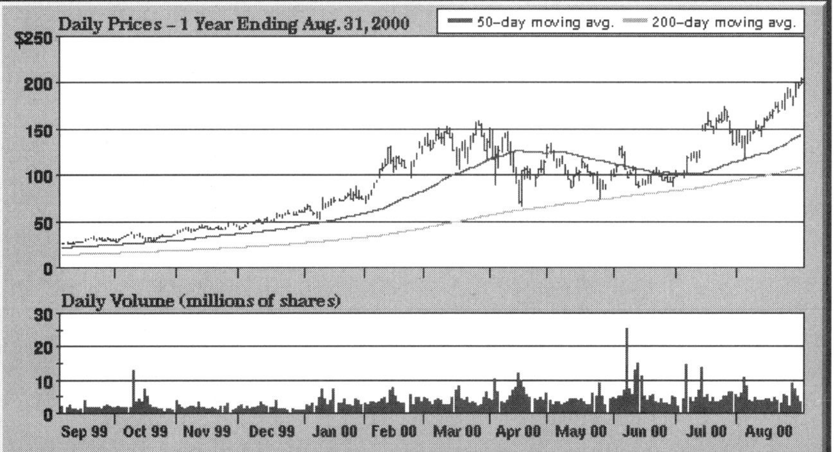

Latest Pricing Data (as of Aug. 31, 2000)		
Close (net change):	$202 15/16 (+5 1/4)	
Day High & Low:	$204 1/2	$197 1/8
Volume & Avg. Volume:	3,564,000	3,952,860
52-Week High:	$204 1/2	Aug. 31, 2000
52-Week Low:	$24 5/8	Sep. 3, 1999
Latest Dividend:	$0.00	
Ind. Ann. Div. & Yield:	$0.00	N.A.
12 Month EPS:	$0.42	June 30, 2000
P/E Ratio & Beta Factor:	483.18	2.017
Shares Outstanding:	125.470 million	
Market Value:	$25.463 billion	
Institutional Holdings:	71.27%	
Number of Institutions:	611	
Primary Market:	Nasdaq NMS	

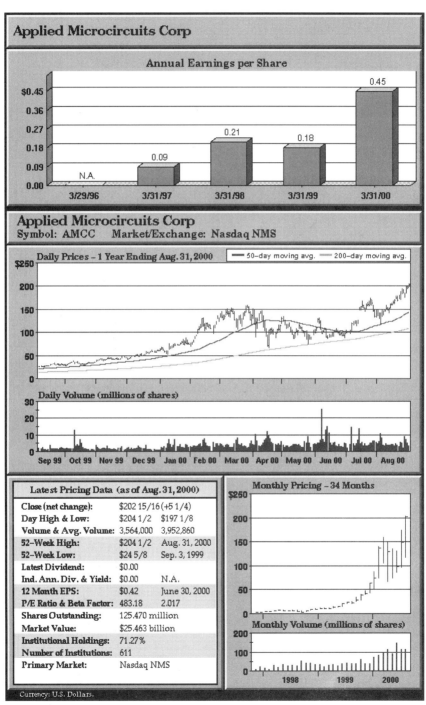

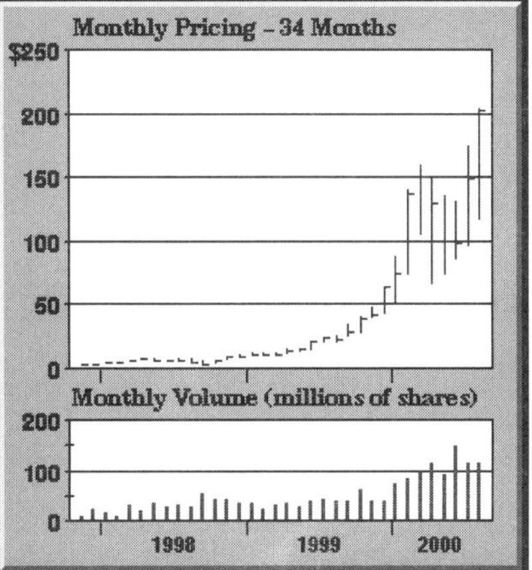

Currency: U.S. Dollars.

Source: Tradeline.Com, a Platinum Equity Holdings Company

Applied Microcircuits Corp

Symbol : AMCC   Market/Exchange : Nasdaq NMS

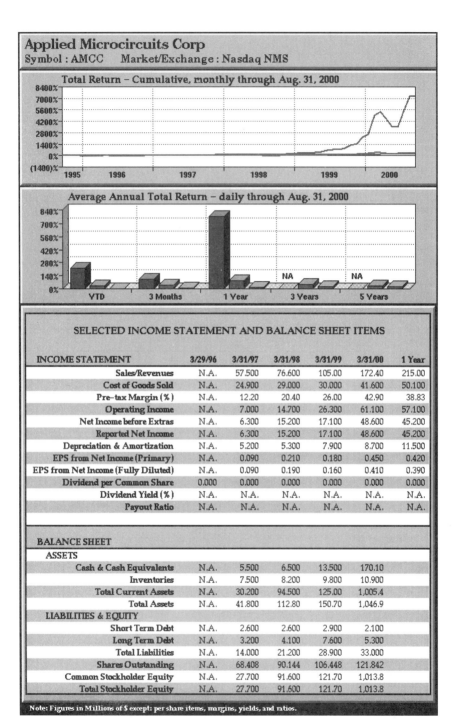

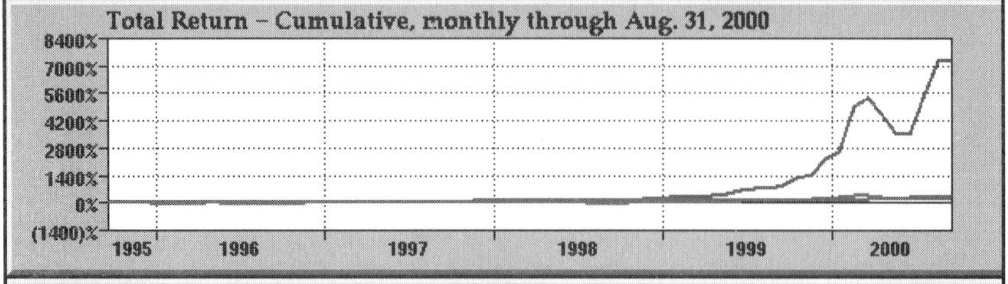

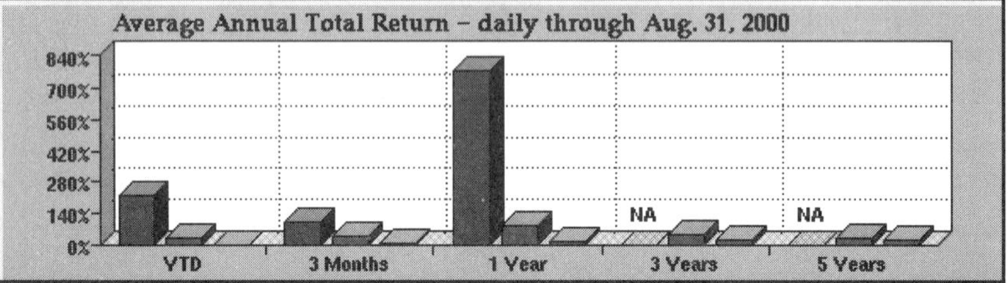

SELECTED INCOME STATEMENT AND BALANCE SHEET ITEMS

INCOME STATEMENT	3/29/96	3/31/97	3/31/98	3/31/99	3/31/00	1 Year
Sales/Revenues	N.A.	57.500	76.600	105.00	172.40	215.00
Cost of Goods Sold	N.A.	24.900	29.000	30.000	41.600	50.100
Pre-tax Margin (%)	N.A.	12.20	20.40	26.00	42.90	38.83
Operating Income	N.A.	7.000	14.700	26.300	61.100	57.100
Net Income before Extras	N.A.	6.300	15.200	17.100	48.600	45.200
Reported Net Income	N.A.	6.300	15.200	17.100	48.600	45.200
Depreciation & Amortization	N.A.	5.200	5.300	7.900	8.700	11.500
EPS from Net Income (Primary)	N.A.	0.090	0.210	0.180	0.450	0.420
EPS from Net Income (Fully Diluted)	N.A.	0.090	0.190	0.160	0.410	0.390
Dividend per Common Share	0.000	0.000	0.000	0.000	0.000	0.000
Dividend Yield (%)	N.A.	N.A.	N.A.	N.A.	N.A.	N.A.
Payout Ratio	N.A.	N.A.	N.A.	N.A.	N.A.	N.A.

BALANCE SHEET					
ASSETS					
Cash & Cash Equivalents	N.A.	5.500	6.500	13.500	170.10
Inventories	N.A.	7.500	8.200	9.800	10.900
Total Current Assets	N.A.	30.200	94.500	125.00	1,005.4
Total Assets	N.A.	41.800	112.80	150.70	1,046.9
LIABILITIES & EQUITY					
Short Term Debt	N.A.	2.600	2.600	2.900	2.100
Long Term Debt	N.A.	3.200	4.100	7.600	5.300
Total Liabilities	N.A.	14.000	21.200	28.900	33.000
Shares Outstanding	N.A.	68.408	90.144	106.448	121.842
Common Stockholder Equity	N.A.	27.700	91.600	121.70	1,013.8
Total Stockholder Equity	N.A.	27.700	91.600	121.70	1,013.8

Note: Figures in Millions of $ except: per share items, margins, yields, and ratios.

Source: Tradeline.Com, a Platinum Equity Holdings Company

CLEAR CHANNEL COMMUNICATIONS

Cappy McGarr
McGarr Capital Management

Company Background

Clear Channel Communications is the largest out-of-home media company in the world. Thanks to its 2000 merger activity, Clear Channel acquired AMFM, Inc. and SFX Entertainment. The new combined company is a media powerhouse with 870 radio stations, 19 television stations, and more than 700,000 outdoor displays. Clear Channel also owns Katz Media Group, a media representation firm, and operates the world's largest diversified promoter, producer, and venue operator for live entertainment events, with 120 live entertainment venues, including 16 in the top ten markets.

The company's radio stations are in 167 markets throughout the U.S. and Puerto Rico. Meanwhile, 87 percent of the U.S. population is exposed to the company's billboards, and an additional 7.5 million people are reached through its television stations. This vast array of offerings across mediums and geographies allows the company to provide its customers with customized bundled advertising packages that are unmatched in the industry.

Reasons for Recommendation

The combined Clear Channel ushers in a renaissance in the out-of-home media space. In the past, national advertisers allocated less of their advertising budget to this space because a national campaign required intense coordination in a fragmented industry. Therefore, radio, which consumes 30 percent of consumer media time, captured only 8 percent of the total $220 billion advertising pie. Clear Channel's "one-stop shop" solves the coordination problem for national campaigns. In addition, the company trades at a discount to its five-year ATCF (after-tax cash flow) growth rate of 26 percent. Growth should continue to be robust because of synergies from the merger, cross-promotion through the unparalleled live music franchise, and real-time inventory management. At 22 times projected 2001 ATCF, Clear Channel's valuation is at the low end of its three-year range, and its business is booming.

Biggest Risks

The biggest risk is a prolonged economic downturn, which could negatively impact Clear Channel's advertising revenue. However, despite several recessions, advertising expenditure has had only one down year over the past 30 years. Another recent concern is a decrease in dot-com advertising revenue. However, this is a misplaced apprehension, as only 5 to 6 percent of Clear Channel's revenue comes from dot-com company advertising.

Bottom Line

Clear Channel could trade around $135 a share by the end of 2001. The company is capable of increasing cash earnings by about 26 percent annually over the next six years, which compounded would imply a 300 percent increase. We believe the stock could appreciate even more over that time frame.

Contact Information: Clear Channel Communications
200 Concord Plaza, Suite 600
San Antonio, TX 78216
210-822-2828
<www.clearchannel.com>

BONUS PICK FOR 2001

VODAFONE AIRTOUCH PLC

Symbol: VOD
Exchange: NYSE

Vodafone is the largest and most profitable wireless operator in the world, with a proportionate customer base of 52 million across 25 countries and 5 continents. On a total aggregate basis, Vodafone's cellular affiliates boast more than 95.2 million customers, with a population footprint worldwide of more than 1 billion customers. In the United States, Vodafone's presence can be seen in Verizon, its joint venture with Bell Atlantic, the largest domestic cellular provider, with service in 96 of the top 100 markets. With the rollout of third-generation cellular technology, Vodafone will provide wireless Internet access, multimedia messaging, wireless data service, and a full range of mobile commerce and financial services. This wireless data explosion is projected to increase the average revenue per user by more than 30 percent. At the same time, Vodafone has estimated EBITDA growth of 30 percent through 2005. This is going to be a very exciting story over the next five years.

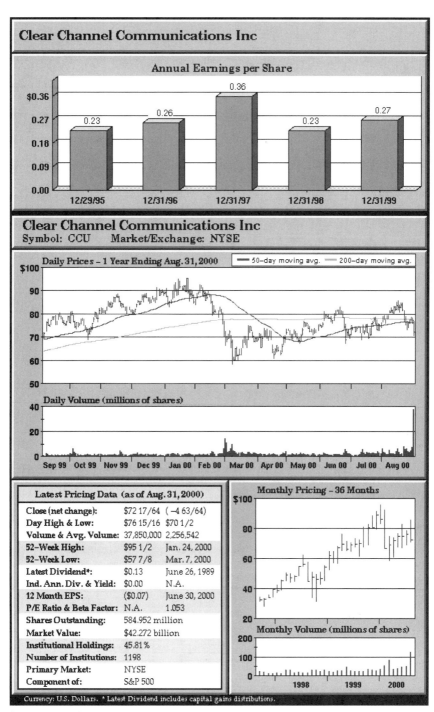

Clear Channel Communications Inc

Clear Channel Communications Inc

Symbol: CCU Market/Exchange: NYSE

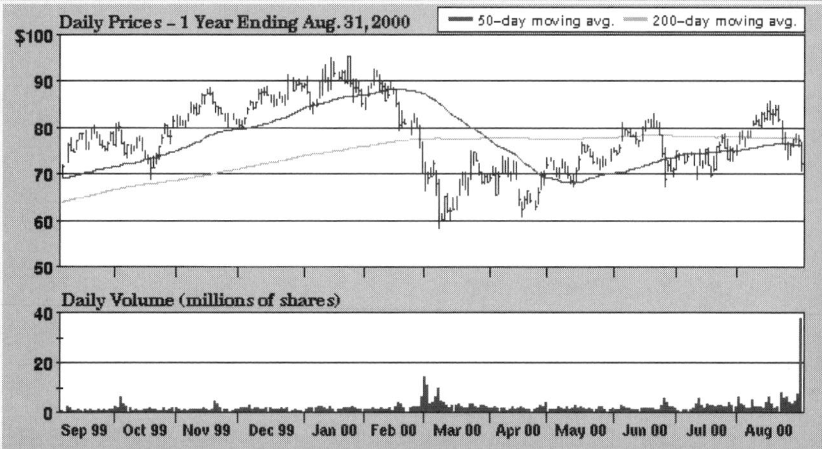

Latest Pricing Data (as of Aug. 31, 2000)		
Close (net change):	$72 17/64	(–4 63/64)
Day High & Low:	$76 15/16	$70 1/2
Volume & Avg. Volume:	37,850,000	2,256,542
52-Week High:	$95 1/2	Jan. 24, 2000
52-Week Low:	$57 7/8	Mar. 7, 2000
Latest Dividend*:	$0.13	June 26, 1989
Ind. Ann. Div. & Yield:	$0.00	N.A.
12 Month EPS:	($0.07)	June 30, 2000
P/E Ratio & Beta Factor:	N.A.	1.053
Shares Outstanding:	584.952 million	
Market Value:	$42.272 billion	
Institutional Holdings:	45.81%	
Number of Institutions:	1198	
Primary Market:	NYSE	
Component of:	S&P 500	

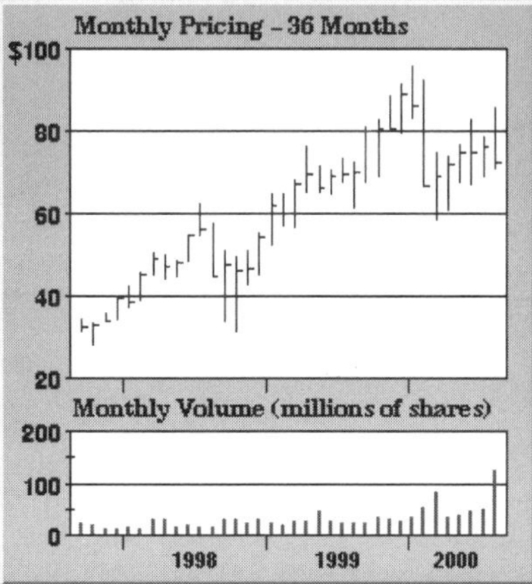

Currency: U.S. Dollars. * Latest Dividend includes capital gains distributions.

Source: Tradeline.Com, a Platinum Equity Holdings Company

Clear Channel Communications Inc
Symbol : CCU   Market/Exchange : NYSE

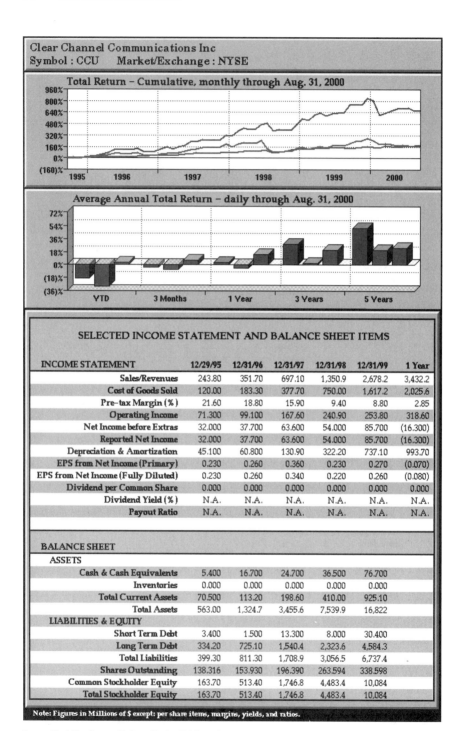

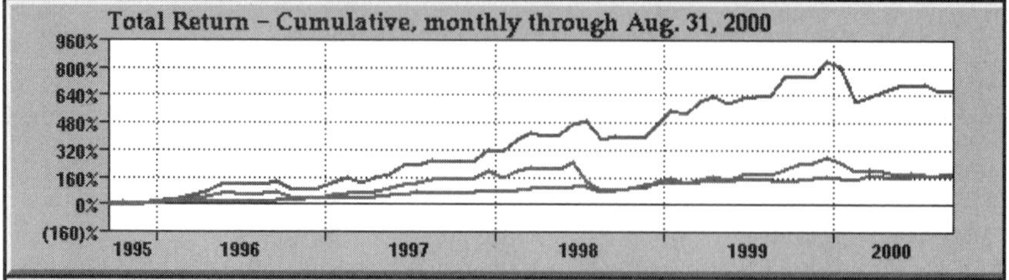

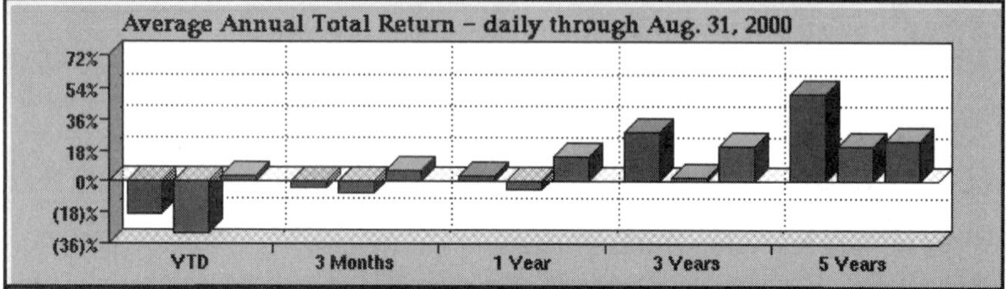

SELECTED INCOME STATEMENT AND BALANCE SHEET ITEMS

INCOME STATEMENT	12/29/95	12/31/96	12/31/97	12/31/98	12/31/99	1 Year
Sales/Revenues	243.80	351.70	697.10	1,350.9	2,678.2	3,432.2
Cost of Goods Sold	120.00	183.30	377.70	750.00	1,617.2	2,025.6
Pre-tax Margin (%)	21.60	18.80	15.90	9.40	8.80	2.85
Operating Income	71.300	99.100	167.60	240.90	253.80	318.60
Net Income before Extras	32.000	37.700	63.600	54.000	85.700	(16.300)
Reported Net Income	32.000	37.700	63.600	54.000	85.700	(16.300)
Depreciation & Amortization	45.100	60.800	130.90	322.20	737.10	993.70
EPS from Net Income (Primary)	0.230	0.260	0.360	0.230	0.270	(0.070)
EPS from Net Income (Fully Diluted)	0.230	0.260	0.340	0.220	0.260	(0.080)
Dividend per Common Share	0.000	0.000	0.000	0.000	0.000	0.000
Dividend Yield (%)	N.A.	N.A.	N.A.	N.A.	N.A.	N.A.
Payout Ratio	N.A.	N.A.	N.A.	N.A.	N.A.	N.A.

BALANCE SHEET					
ASSETS					
Cash & Cash Equivalents	5.400	16.700	24.700	36.500	76.700
Inventories	0.000	0.000	0.000	0.000	0.000
Total Current Assets	70.500	113.20	198.60	410.00	925.10
Total Assets	563.00	1,324.7	3,455.6	7,539.9	16,822
LIABILITIES & EQUITY					
Short Term Debt	3.400	1.500	13.300	8.000	30.400
Long Term Debt	334.20	725.10	1,540.4	2,323.6	4,584.3
Total Liabilities	399.30	811.30	1,708.9	3,056.5	6,737.4
Shares Outstanding	138.316	153.930	196.390	263.594	338.598
Common Stockholder Equity	163.70	513.40	1,746.8	4,483.4	10,084
Total Stockholder Equity	163.70	513.40	1,746.8	4,483.4	10,084

Note: Figures in Millions of $ except: per share items, margins, yields, and ratios.

Source: Tradeline.Com, a Platinum Equity Holdings Company

CORNING

James Collins
Insight Capital Research & Management

Company Background

The first time I ran into Corning was when it was famous for making glass casserole dishes in the 1950s and 1960s. Who knew this would emerge as one of the top fiber-optic companies in the world? Yes, the Corning of today is a global technology company that operates in three broadly based business segments, including telecommunications, advanced materials, and information displays. Corning really invented fiber-optic cable more than two decades ago. The telecommunications unit, which accounts for more than half of all sales, continues to make optical fiber, along with cable and photonic components. The advanced materials unit produces industrial and scientific products, including environmental and semiconductor materials. The display unit is a leading producer of glass products for TVs, VCRs, and the popular new flat-panel monitors.

Corning has changed its strategy a bit. It is out acquiring companies to help round out its telecommunications product line, which is positive from a strategic point of view. I think management is now willing to shed many of the slower-growth components. The fiber-optics business is capacity constrained at the moment, which is good. This is a well-managed company generating a high return on equity with solid growth from one quarter to the next.

Reason for Recommendation

Corning is a company in the right space at the right time. The company has been participating in the huge build-out of the Internet, and is seeing a huge demand for its fiber-optic cable and equipment. It is also constantly adding to its product line. Corning is very well positioned going into 2001.

Biggest Risks

I don't see many risks associated with the fiber-optics part of the business. I think if the company doesn't sell off some of its "older" business units, it might have to continue to deal with Wall Street's distorted image that it is into mundane businesses, which may hold down stock valuations. My reading is that management is quite conservative, so it may be a little slow on moving in that direction. On the other hand, it is actively pursuing the addition of other companies.

Bottom Line

Corning is a good, well-run, solid company. It spends a lot of money on research and development, and is willing to continually add new products to its line. This should spell good returns going forward, even though the stock has run up impressively in recent years.

Contact Information: Corning Incorporated
1 Riverfront Plaza
Corning, NY 14831-0001
607-974-9000
<www.corning.com>

BONUS PICK FOR 2001

APPLIED MATERIALS

Symbol: AMAT
Exchange: Nasdaq

Like Corning, Applied Materials is a company facing a capacity constraint. It is the world's leading maker of semiconductor wafer fabrication equipment. As we make the transition to making thinner and thinner semiconductors, companies that don't buy new equipment to keep up with advances in technolog will be left behind at the gate very quickly. Competitors will eat them alive. Applied Materials has a big share in most industry segments, including deposition, which is the layer film on wafers, and etching, which involves removing excess material during patterning. Another factor driving growth for Applied Materials is the shift from an aluminum interconnect structure on chips to copper. Copper is very difficult to work with, but Applied Materials has the technology to do it. Speed is the name of the game, and companies need equipment from Applied Materials to stay ahead. I think we're probably still in the early stages of the strength in the semiconductor industry, and expect chip orders to remain strong over the next year. If so, this stock should easily get up to $160 per share by the end of 2001.

Corning Inc

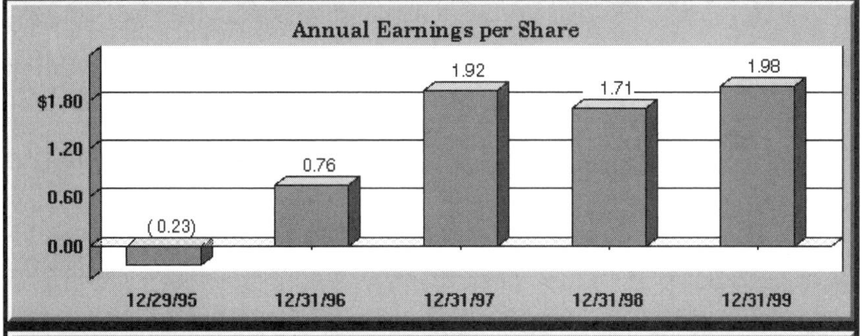

Corning Inc

Symbol: GLW   Market/Exchange: NYSE

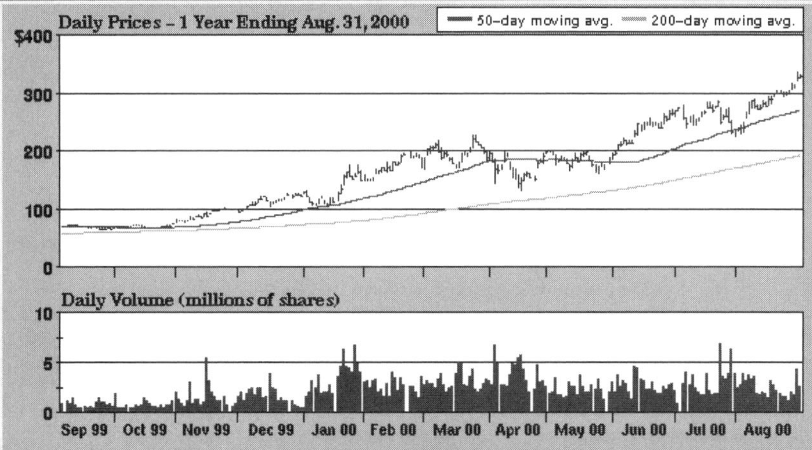

Latest Pricing Data (as of Aug. 31, 2000)		
Close (net change):	$328	(+1)
Day High & Low:	$330	$324 1/2
Volume & Avg. Volume:	2,595,000	2,343,647
52-Week High:	$334 15/16	Aug. 30, 2000
52-Week Low:	$62 5/8	Sep. 22, 1999
Latest Dividend:	$0.18	June 1, 2000
Ind. Ann. Div. & Yield:	$0.72	0.22%
12 Month EPS:	$1.92	June 30, 2000
P/E Ratio & Beta Factor:	170.83	1.348
Shares Outstanding:	293.987 million	
Market Value:	$96.428 billion	
Institutional Holdings:	67.86%	
Number of Institutions:	1518	
Primary Market:	NYSE	
Component of:	S&P 500	

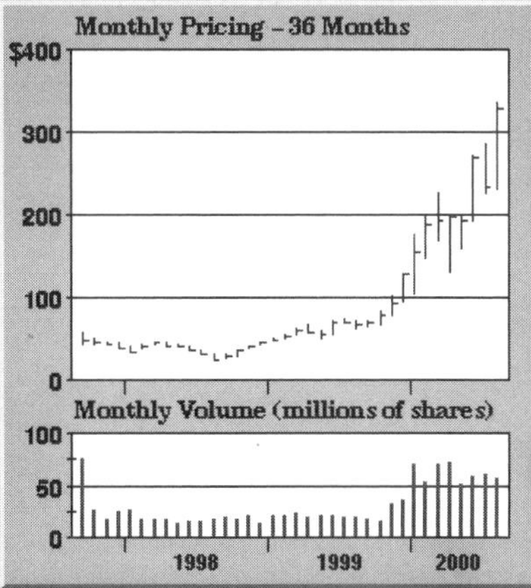

Currency: U.S. Dollars.

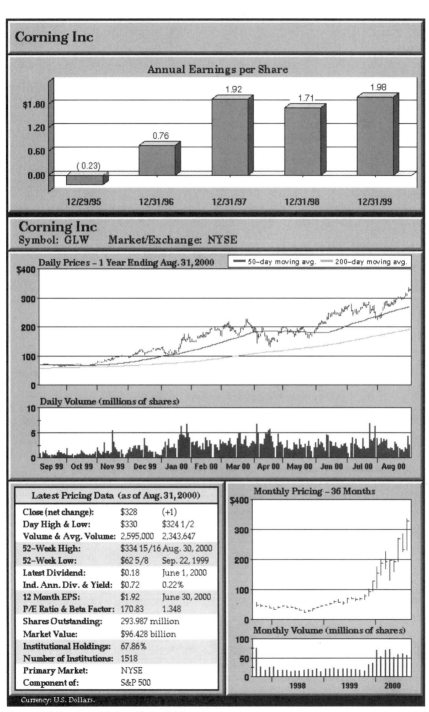

Source: Tradeline.Com, a Platinum Equity Holdings Company

Corning Inc

Symbol : GLW Market/Exchange : NYSE

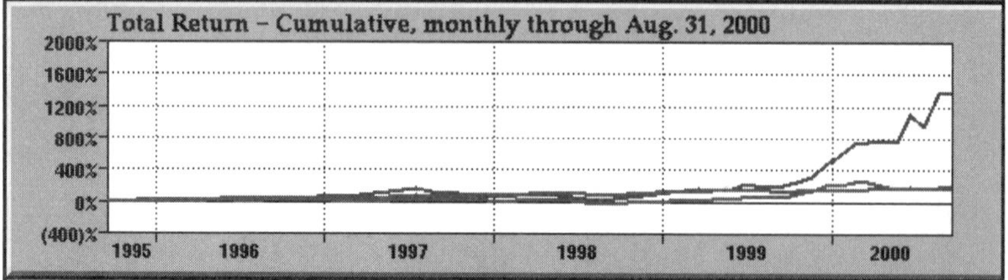

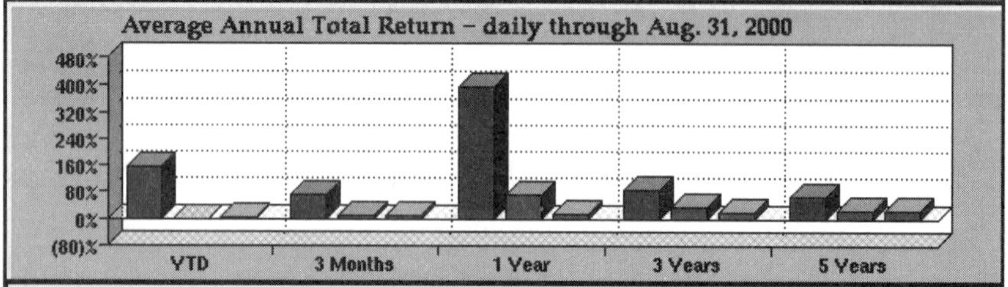

SELECTED INCOME STATEMENT AND BALANCE SHEET ITEMS

INCOME STATEMENT	12/29/95	12/31/96	12/31/97	12/31/98	12/31/99	1 Year
Sales/Revenues	5,313.1	3,651.6	4,089.7	3,484.0	4,297.2	5,569.2
Cost of Goods Sold	3,008.6	1,970.8	2,084.6	1,855.9	2,320.2	2,933.6
Pre-tax Margin (%)	2.00	13.90	16.30	13.20	15.50	14.23
Operating Income	586.90	561.60	761.40	548.50	631.20	915.00
Net Income before Extras	(50.800)	342.90	439.80	327.50	476.90	494.70
Reported Net Income	(50.800)	175.60	439.80	394.00	481.70	499.50
Depreciation & Amortization	377.40	288.10	321.60	298.00	380.70	493.00
EPS from Net Income (Primary)	(0.230)	0.760	1.920	1.710	1.980	1.920
EPS from Net Income (Fully Diluted)	(0.230)	0.780	1.850	1.670	1.930	1.880
Dividend per Common Share	0.605	0.605	0.720	0.720	0.720	0.720
Dividend Yield (%)	2.25	1.56	1.94	1.60	0.56	0.27
Payout Ratio	N.A.	0.80	0.38	0.42	0.36	0.38
BALANCE SHEET						
ASSETS						
Cash & Cash Equivalents	214.90	223.20	101.30	45.400	253.40	
Inventories	467.80	498.50	564.70	458.70	525.30	
Total Current Assets	1,834.3	1,418.7	1,424.2	1,310.3	1,782.5	
Total Assets	5,987.1	4,321.3	4,811.4	4,981.9	6,012.2	
LIABILITIES & EQUITY						
Short Term Debt	146.00	53.900	215.00	204.60	418.50	
Long Term Debt	1,393.0	1,208.5	1,134.1	998.30	1,288.7	
Total Liabilities	3,860.2	3,338.0	3,545.1	3,458.4	3,771.5	
Shares Outstanding	229.800	228.700	231.600	231.500	245.400	
Common Stockholder Equity	2,103.0	961.10	1,246.5	1,505.6	2,227.2	
Total Stockholder Equity	2,126.9	983.30	1,266.3	1,523.5	2,240.7	

Note: Figures in Millions of $ except: per share items, margins, yields, and ratios.

Source: Tradeline.Com, a Platinum Equity Holdings Company

CYPRESS SEMICONDUCTOR

Margarita Perez

Fortaleza Asset Management

Company Background

Cypress Semiconductor makes memory and logic chips (or semiconductors) primarily for the PC market, but is also involved in the telecommunications and instrumentation markets. I like how the company has successfully turned a commodity-type product into a higher-margin item. It has come a long way since 1995, when most of its products were sold into the PC market. In fact, back then PC sales accounted for 65 percent of total revenue. Now, almost 75 percent of Cypress Semiconductor's revenue comes from the telecommunications market, which is a much higher margin business.

One of the company's hottest products is in the SRAM area. SRAM is an acronym for standard random access memory, which is part of the memory chip. The specific product put out by Cypress is referred to as MoBL SRAM. MoBL stands for more battery life. This product is sold into the wireless telecommunications market. It means that customers can get longer talk and standby times thanks to this chip.

Cypress makes more than 400 integrated circuit products in all. Its customers include many blue chip computer, electronics, and telecomunications equipment manufacturers, such as Alcatel, Intel, Cisco, Motorola, Lucent, and Nortel Networks.

Reason for Recommendation

In this current market environment, I'm looking for companies with pricing power. Cypress definitely has this. The company has been increasing prices on its SRAM products. Demand is high, and supply is pretty tight. That's a great place to be. More importantly, I expect this to continue into 2001.

Biggest Risks

Some people still think of this as a company that's heavy into commodities, which used to be true. That has kept some people out of the stock. In addition, the semiconductor industry does go up and down with the economic cycles. Right now, demand is great. But if the economy slows down, this could be an issue. Actually, the company may be more isolated from the economy than others in the tech sector, because it serves the wireless telecommunications market. Growth in this area is very robust. I've heard analysts talk about growth rates of 45 percent-plus through 2003.

Bottom Line

Cypress Semiconductor is expected to earn about $2.35 per share in 2001. Based on this, I think the stock can get to at least $70 per share by the end of the year. Yes, there is competition in this space, but there seems to be plenty of business for everyone. Cypress has its own manufacturing capacity, unlike many of its competitors, with facilities in Texas and Minnesota. The company also has testing facilities in the Philippines. It looks like Cypress has plenty of growth ahead of it.

Contact Information: Cypress Semiconductor Corporation
3901 North 1st Street
San Jose, CA 95134-1599
408-943-02600
<www.cypress.com>

BONUS PICK FOR 2001

POWERWAVE TECHNOLOGIES

Symbol: PWAV
Exchange: Nasdaq

Powerwave is a company that manufactures and markets ultralinear radio frequency power amplifiers primarily for the wireless communications market. These devices increase the signal strength of wireless transmissions while reducing interference. The company controls about 30 percent of what is a pretty captive market. Demand for wireless usage is exploding and is expected to double in the next year. Even if Powerwave simply keeps its current market share, it will be a big player. We're talking about a market that should grow to $30 billion by 2003. If the company can just gain a few percentage points in market share, that will be significant. I'm also impressed with how well Powerwave has transitioned its business. At one point, 90 percent of the company's business came from Korea. Now about 65 percent of its client base is in North America.

Cypress Semiconductor Corp Delaware

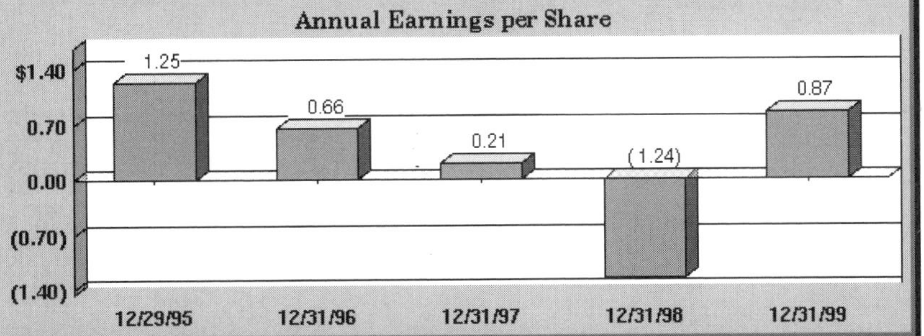

Cypress Semiconductor Corp Delaware

Symbol: CY Market/Exchange: NYSE

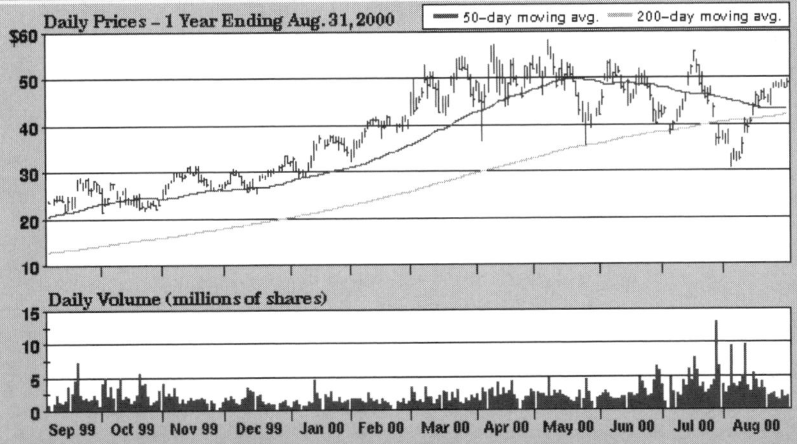

Latest Pricing Data (as of Aug. 31, 2000)

Close (net change):	$49	(+1 1/4)
Day High & Low:	$49 1/2	$47 11/16
Volume & Avg. Volume:	2,006,000	2,406,213
52-Week High:	$58	May 5, 2000
52-Week Low:	$21 5/16	Oct. 21, 1999
Latest Dividend:	$0.00	
Ind. Ann. Div. & Yield:	$0.00	N.A.
12 Month EPS:	$1.72	June 30, 2000
P/E Ratio & Beta Factor:	28.49	1.210
Shares Outstanding:	120.609 million	
Market Value:	$5.910 billion	
Institutional Holdings:	65.90%	
Number of Institutions:	535	
Primary Market:	NYSE	

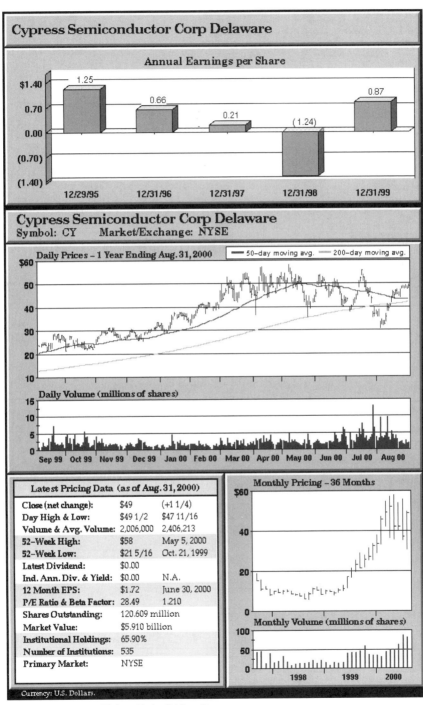

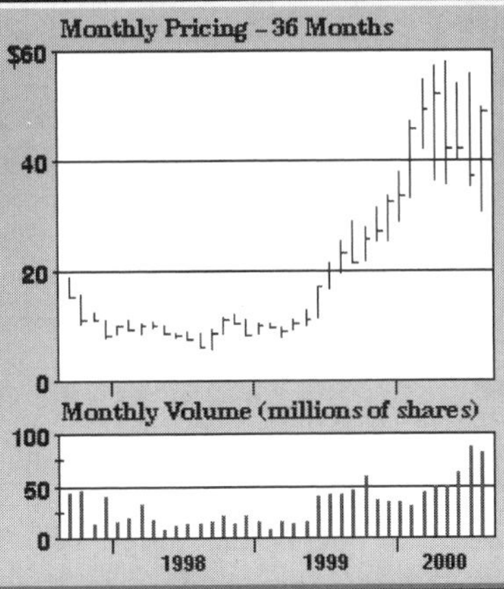

Currency: U.S. Dollars.

Source: Tradeline.Com, a Platinum Equity Holdings Company

Cypress Semiconductor Corp Delaware
Symbol : CY Market/Exchange : NYSE

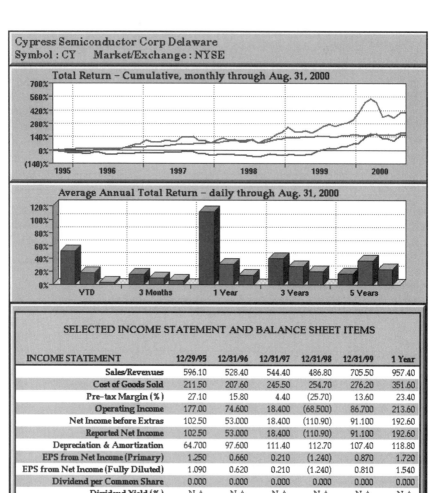

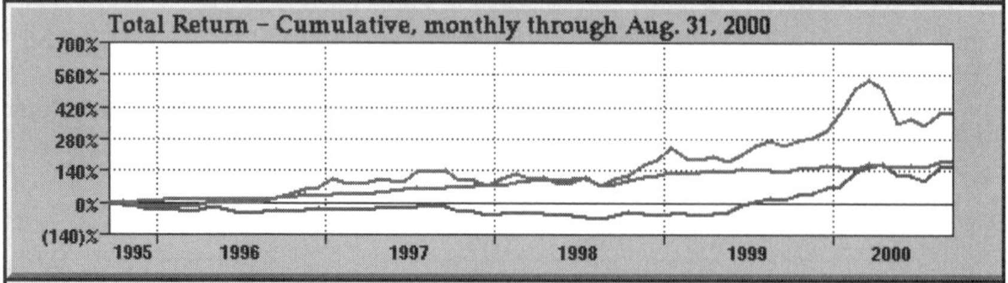

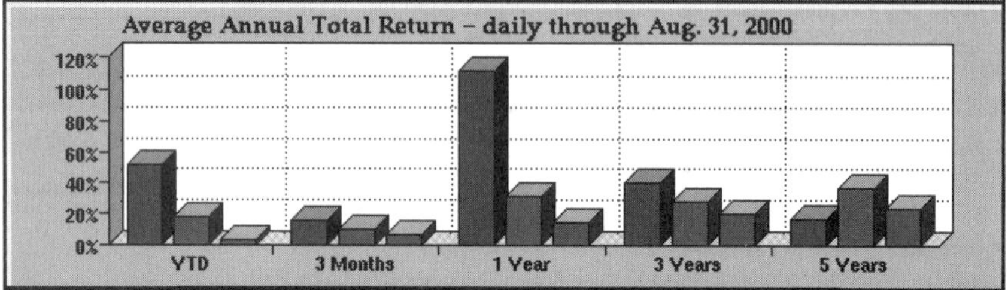

SELECTED INCOME STATEMENT AND BALANCE SHEET ITEMS

INCOME STATEMENT	12/29/95	12/31/96	12/31/97	12/31/98	12/31/99	1 Year
Sales/Revenues	596.10	528.40	544.40	486.80	705.50	957.40
Cost of Goods Sold	211.50	207.60	245.50	254.70	276.20	351.60
Pre-tax Margin (%)	27.10	15.80	4.40	(25.70)	13.60	23.40
Operating Income	177.00	74.600	18.400	(68.500)	86.700	213.60
Net Income before Extras	102.50	53.000	18.400	(110.90)	91.100	192.60
Reported Net Income	102.50	53.000	18.400	(110.90)	91.100	192.60
Depreciation & Amortization	64.700	97.600	111.40	112.70	107.40	118.80
EPS from Net Income (Primary)	1.250	0.660	0.210	(1.240)	0.870	1.720
EPS from Net Income (Fully Diluted)	1.090	0.620	0.210	(1.240)	0.810	1.540
Dividend per Common Share	0.000	0.000	0.000	0.000	0.000	0.000
Dividend Yield (%)	N.A.	N.A.	N.A.	N.A.	N.A.	N.A.
Payout Ratio	N.A.	N.A.	N.A.	N.A.	N.A.	N.A.
BALANCE SHEET						
ASSETS						
Cash & Cash Equivalents	9.500	20.100	151.70	133.80	155.00	
Inventories	29.000	53.100	76.900	58.800	89.400	
Total Current Assets	351.60	281.40	398.10	283.70	537.40	
Total Assets	750.70	794.00	956.30	756.30	1,117.2	
LIABILITIES & EQUITY						
Short Term Debt	0.000	0.000	0.000	0.000	0.000	
Long Term Debt	95.900	98.200	175.00	160.00	160.00	
Total Liabilities	278.60	283.30	312.90	267.20	419.30	
Shares Outstanding	81.501	81.098	90.684	84.859	110.516	
Common Stockholder Equity	472.10	510.70	643.50	489.10	698.00	
Total Stockholder Equity	472.10	510.70	643.50	489.10	698.00	

Note: Figures in Millions of $ except: per share items, margins, yields, and ratios.

Source: Tradeline.Com, a Platinum Equity Holdings Company

D.R. HORTON

Martin Whitman
Third Avenue Funds

Company Background

D.R. Horton is the nation's third-largest homebuilder. The company constructs high-quality, single-family homes, primarily for the entry-level and move-up markets. The majority of its operations are in metropolitan areas of the Mid-Atlantic, Midwest, Southeast, Southwest, and West regions. In fiscal 1999, the company sold 18,395 homes at an average price of $166,000. D.R. Horton also provides title agency and mortgage brokerage services, but that's a small part of its overall business.

Reason for Recommendation

This is a terrific builder with a fantastic record. The company is pretty well financed and management has done a good job running all of the various divisions. The homes D.R. Horton builds are very popular and demand is strong. Management says that as long as consumer confidence remains high, unemployment stays low, and interest rates are in the single digits, this demand should continue. Despite this, the stock is selling around book value, which is a sign to me that it's cheap. Why is the stock down? There is fear that earnings may fall short over the next year, but business is increasing and so are sales prices.

Biggest Risks

If interest rates continue to rise, that could cause the home market to cool down. I think that's one reason you've seen the shares of this stock stall. But here's the deal: You're able to buy this company around book value. (At last check, book value was $12.) Book value represents an estimate of the company's actual net assets based on generally accepted accounting principles. With a price that cheap, the long-term risk ought to be very small.

Bottom Line

I don't know what will happen with the economy. I don't even know what will happen with home sales in 2001. But what I anticipate is that the leading homebuilders, including D.R. Horton, will continue to increase their market penetration. Everything related to real estate is pretty depressed right now. This industry has really been in its own bear market. To make money with this stock, all it has to do is not get cheaper. I think D.R. Horton will do well over time. As long as the outlook doesn't get worse, which I can't imagine why it would, we should make out like bandits.

Contact Information: D.R. Horton Inc.
1901 Ascension Boulevard, Suite 100
Arlington, TX 76006
817-856-8200
<www.drhorton.com>

BONUS PICK FOR 2001

LIBERTY FINANCIAL

Symbol: L
Exchange: NYSE

Liberty Financial is an asset accumulation and management company. It provides a variety of products, including insurance and mutual funds. Among other things, the company owns Stein Roe & Farnham, which is an asset management firm that runs several mutual funds. It also owns Newport Pacific Management, Crabbe Huson, Liberty Asset Management, and Independent Financial Marketing Group, among others. This is a dirt cheap stock, largely because there has been some turmoil among the executive ranks. The mutual fund business, which Liberty is big into, is a license to steal, even when assets under management aren't growing rapidly. The profits are just great. I think one reason this stock sells for such a low price, even compared to some of the competitors, is that the common stock is 72 percent owned by Liberty Mutual Insurance Company. Because of this, there is a perception on Wall Street that it is highly unlikely the company would ever be bought out. I think the "Street" is probably wrong about that. The earnings at this company keep going up, and even if it does half as well going forward, this will be an attractive investment.

D R Horton Inc

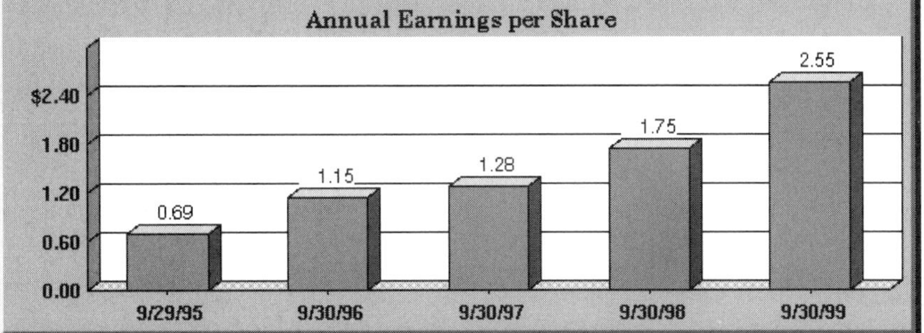

D R Horton Inc

Symbol: DHI Market/Exchange: NYSE

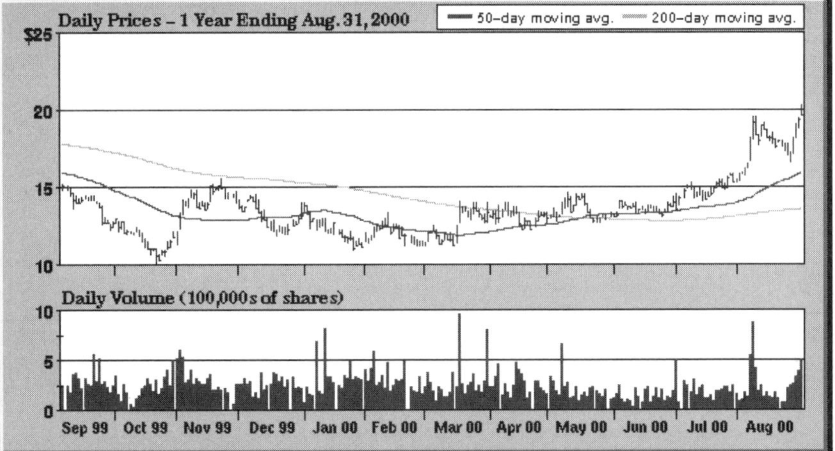

Latest Pricing Data (as of Aug. 31, 2000)

Close (net change):	$19 5/8	(+1/4)
Day High & Low:	$20 1/4	$19 1/2
Volume & Avg. Volume:	499,600	250,009
52-Week High:	$20 1/4	Aug. 31, 2000
52-Week Low:	$10	Oct. 20, 1999
Latest Dividend:	$0.04	Aug. 14, 2000
Ind. Ann. Div. & Yield:	$0.16	0.82%
12 Month EPS:	$2.86	June 30, 2000
P/E Ratio & Beta Factor:	6.86	1.165
Shares Outstanding:	61.832 million	
Market Value:	$1.213 billion	
Institutional Holdings:	63.91%	
Number of Institutions:	313	
Primary Market:	NYSE	

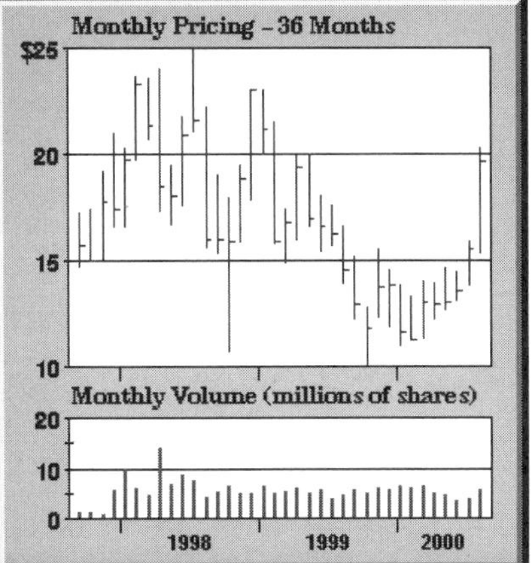

Currency: U.S. Dollars.

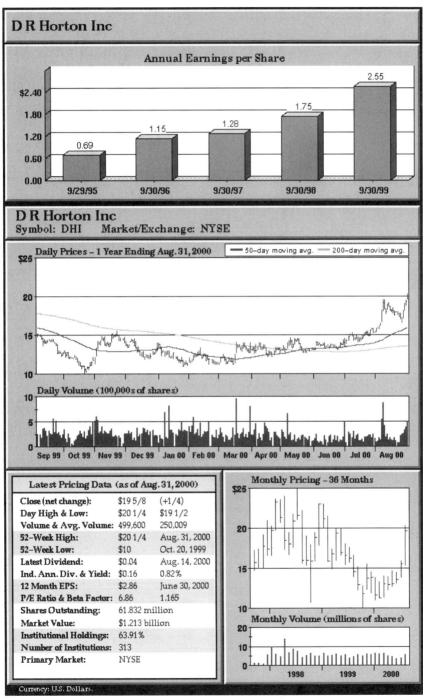

Source: Tradeline.Com, a Platinum Equity Holdings Company

D R Horton Inc

Symbol : DHI   Market/Exchange : NYSE

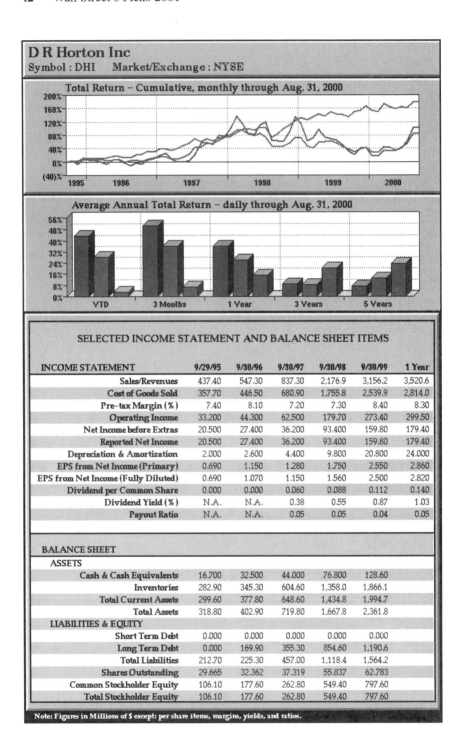

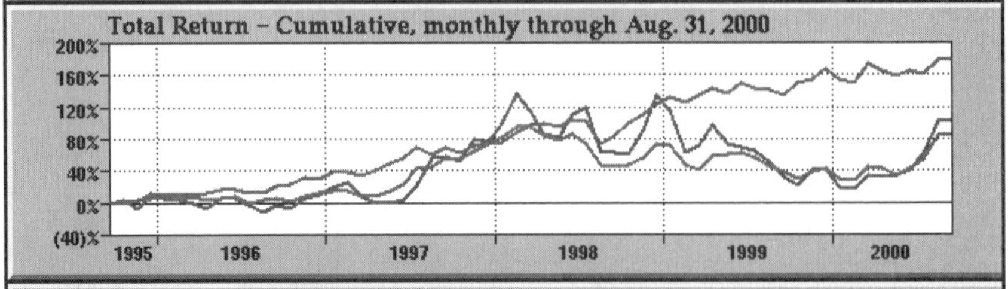

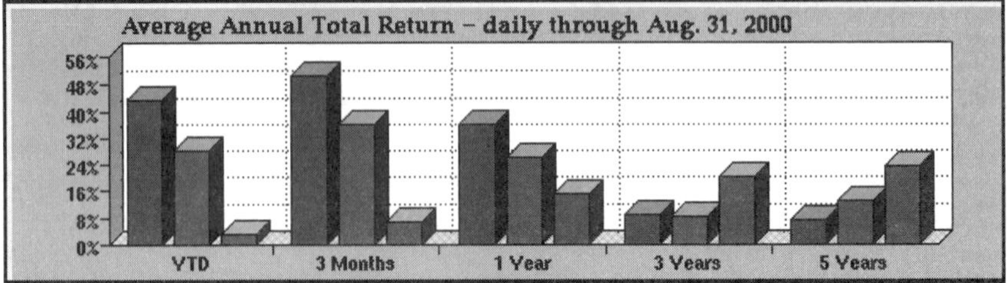

SELECTED INCOME STATEMENT AND BALANCE SHEET ITEMS

INCOME STATEMENT	9/29/95	9/30/96	9/30/97	9/30/98	9/30/99	1 Year
Sales/Revenues	437.40	547.30	837.30	2,176.9	3,156.2	3,520.6
Cost of Goods Sold	357.70	446.50	680.90	1,755.8	2,539.9	2,814.0
Pre-tax Margin (%)	7.40	8.10	7.20	7.30	8.40	8.30
Operating Income	33.200	44.300	62.500	179.70	273.40	299.50
Net Income before Extras	20.500	27.400	36.200	93.400	159.80	179.40
Reported Net Income	20.500	27.400	36.200	93.400	159.80	179.40
Depreciation & Amortization	2.000	2.600	4.400	9.800	20.800	24.000
EPS from Net Income (Primary)	0.690	1.150	1.280	1.750	2.550	2.860
EPS from Net Income (Fully Diluted)	0.690	1.070	1.150	1.560	2.500	2.820
Dividend per Common Share	0.000	0.000	0.060	0.088	0.112	0.140
Dividend Yield (%)	N.A.	N.A.	0.38	0.55	0.87	1.03
Payout Ratio	N.A.	N.A.	0.05	0.05	0.04	0.05
BALANCE SHEET						
ASSETS						
Cash & Cash Equivalents	16.700	32.500	44.000	76.800	128.60	
Inventories	282.90	345.30	604.60	1,358.0	1,866.1	
Total Current Assets	299.60	377.80	648.60	1,434.8	1,994.7	
Total Assets	318.80	402.90	719.80	1,667.8	2,361.8	
LIABILITIES & EQUITY						
Short Term Debt	0.000	0.000	0.000	0.000	0.000	
Long Term Debt	0.000	169.90	355.30	854.60	1,190.6	
Total Liabilities	212.70	225.30	457.00	1,118.4	1,564.2	
Shares Outstanding	29.665	32.362	37.319	55.837	62.783	
Common Stockholder Equity	106.10	177.60	262.80	549.40	797.60	
Total Stockholder Equity	106.10	177.60	262.80	549.40	797.60	

Note: Figures in Millions of $ except: per share items, margins, yields, and ratios.

Source: Tradeline.Com, a Platinum Equity Holdings Company

DUKE ENERGY

David Williams
US Trust

Company Background

One of the biggest appeals of Duke Energy is that it is involved in an industry in the midst of deregulation. I think the company has more growth potential than Wall Street gives it credit for. It won't happen overnight, because the benefits of deregulation are gradual. But I believe it's coming.

Duke is an integrated energy and energy services provider that offers the physical delivery and management of both electricity and natural gas. The company runs its regular utility service in North Carolina, which is growing revenue at around 5 percent a year. This is a regulated and boring business. The exciting part is the unregulated operations of the company. Duke management seems to have the wherewithal and model to be successful as either the industry deregulates itself or the government deregulates the industry.

Reason for Recommendation

I always like to compare one industry participant with another and give the poorer performing of the two stocks the same multiple as the better performer. If you take a company like Enron, which does wholesale energy marketing—the deregulated part of the utility business—you'll see it has a much higher multiple than Duke. Duke is also involved in deregulated wholesale marketing. My sense is that Duke has the ability to achieve this same kind of multiple appreciation.

Biggest Risks

One risk is that Duke is essentially getting into a new business, although it has been gearing up for this for a number a years. Still, it's essentially a different business. Deregulation is often difficult for huge monopolistic companies like this. Think back to what happened with AT&T and the airlines when they were first deregulated. These companies are, for the most part, run by bureaucrats who don't have the mind-set to be competitive and earn a high rate of return on invested capital. That's something you have to learn, and it's a risk that Duke management will continue to work as if they are still in a regulated business. On the other hand, the stock is cheap and has a nice dividend. There is a risk of execution, but I don't think the stock itself is particularly risky. If they don't do well at growing the unregulated part of the business, Duke will probably remain a number-three player, as it is now.

Bottom Line

Right now, Duke trades for around 13 times earnings. I think it could sell for at least 20 times earnings off the top, and that's assuming it doesn't even achieve the higher growth I foresee. There are definitely some stodgy utility stocks out there, but I don't believe this is one of them. Duke is a cut above your local utility. It has a game plan in place to be competitive, to take market share, and to really grow its business.

Contact Information: Duke Energy Corporation
526 South Church Street
Charlotte, NC 28202
704-594-6200
<www.duke-energy.com>

BONUS PICK FOR 2001

AT&T

Symbol: T
Exchange: NYSE

AT&T is a sum of the parts business. It has everything I look for in a company: good management, a vibrant industry, and solid growth prospects. The company is essentially in three separate businesses: long distance, wireless, and broadband. I don't think people give AT&T enough credit for its ability to execute and refocus itself away from the long distance market to these other, more lucrative areas. I believe management is doing it right and over time will improve the growth rate to get a cash flow model in line with other broadband and wireless companies. It's a stock with limited downside, and a lot of upside. I think in the best of all worlds, AT&T stock should at least double from here.

Duke Energy Corp

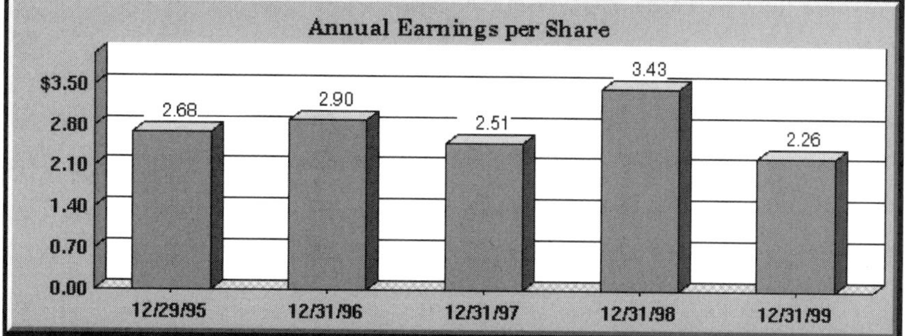

Duke Energy Corp

Symbol: DUK Market/Exchange: NYSE

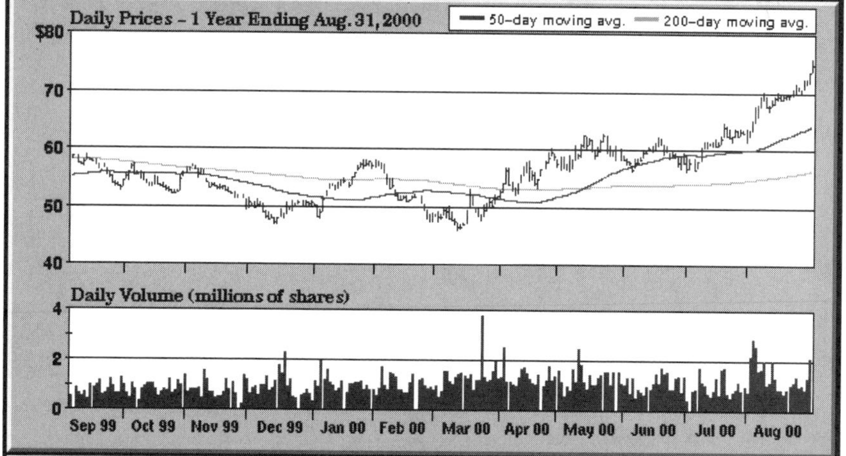

Latest Pricing Data (as of Aug. 31, 2000)

Close (net change):	$74 53/64	(+1 21/64)
Day High & Low:	$75 13/16	$73 1/2
Volume & Avg. Volume:	2,096,000	1,082,298
52-Week High:	$75 13/16	Aug. 31, 2000
52-Week Low:	$45 3/4	Mar. 10, 2000
Latest Dividend:	$0.55	Aug. 9, 2000
Ind. Ann. Div. & Yield:	$2.20	2.94%
12 Month EPS:	$2.60	June 30, 2000
P/E Ratio & Beta Factor:	28.78	N.A.
Shares Outstanding:	368.066 million	
Market Value:	$27.542 billion	
Institutional Holdings:	59.55%	
Number of Institutions:	1191	
Primary Market:	NYSE	
Component of:	DJUA, S&P 500	

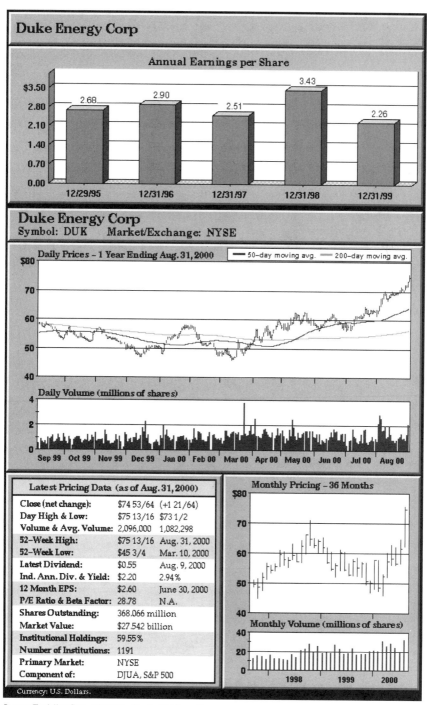

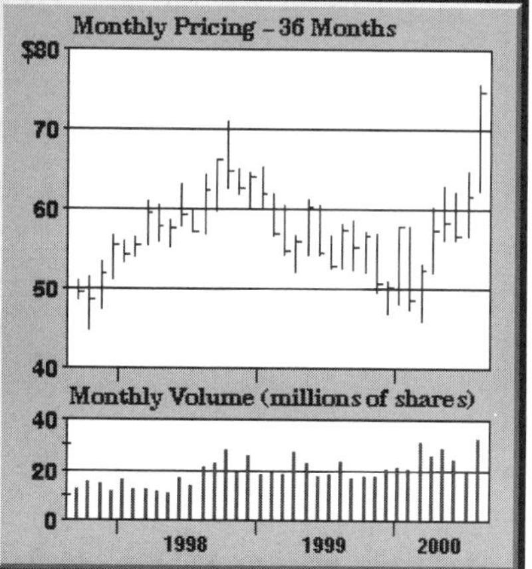

Currency: U.S. Dollars.

Source: Tradeline.Com, a Platinum Equity Holdings Company

Duke Energy Corp

Symbol : DUK Market/Exchange : NYSE

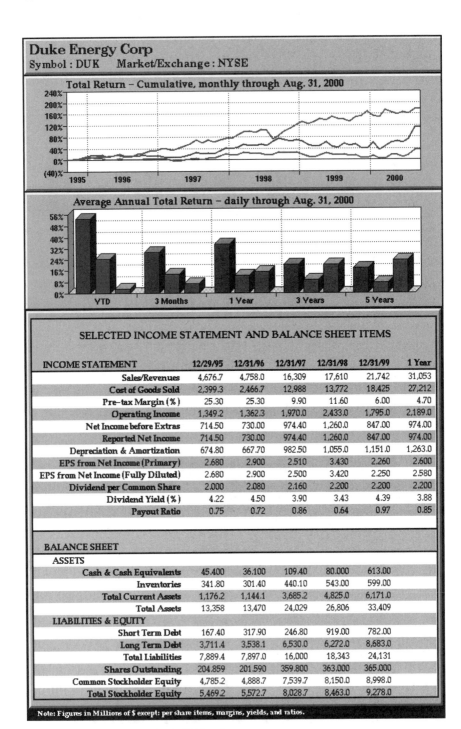

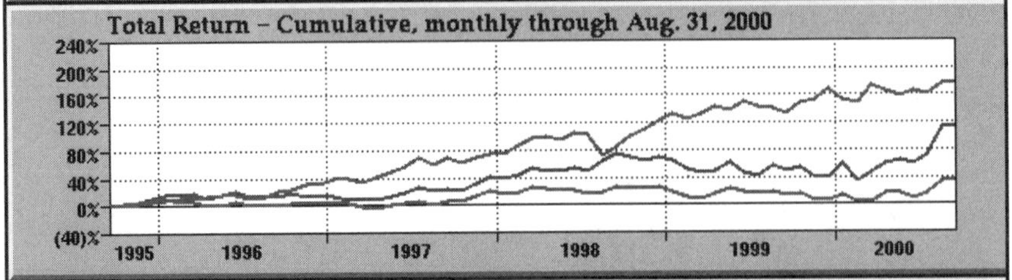

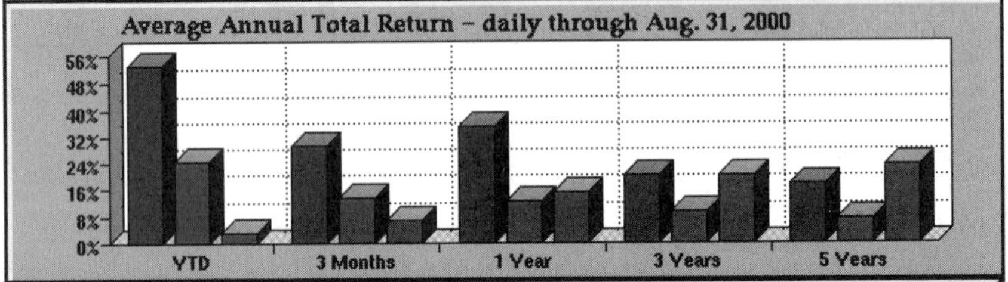

SELECTED INCOME STATEMENT AND BALANCE SHEET ITEMS

INCOME STATEMENT	12/29/95	12/31/96	12/31/97	12/31/98	12/31/99	1 Year
Sales/Revenues	4,676.7	4,758.0	16,309	17,610	21,742	31,053
Cost of Goods Sold	2,399.3	2,466.7	12,988	13,772	18,425	27,212
Pre-tax Margin (%)	25.30	25.30	9.90	11.60	6.00	4.70
Operating Income	1,349.2	1,362.3	1,970.0	2,433.0	1,795.0	2,189.0
Net Income before Extras	714.50	730.00	974.40	1,260.0	847.00	974.00
Reported Net Income	714.50	730.00	974.40	1,260.0	847.00	974.00
Depreciation & Amortization	674.80	667.70	982.50	1,055.0	1,151.0	1,263.0
EPS from Net Income (Primary)	2.680	2.900	2.510	3.430	2.260	2.600
EPS from Net Income (Fully Diluted)	2.680	2.900	2.500	3.420	2.250	2.580
Dividend per Common Share	2.000	2.080	2.160	2.200	2.200	2.200
Dividend Yield (%)	4.22	4.50	3.90	3.43	4.39	3.88
Payout Ratio	0.75	0.72	0.86	0.64	0.97	0.85

BALANCE SHEET					
ASSETS					
Cash & Cash Equivalents	45.400	36.100	109.40	80.000	613.00
Inventories	341.80	301.40	440.10	543.00	599.00
Total Current Assets	1,176.2	1,144.1	3,685.2	4,825.0	6,171.0
Total Assets	13,358	13,470	24,029	26,806	33,409
LIABILITIES & EQUITY					
Short Term Debt	167.40	317.90	246.80	919.00	782.00
Long Term Debt	3,711.4	3,538.1	6,530.0	6,272.0	8,683.0
Total Liabilities	7,889.4	7,897.0	16,000	18,343	24,131
Shares Outstanding	204.859	201.590	359.800	363.000	365.000
Common Stockholder Equity	4,785.2	4,888.7	7,539.7	8,150.0	8,998.0
Total Stockholder Equity	5,469.2	5,572.7	8,028.7	8,463.0	9,278.0

Note: Figures in Millions of $ except: per share items, margins, yields, and ratios.

Source: Tradeline.Com, a Platinum Equity Holdings Company

GENERAL ELECTRIC

Robert Stovall
Prudential Securities

Company Background

General Electric (GE) is the only stock among the original Dow 30 that's still in the index, going back more than 100 years. This is a huge company that continues to grow earnings year after year by at least 15 percent. The company is involved in a number of industries, including manufacturing, technology, and services. GE has operations in aircraft engines, appliances, capital services, lighting, plastics, information services, electrical distribution, power, motors, and transportation. GE also owns the National Broadcasting Company (NBC). Despite this diversity, GE has always managed to have a collegiate style of management where all of the various regents seem to communicate and share goals well.

The company also pays a dividend, which it increased by 17 percent recently. That's unusual these days because most companies don't consider the dividend to be important anymore.

Reason for Recommendation

I believe that GE should be thought of as a stock that can deliver two additional sources of growth in the new economy: as a provider of e-business conversion software and services, and as one of the first companies to leverage e-business across an exceptional $125 to $130 billion base. Going into 2001, GE appears poised to experience a whole new wave of accelerated growth. It is one of the strongest magnets for intellectual capital, has one of the best work cultures, and continues to implement the most capital-efficient ways to conduct business. The company is also buying back stock at an impressive rate.

Biggest Risks

As most people know, CEO Jack Welch has announced he is retiring in early 2001. One risk is that the new management regime won't be as successful at running this mammoth company as Welch was. There's also the possibility that Wall Street won't receive the transition well. Furthermore, anytime you have a company this diversified, you run the risk that there will be too many egos and differences to keep things running smoothly. GE is really one of the only companies to be this successful running such a diversified operation.

Bottom Line

I estimate that GE will earn around $4.35 per share in 2001, and expect revenues to grow by 12 to 17 percent going forward. This is one of those stocks that I think belongs in almost every portfolio.

Contact Information: General Electric Company
3135 Easton Turnpike
Fairfield, CT 06431
203-373-2211
<www.ge.com>

BONUS PICK FOR 2001

GENERAL DYNAMICS

Symbol: GD
Exchange: NYSE

General Dynamics is the fourth-largest U.S. defense contractor. It produces main battle tanks, nuclear submarines, business jets, and information technology products and services. The company produces core products for the Army and Navy. It has also entered the business jet market by purchasing Gulfstream. This diverse business base should yield impressive results going forward. General Dynamics has been out of favor lately, largely because some of its prime competitors have experienced various negative catalysts. But I don't think General Dynamics faces these same problems. In addition, the company's aerospace division is being driven by manufacturing process optimization, which will be a significant source of future savings and should help drive operating margins above 20 percent by 2001. Plus, the company is getting new orders from other countries, including contracts to build battle tanks for Saudi Arabia, Greece, and Turkey.

General Electric Co

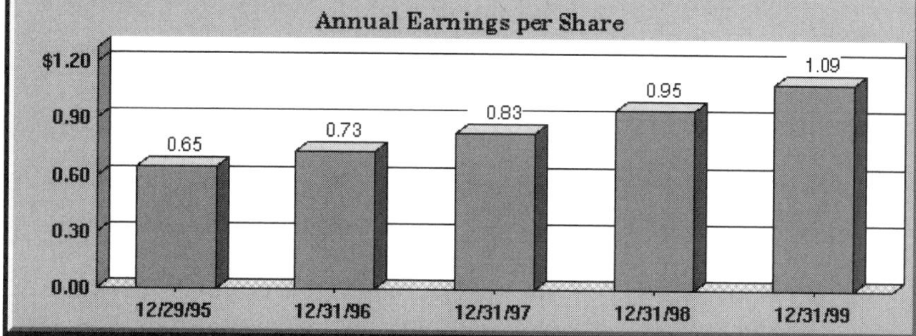

General Electric Co

Symbol: GE Market/Exchange: NYSE

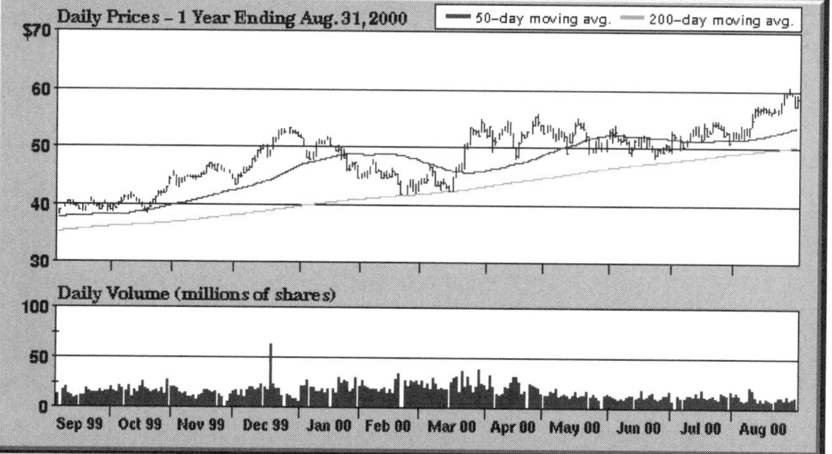

Latest Pricing Data (as of Aug. 31, 2000)		
Close (net change):	$58 45/64	(+1 13/64)
Day High & Low:	$59 5/16	$57 3/16
Volume & Avg. Volume:	11,900,000	16,667,163
52-Week High:	$60 1/2	Aug. 28, 2000
52-Week Low:	$37 51/64	Sep. 3, 1999
Latest Dividend:	$0.14	July 5, 2000
Ind. Ann. Div. & Yield:	$0.55	0.93%
12 Month EPS:	$1.18	June 30, 2000
P/E Ratio & Beta Factor:	49.75	1.231
Shares Outstanding:	9.902 billion	
Market Value:	$581.254 billion	
Institutional Holdings:	130.62%	
Number of Institutions:	3023	
Primary Market:	NYSE	
Component of:	DJIA, S&P 500	

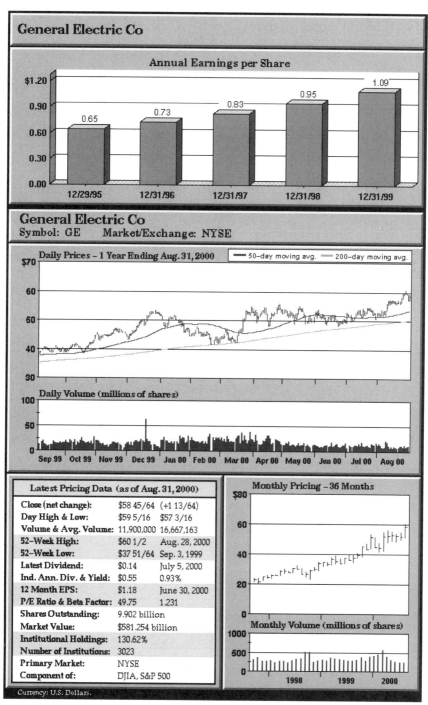

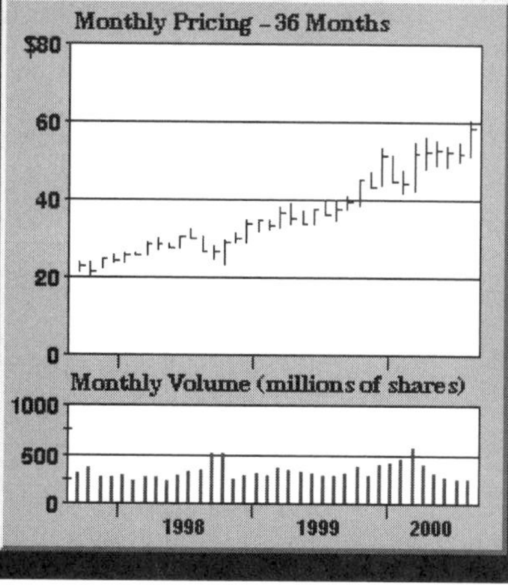

Currency: U.S. Dollars.

Source: Tradeline.Com, a Platinum Equity Holdings Company

General Electric Co

Symbol : GE   Market/Exchange : NYSE

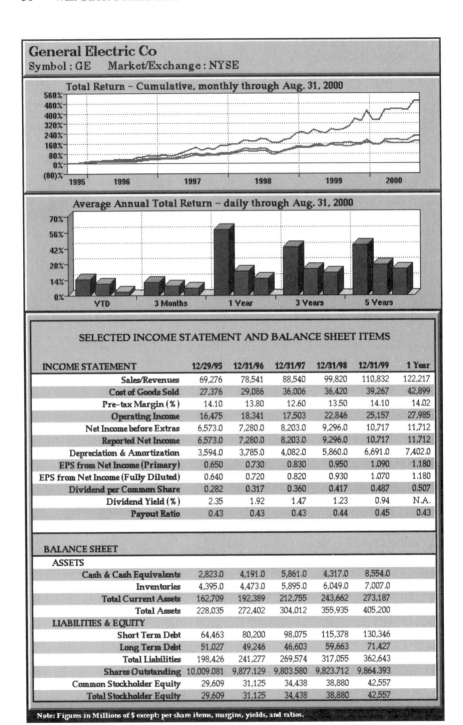

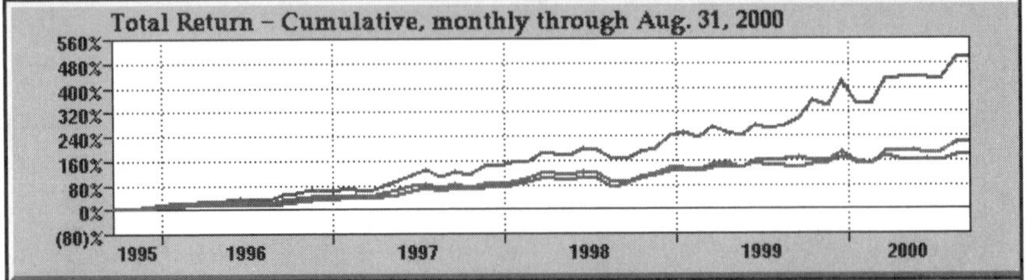

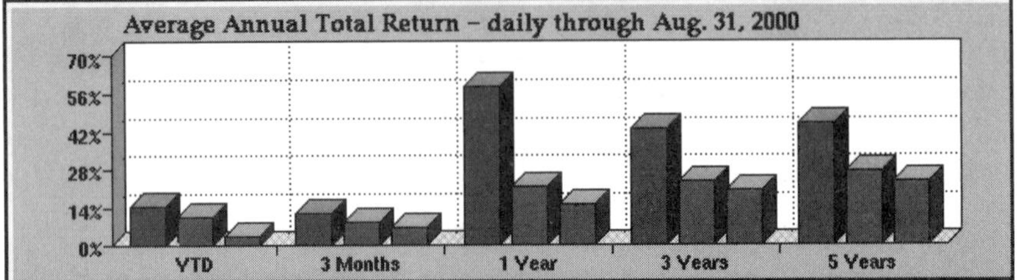

SELECTED INCOME STATEMENT AND BALANCE SHEET ITEMS

INCOME STATEMENT	12/29/95	12/31/96	12/31/97	12/31/98	12/31/99	1 Year
Sales/Revenues	69,276	78,541	88,540	99,820	110,832	122,217
Cost of Goods Sold	27,376	29,086	36,006	36,420	39,267	42,899
Pre-tax Margin (%)	14.10	13.80	12.60	13.50	14.10	14.02
Operating Income	16,475	18,341	17,503	22,846	25,157	27,985
Net Income before Extras	6,573.0	7,280.0	8,203.0	9,296.0	10,717	11,712
Reported Net Income	6,573.0	7,280.0	8,203.0	9,296.0	10,717	11,712
Depreciation & Amortization	3,594.0	3,785.0	4,082.0	5,860.0	6,691.0	7,402.0
EPS from Net Income (Primary)	0.650	0.730	0.830	0.950	1.090	1.180
EPS from Net Income (Fully Diluted)	0.640	0.720	0.820	0.930	1.070	1.180
Dividend per Common Share	0.282	0.317	0.360	0.417	0.487	0.507
Dividend Yield (%)	2.35	1.92	1.47	1.23	0.94	N.A.
Payout Ratio	0.43	0.43	0.43	0.44	0.45	0.43

BALANCE SHEET					
ASSETS					
Cash & Cash Equivalents	2,823.0	4,191.0	5,861.0	4,317.0	8,554.0
Inventories	4,395.0	4,473.0	5,895.0	6,049.0	7,007.0
Total Current Assets	162,709	192,389	212,755	243,662	273,187
Total Assets	228,035	272,402	304,012	355,935	405,200
LIABILITIES & EQUITY					
Short Term Debt	64,463	80,200	98,075	115,378	130,346
Long Term Debt	51,027	49,246	46,603	59,663	71,427
Total Liabilities	198,426	241,277	269,574	317,055	362,643
Shares Outstanding	10,009.081	9,877.129	9,803.580	9,823.712	9,864.393
Common Stockholder Equity	29,609	31,125	34,438	38,880	42,557
Total Stockholder Equity	29,609	31,125	34,438	38,880	42,557

Note: Figures in Millions of $ except: per share items, margins, yields, and ratios.

Source: Tradeline.Com, a Platinum Equity Holdings Company

HARTE-HANKS

Elizabeth Dater
Warburg Pincus Asset Management

Company Background

Harte-Hanks is a media company. It offers one-stop shopping for direct marketing services. This is a company that has been overlooked in the marketplace, but will benefit significantly from the integration of Internet technology with database marketing.

Harte-Hanks uses various technologies that enable its clients to identify and influence customers. It is big in three areas: First is marketing services, which includes labeling, inserting, and fulfillment. I believe this will be a very big area for the Internet down the road. Second is database marketing, which includes market research and development, plus management of data and modeling. The third area is response management. Harte-Hanks provides call center consulting, and does Web site design and management. The company is also involved with media planning, particularly in the interactive area, and publishes weekly shoppers in some parts of California and Florida, including the popular *Pennysaver.*

Harte-Hanks used to be primarily a newspaper company. Now, however, 67 percent of its business comes from direct marketing, with only about 26 percent from the shoppers. The company has a very consistent record of revenue growth. Revenues and earnings have been growing by about 15 percent, while cash flow growth has been about 26 percent EBITDA. The company has no debt. I continue to believe it can grow sales in the low double digits and earnings above 20 percent.

Reason for Recommendation

The company's gross margins will no doubt be enhanced by the application of Internet technology. I also like the fact that Harte-Hanks has real sales and earnings, plus a strong franchise. The company can either continue to integrate backwards into Internet services, or it's possible that a large Internet company might use its inflated stock to acquire the company. If that happened, it would no doubt occur at a much higher price. This stock is certainly not being viewed by the market as an Internet company, which is why it is priced at a much lower PE multiple. I expect earnings to come in at around $1.40 per share next year, which represents growth of around 20 percent.

Biggest Risks

The biggest risk is that we have an economic slowdown in the U.S. Because direct marketing is economically sensitive, this would hurt the company. But we're talking about a company selling at less than 20 times earnings in an industry where other firms have been acquired for 35 to 50 times earnings. That gives you some price protection.

Bottom Line

I believe the strategic value of this company is around $40 a share. It has no debt, huge cash flow, and has self-financed its growth. Harte-Hanks is also positioned to benefit from the true sweet spot of the Internet.

Contact Information: Harte-Hanks, Inc.
200 Concord Plaza Drive
San Antonio, TX 78216
210-829-9000
<www.harte-hanks.com>

BONUS PICK FOR 2001

EXCITE@HOME

Symbol: ATHM
Exchange: Nasdaq

Excite@Home provides Internet services to both consumers and businesses using the cable television infrastructure. The company has distribution agreements with 16 cable partners throughout North America, which collectively reach 57 million homes. It feeds right in to the public's demand for faster Internet access. The company merged with search engine Excite in 1999. While many of Excite@Home's exclusive cable contracts will expire soon, I expect many of them to be renewed or extended. This is a very interesting asset that, if the value is not realized by the market, may be an enormous strategic acquisition for another media provider.

Harte-Hanks Inc

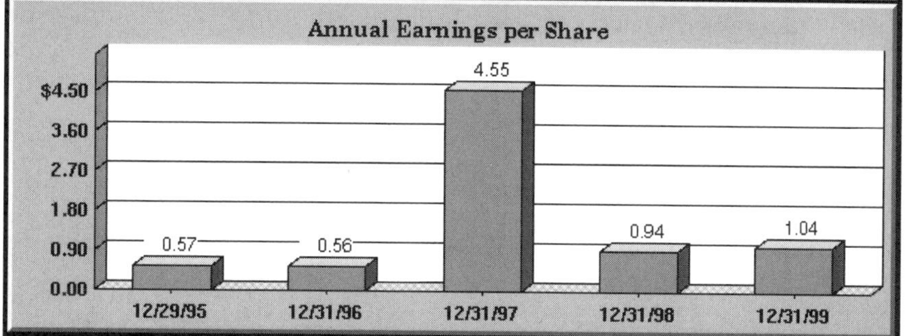

Harte-Hanks Inc

Symbol: HHS   Market/Exchange: NYSE

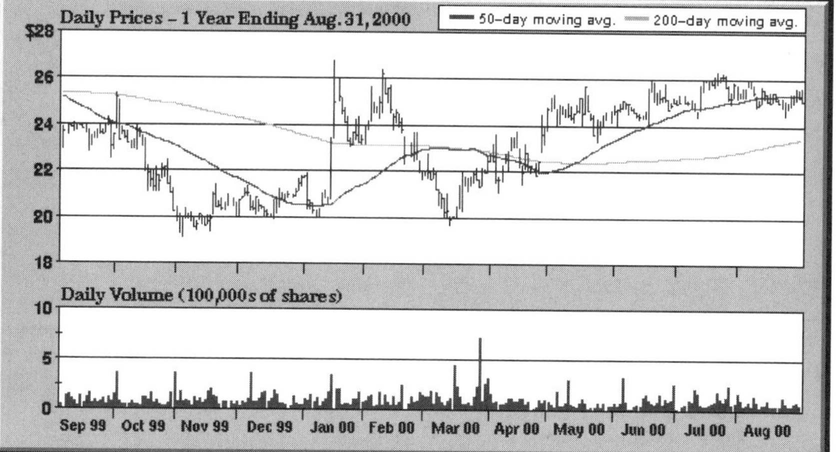

Latest Pricing Data (as of Aug. 31, 2000)		
Close (net change):	$25 1/8	(–3/16)
Day High & Low:	$25 5/8	$25 1/8
Volume & Avg. Volume:	54,000	98,467
52-Week High:	$26 3/4	Jan. 14, 2000
52-Week Low:	$19 1/16	Nov. 2, 1999
Latest Dividend:	$0.03	Aug. 30, 2000
Ind. Ann. Div. & Yield:	$0.10	0.40%
12 Month EPS:	$1.13	June 30, 2000
P/E Ratio & Beta Factor:	22.23	0.407
Shares Outstanding:	67.746 million	
Market Value:	$1.702 billion	
Institutional Holdings:	49.93%	
Number of Institutions:	272	
Primary Market:	NYSE	

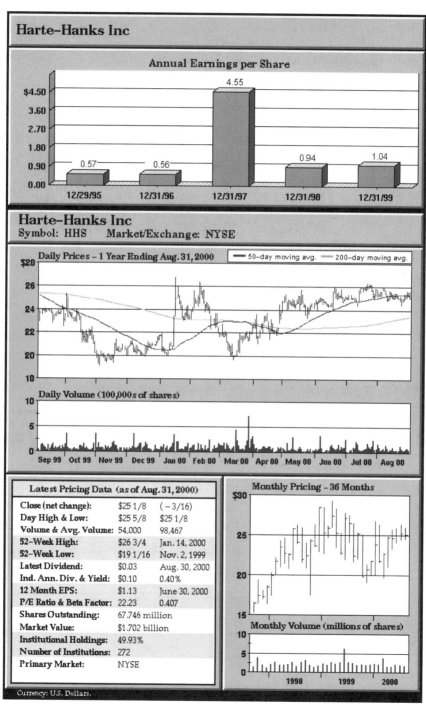

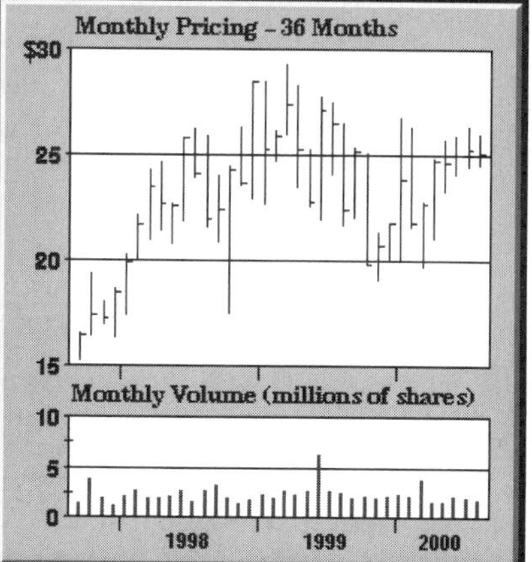

Currency: U.S. Dollars.

Source: Tradeline.Com, a Platinum Equity Holdings Company

Harte-Hanks Inc

Symbol : HHS Market/Exchange : NYSE

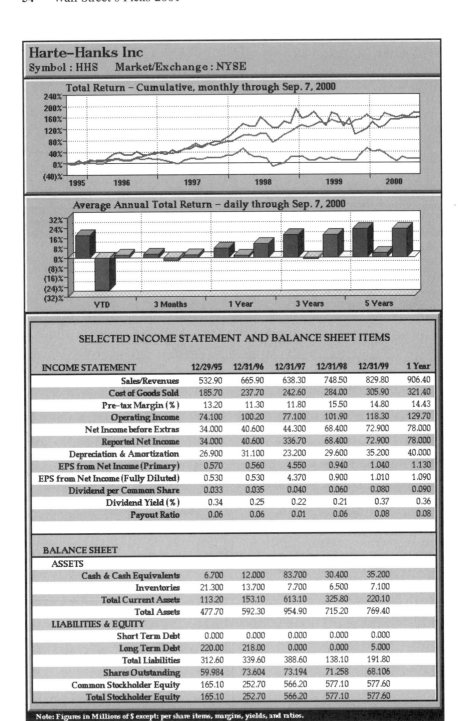

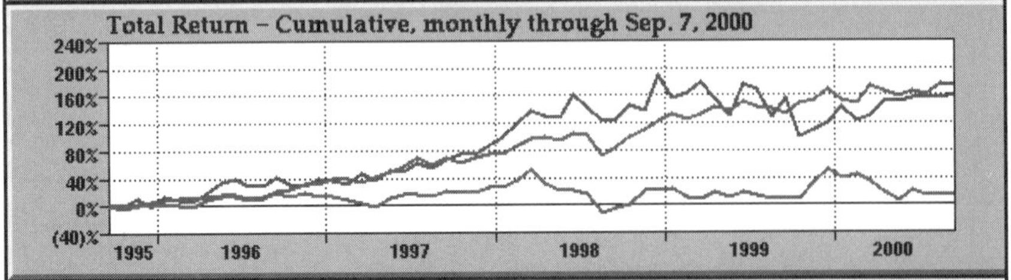

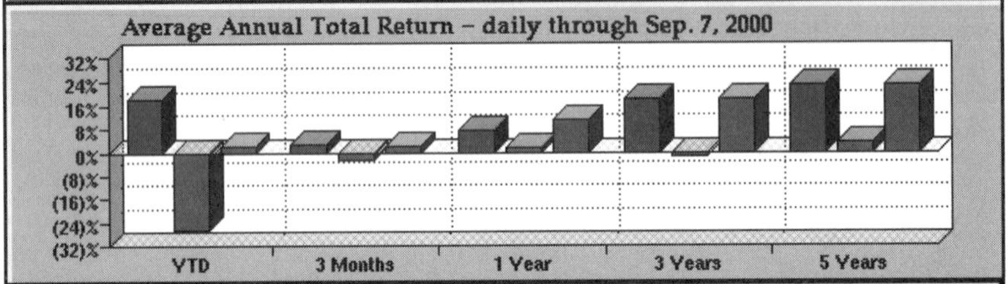

SELECTED INCOME STATEMENT AND BALANCE SHEET ITEMS

INCOME STATEMENT	12/29/95	12/31/96	12/31/97	12/31/98	12/31/99	1 Year
Sales/Revenues	532.90	665.90	638.30	748.50	829.80	906.40
Cost of Goods Sold	185.70	237.70	242.60	284.00	305.90	321.40
Pre-tax Margin (%)	13.20	11.30	11.80	15.50	14.80	14.43
Operating Income	74.100	100.20	77.100	101.90	118.30	129.70
Net Income before Extras	34.000	40.600	44.300	68.400	72.900	78.000
Reported Net Income	34.000	40.600	336.70	68.400	72.900	78.000
Depreciation & Amortization	26.900	31.100	23.200	29.600	35.200	40.000
EPS from Net Income (Primary)	0.570	0.560	4.550	0.940	1.040	1.130
EPS from Net Income (Fully Diluted)	0.530	0.530	4.370	0.900	1.010	1.090
Dividend per Common Share	0.033	0.035	0.040	0.060	0.080	0.090
Dividend Yield (%)	0.34	0.25	0.22	0.21	0.37	0.36
Payout Ratio	0.06	0.06	0.01	0.06	0.08	0.08

BALANCE SHEET					
ASSETS					
Cash & Cash Equivalents	6.700	12.000	83.700	30.400	35.200
Inventories	21.300	13.700	7.700	6.500	7.100
Total Current Assets	113.20	153.10	613.10	325.80	220.10
Total Assets	477.70	592.30	954.90	715.20	769.40
LIABILITIES & EQUITY					
Short Term Debt	0.000	0.000	0.000	0.000	0.000
Long Term Debt	220.00	218.00	0.000	0.000	5.000
Total Liabilities	312.60	339.60	388.60	138.10	191.80
Shares Outstanding	59.984	73.604	73.194	71.258	68.106
Common Stockholder Equity	165.10	252.70	566.20	577.10	577.60
Total Stockholder Equity	165.10	252.70	566.20	577.10	577.60

Note: Figures in Millions of $ except: per share items, margins, yields, and ratios.

Source: Tradeline.Com, a Platinum Equity Holdings Company

HENRY SCHEIN

William Nasgovitz
Heartland Advisors

Company Background

At one point, the stock market was absolutely in love with Henry Schein. This is a dental distributor with worldwide operations in more than 120 countries. The dental business is a growth business. But the stock dropped out of favor after missing its earnings numbers in 1999 as a result of two acquisitions. Schein had a tough time integrating these acquisitions, including systems problems, which caused the company to lose customers. But Schein is still number one in its space.

Here's the beautiful thing: Right now, the stock has a market capitalization of around $690 million, which would be considered small-cap by almost any market watcher. But the company is doing $2.3 billion in business, and should grow earnings at an annual rate of 15 percent. This is a true growth story. Schein also has its own dental practice software system, which is installed in 35,000 dental offices. In addition, it has moved into the areas of training and equipment service, which at one point were its prime competitor's main strengths. Schein markets through a combination of catalogs, telemarketing, and the Internet. Internet sales alone, at $200 million, are growing at 100 percent a year.

Reason for Recommendation

I love the valuation of this company. When you can find an industry leader selling at a fraction of both sales and its historic valuation, you've got to get excited. This company is growing at around 15 percent a year, yet trades for a PE multiple of around 9. So, unlike today's mega-cap growth favorites that sell at maybe three times their growth rate, this is a company selling at just 60 percent of its growth rate.

Biggest Risks

The opportunity risk that the stock will continue to remain out of favor is probably the biggest risk with this stock. Is Internet competition something to worry about? I don't think so. There are at least a half dozen small Internet companies trying to duplicate what Schein is doing, but I don't think they'll make it. The company does have a little more debt on the balance sheet than I normally like to see. But it has tremendous free cash flow and should be paying down debt. There is one more risk: This is still an earnings momentum market, so if this company misses its numbers again, it could get whacked. But I doubt that will happen.

Bottom Line

Shares of Henry Schein got as high as $51 and are down considerably from this price. I think you have tremendous upside potential with little risk. We're talking about an industry leader in a growing profession trading at a fraction of its true value.

Contact Information: Henry Schein, Inc.
135 Duryea Road
Melville, NY 11747
516-843-5500
<www.henryschein.com>

BONUS PICK FOR 2001

ANSYS

Symbol: ANSS
Exchange: Nasdaq

Ansys is a software company that is a leader in computerized assisted engineering. Its customers include Volvo, Intel, Motorola, Microsoft, Procter & Gamble, and DuPont. You can see it's diversified across many different industries. Ansys develops software solutions for design analysis and optimization to accelerate product time to market, improve the engineering process, and optimize product quality and safety. If somebody wants to come out with a new redesigned Bic lighter, for example, they might turn to Ansys or use its software. This company has no debt, and plenty of cash. Just like Henry Schein, it's an industry leader with a client list you can't beat, plus a superb balance sheet. Ansys should grow earnings by more than 15 percent this year and next, yet sells at a PE of only 10. When this undiscovered gem gets recognized, it should be a big winner.

Schein (Henry) Inc

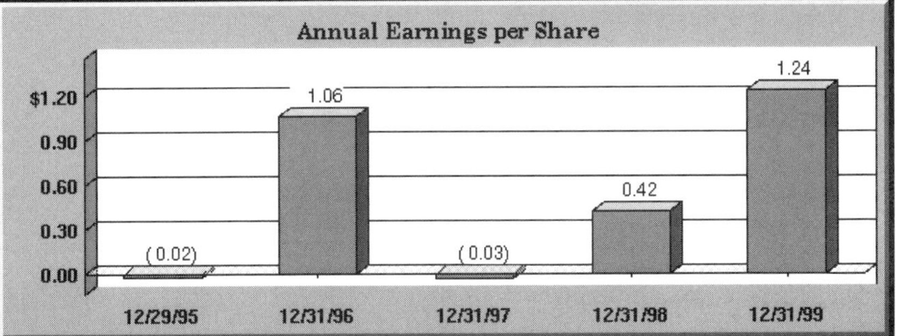

Schein (Henry) Inc

Symbol: HSIC Market/Exchange: Nasdaq NMS

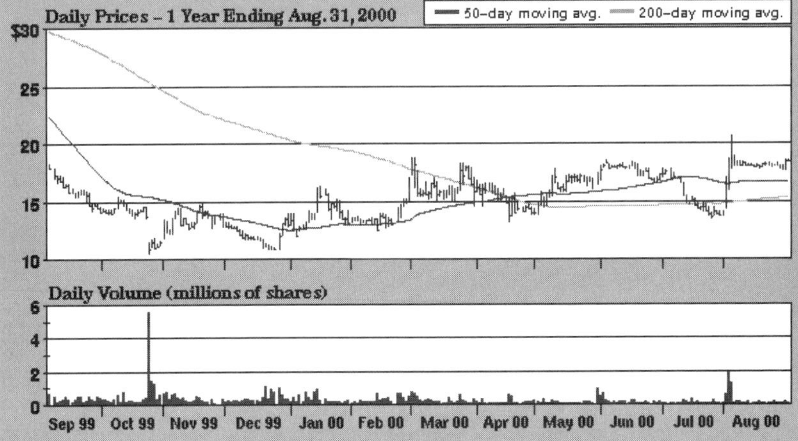

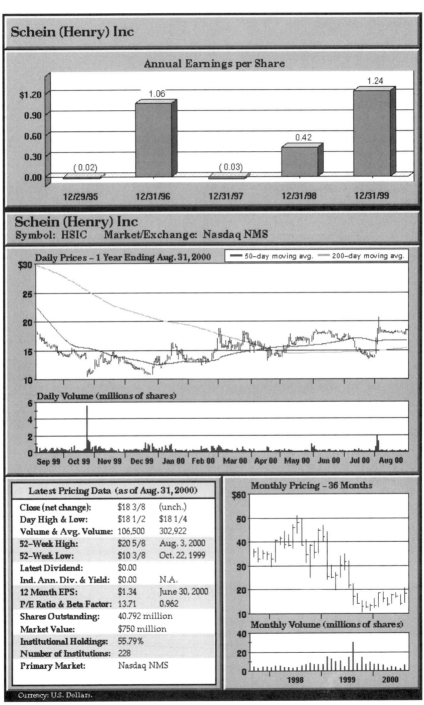

Latest Pricing Data (as of Aug. 31, 2000)

Close (net change):	$18 3/8	(unch.)
Day High & Low:	$18 1/2	$18 1/4
Volume & Avg. Volume:	106,500	302,922
52-Week High:	$20 5/8	Aug. 3, 2000
52-Week Low:	$10 3/8	Oct. 22, 1999
Latest Dividend:	$0.00	
Ind. Ann. Div. & Yield:	$0.00	N.A.
12 Month EPS:	$1.34	June 30, 2000
P/E Ratio & Beta Factor:	13.71	0.962
Shares Outstanding:	40.792 million	
Market Value:	$750 million	
Institutional Holdings:	55.79%	
Number of Institutions:	228	
Primary Market:	Nasdaq NMS	

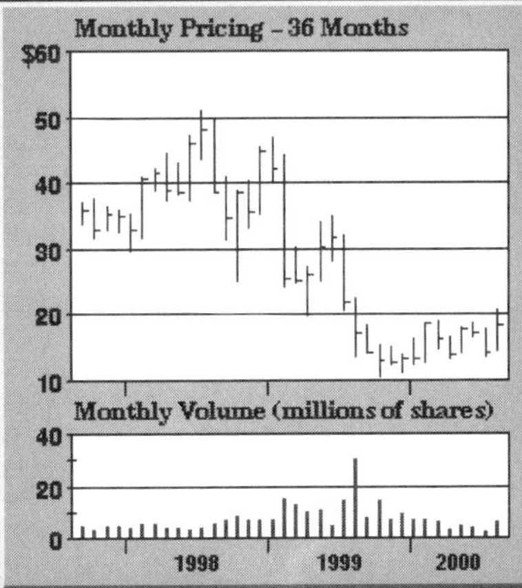

Currency: U.S. Dollars.

Source: Tradeline.Com, a Platinum Equity Holdings Company

Schein (Henry) Inc

Symbol : HSIC   Market/Exchange : Nasdaq NMS

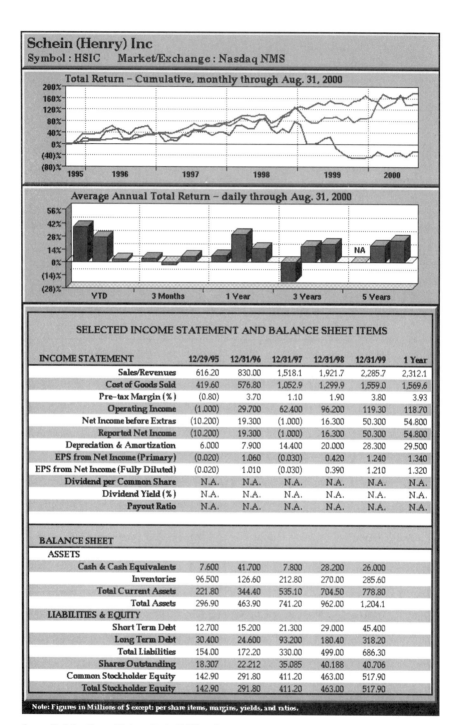

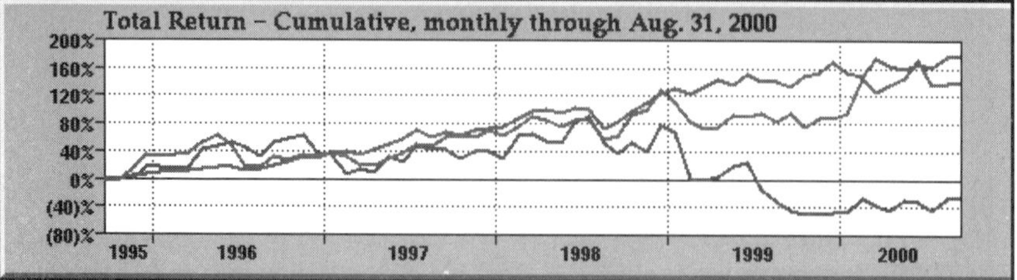

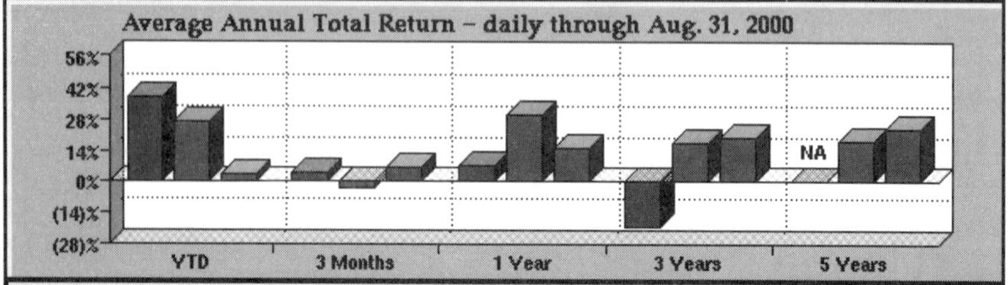

SELECTED INCOME STATEMENT AND BALANCE SHEET ITEMS

INCOME STATEMENT	12/29/95	12/31/96	12/31/97	12/31/98	12/31/99	1 Year
Sales/Revenues	616.20	830.00	1,518.1	1,921.7	2,285.7	2,312.1
Cost of Goods Sold	419.60	576.80	1,052.9	1,299.9	1,559.0	1,569.6
Pre-tax Margin (%)	(0.80)	3.70	1.10	1.90	3.80	3.93
Operating Income	(1.000)	29.700	62.400	96.200	119.30	118.70
Net Income before Extras	(10.200)	19.300	(1.000)	16.300	50.300	54.800
Reported Net Income	(10.200)	19.300	(1.000)	16.300	50.300	54.800
Depreciation & Amortization	6.000	7.900	14.400	20.000	28.300	29.500
EPS from Net Income (Primary)	(0.020)	1.060	(0.030)	0.420	1.240	1.340
EPS from Net Income (Fully Diluted)	(0.020)	1.010	(0.030)	0.390	1.210	1.320
Dividend per Common Share	N.A.	N.A.	N.A.	N.A.	N.A.	N.A.
Dividend Yield (%)	N.A.	N.A.	N.A.	N.A.	N.A.	N.A.
Payout Ratio	N.A.	N.A.	N.A.	N.A.	N.A.	N.A.
BALANCE SHEET						
ASSETS						
Cash & Cash Equivalents	7.600	41.700	7.800	28.200	26.000	
Inventories	96.500	126.60	212.80	270.00	285.60	
Total Current Assets	221.80	344.40	535.10	704.50	778.80	
Total Assets	296.90	463.90	741.20	962.00	1,204.1	
LIABILITIES & EQUITY						
Short Term Debt	12.700	15.200	21.300	29.000	45.400	
Long Term Debt	30.400	24.600	93.200	180.40	318.20	
Total Liabilities	154.00	172.20	330.00	499.00	686.30	
Shares Outstanding	18.307	22.212	35.085	40.188	40.706	
Common Stockholder Equity	142.90	291.80	411.20	463.00	517.90	
Total Stockholder Equity	142.90	291.80	411.20	463.00	517.90	

Note: Figures in Millions of $ except: per share items, margins, yields, and ratios.

Source: Tradeline.Com, a Platinum Equity Holdings Company

HEWLETT-PACKARD

Elizabeth Bramwell
Bramwell Capital Management

Company Background

When people think of computer printers, they most often think of Hewlett-Packard (HP). Though the company is a global provider of computing solutions for both business and home, what I like most is its printing businesses. In fact, printing and imaging accounted for roughly 60 percent of operating earnings in the most recent fiscal year. I believe the outlook for the printing industry is quite attractive. Buying HP is a way to participate in one of my primary investment themes—that we're moving from a world where we print things first and then distribute, to one where we distribute information electronically and then print. HP has one of the largest installed bases and stands to benefit from and drive this secular change.

Reason for Recommendation

People get a lot of information from the Internet these days, and they print much of it out. It takes a lot of ink to do this, and that's where things for HP get really interesting. People are constantly buying new ink to fill their HP printers. And, as technology improves and we have more broadband delivery, the ink used for graphics (which is ink-intensive) will increase even more. The electronic delivery of books, manuals, and other items is very favorable for the printing industry. Plus, as we go forward, the use of color and the sophistication of what is available should improve. The company is developing a whole line of printers that work off TVs and handheld devices, as well as personal computers. That's my main drive in picking this stock. One more thing: HP has an interesting Internet portfolio. It has invested in several start-ups, such as Mimeo.com. The company also just spun off its Agilent Technologies testing and measurement business, following a very successful IPO.

Biggest Risks

I think we're moving away from a PC-centric world, to one that is Internet centered. That shouldn't hurt the printer business though. Yes, there are competitors in this space, but HP has the brand name, financial strength, and investment in innovative research and development.

Bottom Line

HP is really a razor blade stock. You may not make a lot of money selling razors, but you make a ton selling the blades that go in them. The same thing is true for the printing industry. HP has about 50 percent of the ink jet market, 75 to 80 percent of the monochrome laser market, and about 70 percent of the rapidly growing and highly profitable color laser market. I expect the company to be more streamlined and focused under its new president and CEO, Carly Fiorina. If you can buy HP at roughly its forward earnings market multiple, you have a good chance of picking up a great investment.

Contact Information: Hewlett-Packard Company
3000 Hanover Street
Palo Alto, CA 94304
650-857-1501
<www.hp.com>

BONUS PICK FOR 2001

MOLEX

Symbol: MOLX (class A)
Exchange: Nasdaq

Molex is a play on globalization. It is a major participant in the connector industry, which is estimated to be a $27 billion market. Connectors are omnipresent in computers, communications, consumer goods, and automotive electronics, and Molex components are in all of these categories. Molex makes the components that go into many of the devices that we own. We may not know that they contain Molex products, but they do. The telecommunications industry, especially wireless, is booming, and accounted for 21 percent of sales during the most recent period. Computer games are also a big category. Molex products are sold around the world. Forty-one percent of sales are in Asia, 20 percent in Europe, and 39 percent in the Americas. Here's a company providing the products for building the backbone in some of the world's fastest growing industries.

Hewlett Packard Co

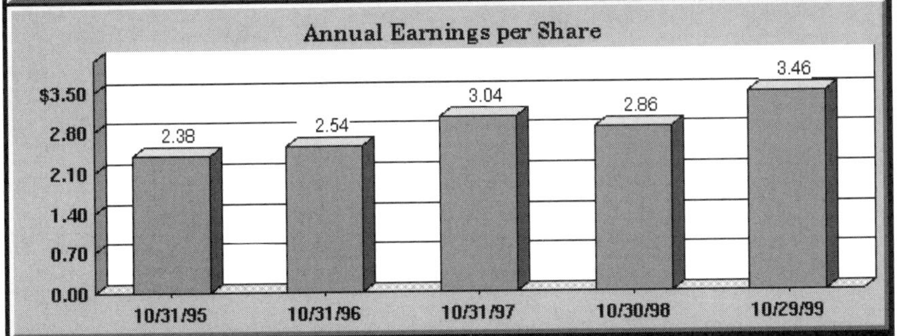

Hewlett Packard Co

Symbol: HWP Market/Exchange: NYSE

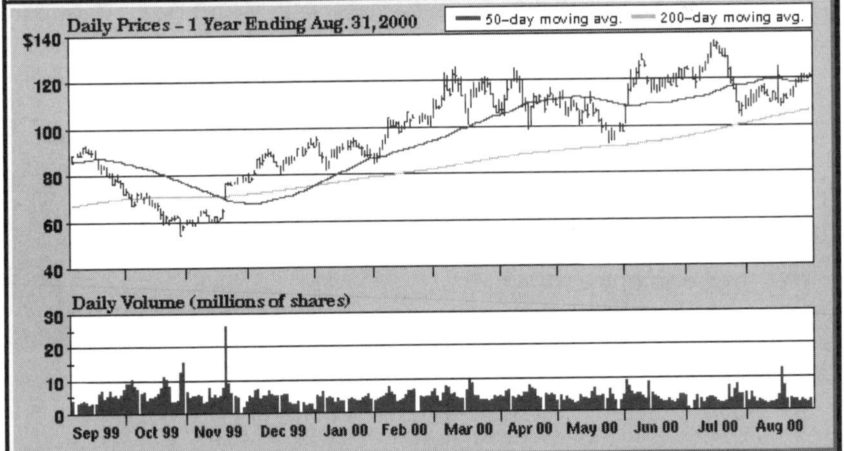

Latest Pricing Data (as of Aug. 31, 2000)		
Close (net change):	$120 41/64 (+45/64)	
Day High & Low:	$121 1/2	$119 9/16
Volume & Avg. Volume:	3,081,000	4,826,506
52-Week High:	$136 3/16	July 14, 2000
52-Week Low:	$54 17/64	Oct. 27, 1999
Latest Dividend:	$0.16	June 19, 2000
Ind. Ann. Div. & Yield:	$0.64	0.53%
12 Month EPS:	$3.59	July 31, 2000
P/E Ratio & Beta Factor:	33.60	1.157
Shares Outstanding:	997.000 million	
Market Value:	$120.279 billion	
Institutional Holdings:	55.36%	
Number of Institutions:	2302	
Primary Market:	NYSE	
Component of:	DJIA, S&P 500	

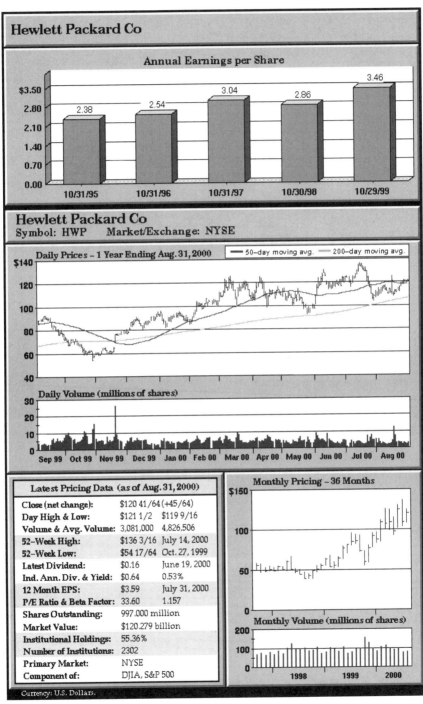

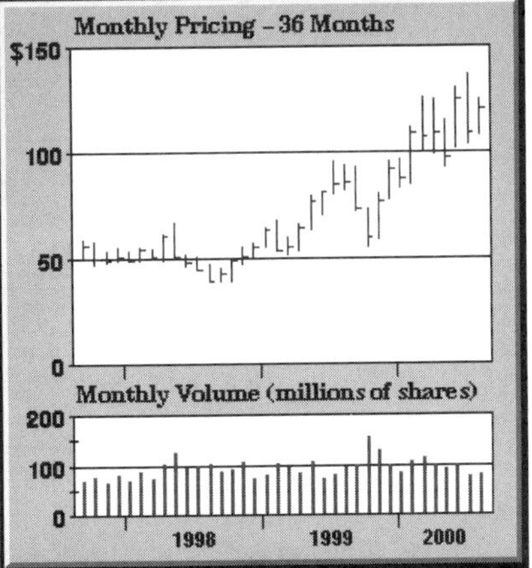

Currency: U.S. Dollars.

Source: Tradeline.Com, a Platinum Equity Holdings Company

Hewlett Packard Co

Symbol : HWP   Market/Exchange : NYSE

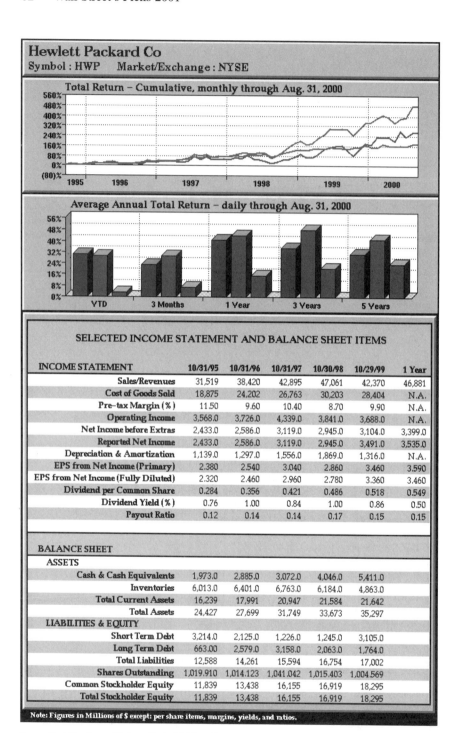

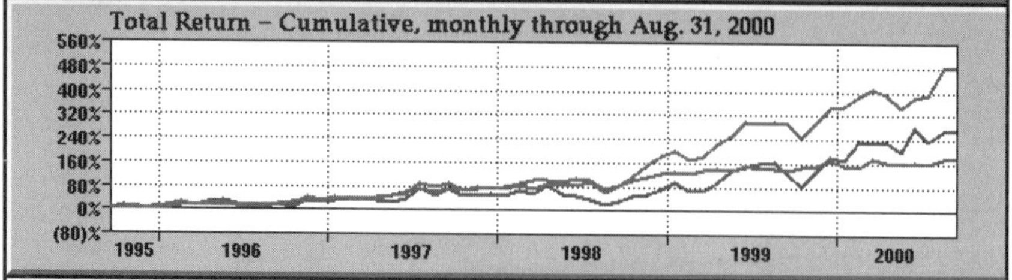

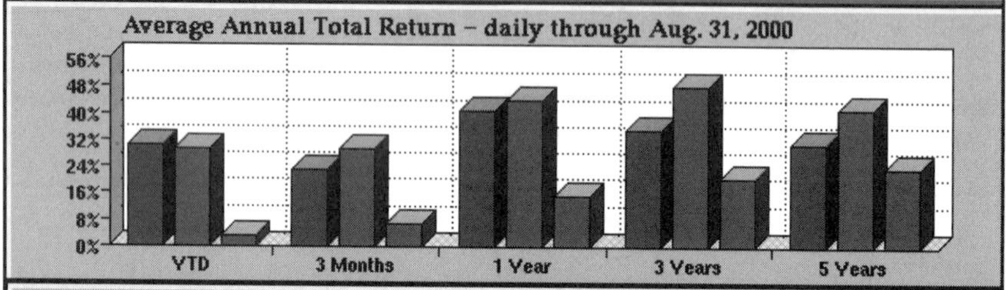

SELECTED INCOME STATEMENT AND BALANCE SHEET ITEMS

INCOME STATEMENT	10/31/95	10/31/96	10/31/97	10/30/98	10/29/99	1 Year
Sales/Revenues	31,519	38,420	42,895	47,061	42,370	46,881
Cost of Goods Sold	18,875	24,202	26,763	30,203	28,404	N.A.
Pre-tax Margin (%)	11.50	9.60	10.40	8.70	9.90	N.A.
Operating Income	3,568.0	3,726.0	4,339.0	3,841.0	3,688.0	N.A.
Net Income before Extras	2,433.0	2,586.0	3,119.0	2,945.0	3,104.0	3,399.0
Reported Net Income	2,433.0	2,586.0	3,119.0	2,945.0	3,491.0	3,535.0
Depreciation & Amortization	1,139.0	1,297.0	1,556.0	1,869.0	1,316.0	N.A.
EPS from Net Income (Primary)	2.380	2.540	3.040	2.860	3.460	3.590
EPS from Net Income (Fully Diluted)	2.320	2.460	2.960	2.780	3.360	3.460
Dividend per Common Share	0.284	0.356	0.421	0.486	0.518	0.549
Dividend Yield (%)	0.76	1.00	0.84	1.00	0.86	0.50
Payout Ratio	0.12	0.14	0.14	0.17	0.15	0.15

BALANCE SHEET					
ASSETS					
Cash & Cash Equivalents	1,973.0	2,885.0	3,072.0	4,046.0	5,411.0
Inventories	6,013.0	6,401.0	6,763.0	6,184.0	4,863.0
Total Current Assets	16,239	17,991	20,947	21,584	21,642
Total Assets	24,427	27,699	31,749	33,673	35,297
LIABILITIES & EQUITY					
Short Term Debt	3,214.0	2,125.0	1,226.0	1,245.0	3,105.0
Long Term Debt	663.00	2,579.0	3,158.0	2,063.0	1,764.0
Total Liabilities	12,588	14,261	15,594	16,754	17,002
Shares Outstanding	1,019.910	1,014.123	1,041.042	1,015.403	1,004.569
Common Stockholder Equity	11,839	13,438	16,155	16,919	18,295
Total Stockholder Equity	11,839	13,438	16,155	16,919	18,295

Note: Figures in Millions of $ except: per share items, margins, yields, and ratios.

Source: Tradeline.Com, a Platinum Equity Holdings Company

HORACE MANN EDUCATORS

Ed Walczak
Vontobel USA

Company Background

Horace Mann, headquartered in Springfield, Illionis, is a multiline insurance company that targets U.S. educators and other school employees. The sales force is basically comprised of retired teachers selling policies to employed teachers. This probably doesn't sound like a sexy industry, but it's a great franchise. In order to sell to the educational market, you must have state government approval. It's not like anyone can do it. Obviously, the best people to sell to teachers are those who have been through the system themselves and know what it's like. These retired teachers can also go back to their old buddies and make sales that way.

Horace Mann offers life, homeowners, and automobile insurance. It also sells annuities. What's more interesting is to whom it sells and who is doing the selling. Teachers are relatively conservative. They buy annuities, usually fixed-income annuities, because they are less likely to have exposure to the equity markets. Teachers also like to deal with agents face to face, instead of by phone or online.

Reason for Recommendation

In addition to the ingenious sales network, Horace Mann's policies come with higher premiums than other insurers. Teachers don't seem to mind that, because they're getting great service and supporting people they like. As a result, if you look at the history of this company, it has been like a tortoise in its dependability. It grows slowly and steadily over time. In the early days, returns on equity were in the 18 to 20 percent range. Now we're looking at growth of around 16 to 17 percent annually, which is still respectable. The sales force increases by around 5 percent a year. All sales agents must work exclusively for the company. They can't write policies for anyone else. The company has a clear, defensible, reliable, and dependable niche. This company is so good at managing its books, it has a combined ratio in the mid-90s. (A number of 100 or less is excellent.) This means the company not only makes money on the underwriting process, but also on its investments. And its retention rate varies between 89 and 94 percent.

Biggest Risks

Rightly or wrongly, most insurance stocks are perceived as being interest sensitive. When rates go up, people tend to have a knee-jerk reaction and sell off insurance stocks. Also, the market for automobile insurance policies is very competitive. Companies like Geico are growing nationally and doing a lot of advertising. Even though teachers have been less price sensitive in the past, you never know what will happen in the future. Finally, the company does sell some annuities tied to the equity market, so if stocks don't do well, these investments probably will be more difficult to sell.

Bottom Line

This is truly a predictable old business with an interesting franchise that could be an attractive takeover candidate. You can buy it right now for less than ten times trailing estimates, and once the interest rate environment improves, as it should in 2001, this stock should do very well.

Contact Information: Horace Mann Educators Corporation
1 Horace Mann Plaza
Springfield, IL 62715-0001
217-789-2500
<www.horacemann.com>

BONUS PICK FOR 2001

WATTS INDUSTRIES

Symbol: WTS
Exchange: NYSE

Watts Industries manufactures and sells an extensive line of valves for the plumbing, heating, and water quality markets. It has been a slow and steady grower for many years. In this volatile market, I like to keep my business risks low. Here's a company trading at a low PE multiple with a reliable business and steady earnings growth. The company has a strong distribution network and a nice brand name. Also, the company just struck a deal to do business with Home Depot, which should serve it well in 2001.

Horace Mann Educators Corp New

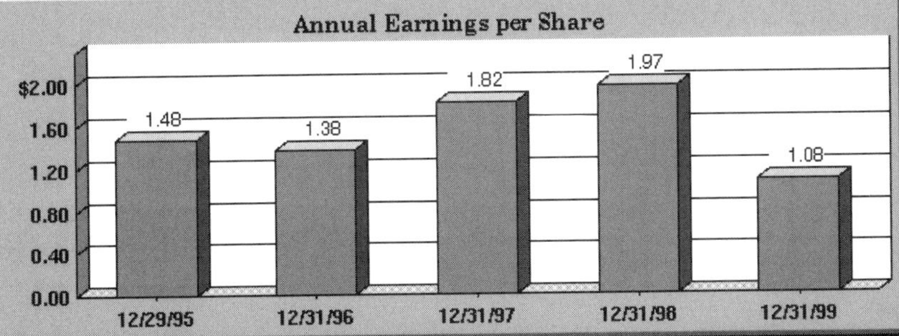

Horace Mann Educators Corp New

Symbol: HMN   Market/Exchange: NYSE

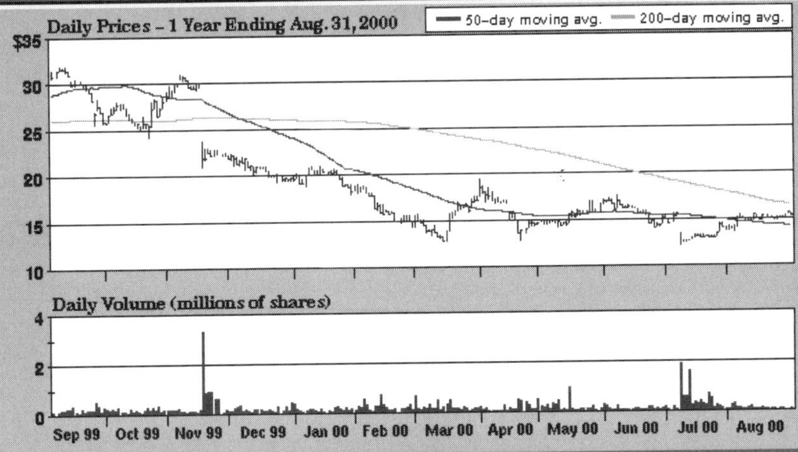

Latest Pricing Data (as of Aug. 31, 2000)		
Close (net change):	$15 1/4	(−1/4)
Day High & Low:	$15 3/8	$15 1/8
Volume & Avg. Volume:	51,200	219,857
52-Week High:	$31 15/16	Sep. 10, 1999
52-Week Low:	$12	July 7, 2000
Latest Dividend:	$0.10	June 1, 2000
Ind. Ann. Div. & Yield:	$0.42	2.75%
12 Month EPS:	$0.97	June 30, 2000
P/E Ratio & Beta Factor:	15.72	0.377
Shares Outstanding:	40.516 million	
Market Value:	$618 million	
Institutional Holdings:	87.04%	
Number of Institutions:	291	
Primary Market:	NYSE	

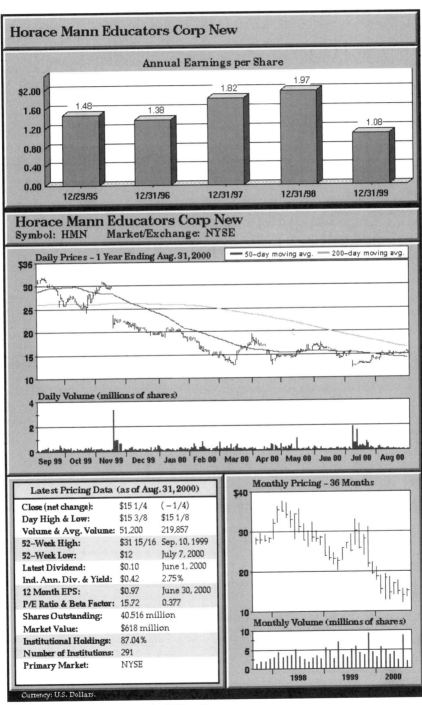

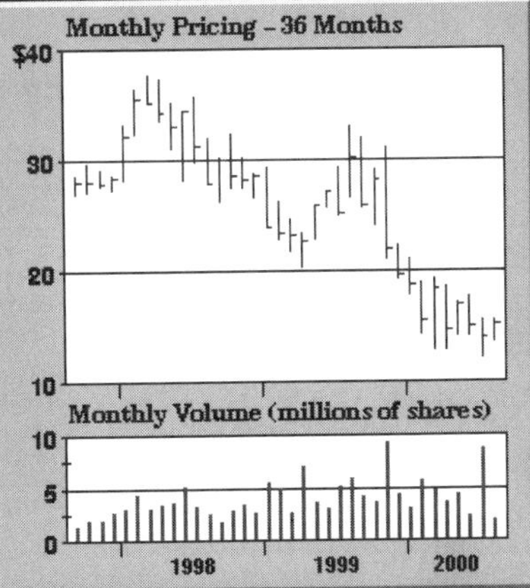

Currency: U.S. Dollars.

Source: Tradeline.Com, a Platinum Equity Holdings Company

Horace Mann Educators Corp New
Symbol : HMN Market/Exchange : NYSE

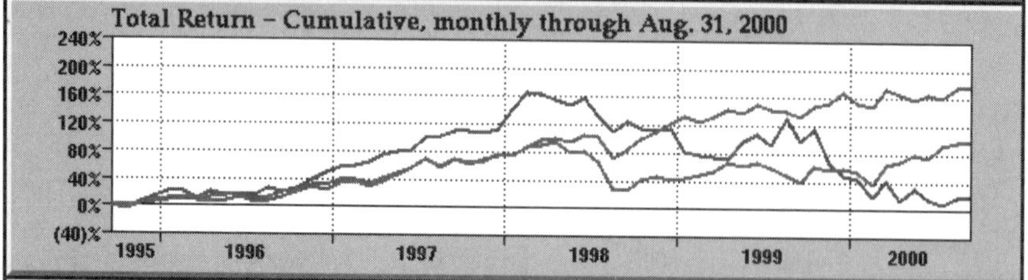

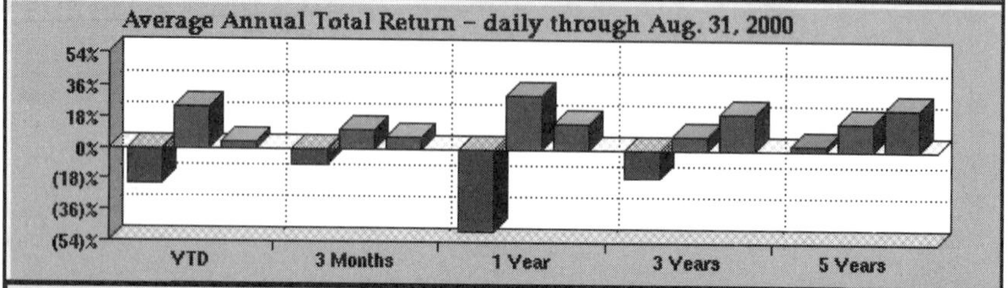

SELECTED INCOME STATEMENT AND BALANCE SHEET ITEMS

INCOME STATEMENT	12/29/95	12/31/96	12/31/97	12/31/98	12/31/99	1 Year
Sales/Revenues	740.60	703.80	747.00	779.40	775.40	785.90
Cost of Goods Sold	N.A.	N.A.	N.A.	N.A.	N.A.	N.A.
Pre-tax Margin (%)	13.70	14.30	16.00	15.00	12.00	10.90
Operating Income	113.30	111.20	129.10	126.20	103.10	95.800
Net Income before Extras	73.900	73.800	87.100	85.300	44.500	39.400
Reported Net Income	73.900	64.600	83.600	85.300	44.500	39.400
Depreciation & Amortization	N.A.	N.A.	N.A.	N.A.	N.A.	N.A.
EPS from Net Income (Primary)	1.480	1.380	1.820	1.970	1.080	0.970
EPS from Net Income (Fully Diluted)	1.390	1.360	1.800	1.950	1.070	0.960
Dividend per Common Share	0.180	0.220	0.243	0.332	0.382	0.407
Dividend Yield (%)	1.15	1.09	0.85	1.17	1.95	2.72
Payout Ratio	0.12	0.16	0.13	0.17	0.35	0.42

BALANCE SHEET					
ASSETS					
Cash & Cash Equivalents	N.A.	N.A.	N.A.	N.A.	N.A.
Inventories	N.A.	N.A.	N.A.	N.A.	N.A.
Total Current Assets	N.A.	N.A.	N.A.	N.A.	N.A.
Total Assets	3,662.3	3,861.0	4,131.9	4,395.5	4,253.8
LIABILITIES & EQUITY					
Short Term Debt	75.000	34.000	42.000	50.000	49.000
Long Term Debt	100.60	99.600	99.600	99.600	99.700
Total Liabilities	3,192.1	3,376.7	3,626.0	3,898.8	3,853.7
Shares Outstanding	46.778	47.250	44.264	42.091	42.108
Common Stockholder Equity	470.20	484.40	506.00	496.60	400.10
Total Stockholder Equity	470.20	484.40	506.00	496.60	400.10

Note: Figures in Millions of $ except: per share items, margins, yields, and ratios.

Source: Tradeline.Com, a Platinum Equity Holdings Company

ICICI LIMITED

Vivian Lewis
Global Investing

Company Background

ICICI Limited is a financial services company in India. It was founded by the World Bank, India's government, and private investors in 1955. The company owns a bank, among other things, and is involved in financing, brokerage services, credit cards, and venture capital funding. There really isn't a U.S. company that compares, in terms of the breadth of financial services ICICI offers. ICICI stands for Industrial Credit and Investment Corporation of India. It was initially started as a financier of industrial projects, then it branched into retail banking, and now it is really getting involved in the brokerage and venture capital area. It even operates an asset management company.

Although based in Bombay, you can purchase shares of the stock as an American depositary receipt (ADR) on the New York Stock Exchange. The stock began trading in late 1999 and immediately took off like a rocket. But it has since come down quite a bit, primarily because it fell in sympathy with a number of technology stocks headquartered in India. It's currently trading at a PE multiple of less than ten times last years earnings and it pays a dividend that, by next year, should amount to around 5 percent. Not bad, considering the stock is also appreciating smartly.

Reason for Recommendation

I love the idea of owning such a huge and powerful company in any country, and especially India. ICICI is involved in so many exciting things right now, this only adds to my enthusiasm. It is creating a way to access your bank by telephone, meaning you won't have to bother with visiting an ATM. This is a revolutionary concept that is spreading through Europe, but hasn't quite made its way to the U.S. yet.

Biggest Risks

I think the biggest risk is India itself. The country is prone to political turmoil. Some also worry about owning stock traded in a foreign country. But because you're buying an ADR, the company has to conform to U.S. generally accepted accounting standards.

Bottom Line

Earnings at this company are growing like crazy, and I think the future for the financial services industry in India is extremely bright. I expect this stock will at least get back to $46 per share, which is where it was in early 2000. And, remember, you also get that fat dividend while you wait for the appreciation.

Contact Information: ICICI Limited
ICICI Towers
Bandra Kurla Complex, Bandra
Bombay 400 051, India
91 22 653-1414
<www.icici.com>

BONUS PICK FOR 2001

BANCO LATINOAMERICANO DE EXPORTACIONES, S.A.

Symbol: BLX
Exchange: NYSE

This is another financial services stock in a different emerging market—Panama. Banco Latinoamericano de Exportaciones, which is often referred to as BLADEX, specializes in financing foreign trade for Latin American and Caribbean countries. In other words, it mainly lends money to both government and private export financing banks, which in turn make loans to private companies. BLADEX trades at a mere five times earnings and yields around 5 percent. I expect this company may soon grow and branch into other areas, just like ICICI. BLADEX already is expanding its office in New York and has established a presence in Mexico City as well. To get more information on this company, I recommend you visit the BLADEX Web site at <www.blx.com>.

Tradeline.Com annual earnings per share chart unavailable for this security.

Icici Ltd-INR Spons ADR 2000 Dividend
Symbol: IC Market/Exchange: NYSE

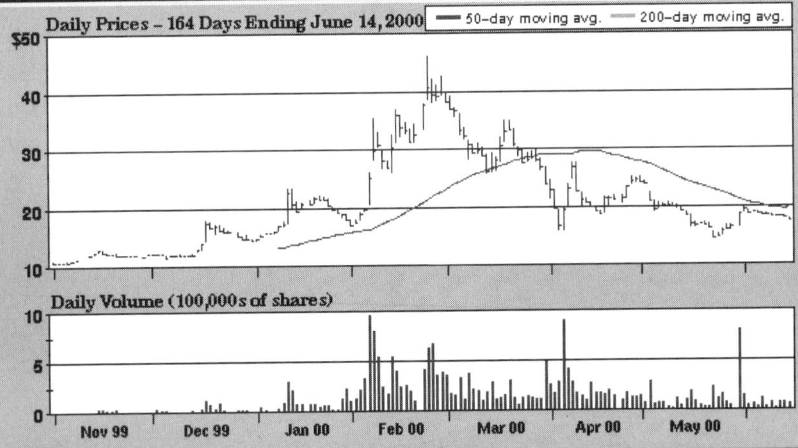

Latest Pricing Data (as of June 14, 2000)

Close (net change):	$17 1/2	(-5/16)
Day High & Low:	$17 3/4	$17 5/16
Volume & Avg. Volume:	52,800	140,025
52-Week High:	$46	Feb. 23, 2000
52-Week Low:	$10 5/8	Nov. 1, 1999
Latest Dividend:	$0.00	
Ind. Ann. Div. & Yield:	$0.63	3.60%
12 Month EPS:	N.A.	
P/E Ratio & Beta Factor:	N.A.	N.A.
Shares Outstanding:	95.676 million	
Market Value:	$1.674 billion	
Institutional Holdings:	15.01%	
Number of Institutions:	43	
Primary Market:	NYSE	

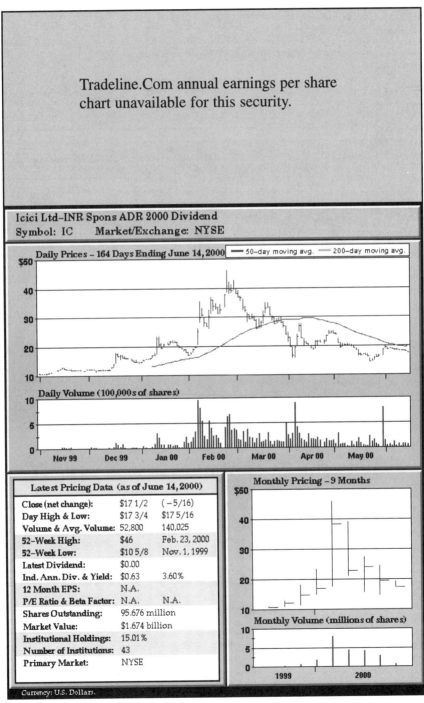

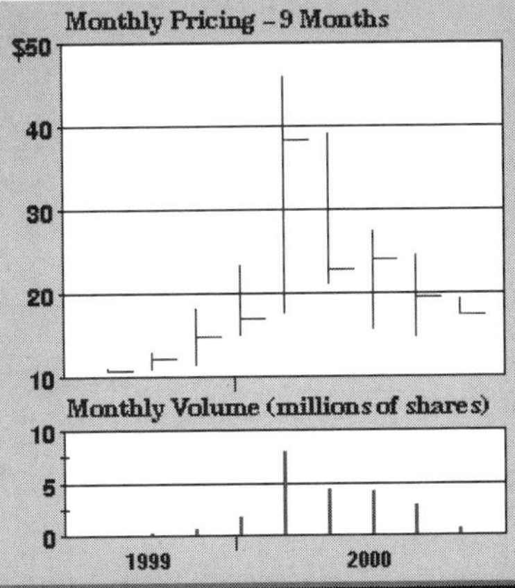

Currency: U.S. Dollars.

Source: Tradeline.Com, a Platinum Equity Holdings Company

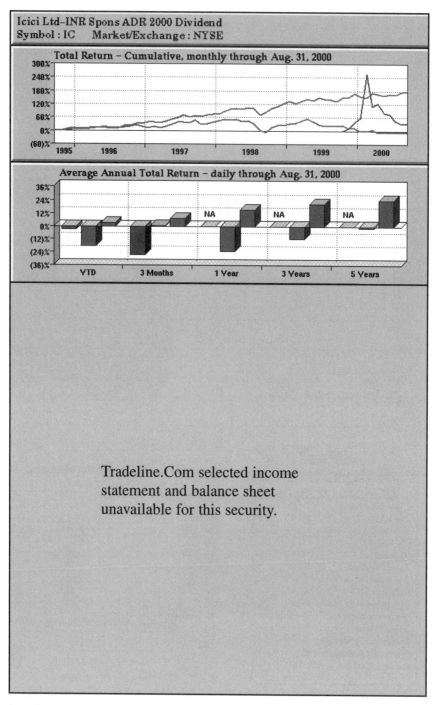

Icici Ltd-INR Spons ADR 2000 Dividend
Symbol : IC Market/Exchange : NYSE

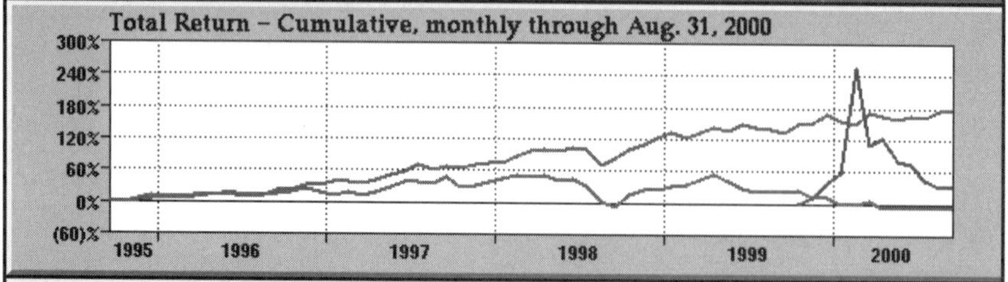

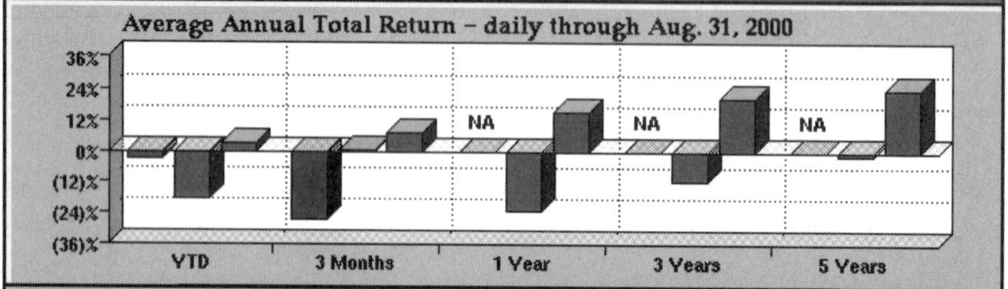

Tradeline.Com selected income statement and balance sheet unavailable for this security.

Source: Tradeline.Com, a Platinum Equity Holdings Company

INTEL

L. Roy Papp
L. Roy Papp & Associates

Company Background

Intel is the premier maker of semiconductor chips. It also supplies the computing and communications industries with boards, chips, systems, and software essential in computers, servers, and networking products. The company has moved from making simple chips to manufacturing mega-brain centers. Intel beats everybody else when it comes to quality and just about everything else. I'm also pleased with how the company has made a successful transition from computers to the Internet. I believe it will be the dominant player in chips and equipment for the Internet. Intel will certainly have competition from others making parts for the Internet, but I'm convinced it will win hands down.

Not long ago, Intel forecast that it would do at least $1 billion a month in business over the Internet, and it is already way ahead of that. I heard (cofounder and chairman) Andy Grove say at a conference recently that more than 90 percent of the servers that will be used on the Internet in 2005 have not even been built yet. That translates into plenty of business for Intel.

Reason for Recommendation

In addition to the company's great prospects, I really feel that all of the people in top management are farsighted and gifted. I admire their ability not to get upset over little things. The company doesn't have much competition. Advanced Micro Devices keeps trying to compete, but, in my opinion, never comes through with the products. What's more, Intel's PE ratio is far below some of the other big technology giants because it is incorrectly viewed as a cyclical stock. Plus, the company has a new chip coming out soon that offers an enormous increase in capacity and ability, yet will be moderately priced.

Biggest Risks

The biggest risk is that somebody else comes out and leapfrogs the company to market. I think that's hard to do, because the company's lead has grown so big. Of course, a slowdown in computer buying would also hurt, but it would have to be across the board, from PCs to Internet servers, which I just can't see happening in the near term.

Bottom Line

Intel is a global technology powerhouse that I think has a great future. While I don't have a specific target price for the stock, I believe it will be a lot higher a year from now than it is today.

Contact Information: Intel Corporation
2200 Mission College Boulevard
Santa Clara, CA 95052
408-765-8080
<www.intel.com>

BONUS PICK FOR 2001

MERCK

Symbol: MRK
Exchange: NYSE

Merck is a pharmaceutical powerhouse with a number of big products in the pipeline. Unfortunately, it also has several drugs that are coming off patent soon, and the market hasn't been very happy about that. As a result, you can get this stock at a decent price. I believe that pharmaceutical stocks will continue to do well for at least the next 10 to 15 years. This company is investing a lot of money in research and development, which comes out of current earnings. But this move should pay high dividends in the future. It appears that the political environment for pharmaceutical companies going forward may be more favorable than it has been in the past, and this should be another positive that can move Merck shares higher.

Intel Corp

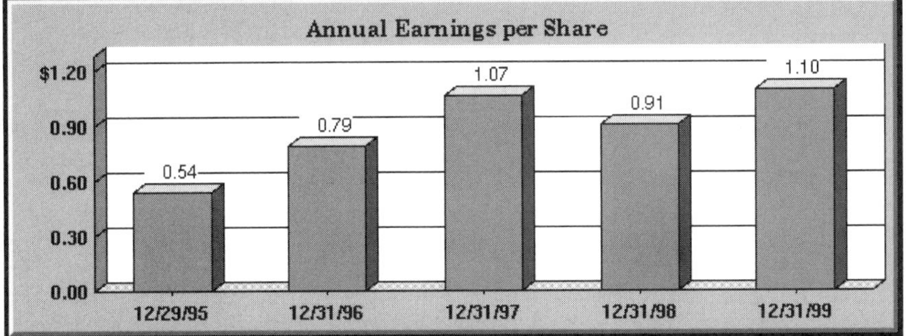

Intel Corp

Symbol: INTC Market/Exchange: Nasdaq NMS

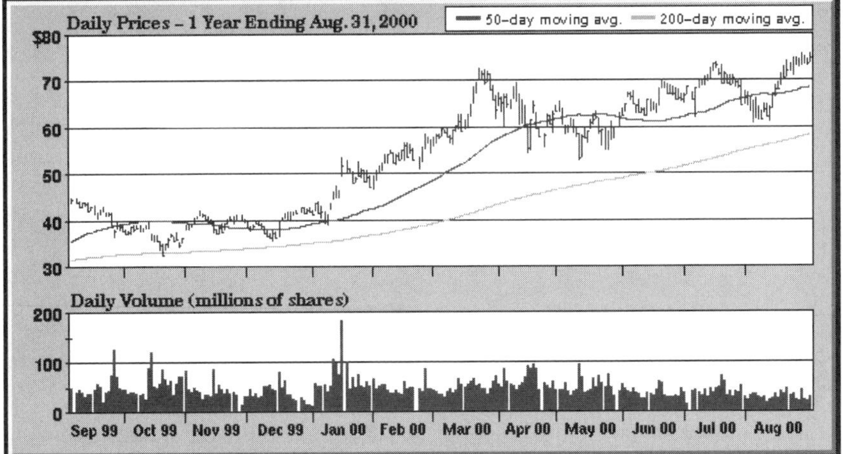

Latest Pricing Data (as of Aug. 31, 2000)		
Close (net change):	$74 7/8	(+1 3/8)
Day High & Low:	$75 5/8	$73 5/8
Volume & Avg. Volume:	28,000,000	46,950,332
52-Week High:	$75 13/16	Aug. 28, 2000
52-Week Low:	$32 1/2	Oct. 19, 1999
Latest Dividend:	$0.02	Aug. 3, 2000
Ind. Ann. Div. & Yield:	$0.06	0.08%
12 Month EPS:	$1.42	June 30, 2000
P/E Ratio & Beta Factor:	52.73	1.172
Shares Outstanding:	6.698 billion	
Market Value:	$501.513 billion	
Institutional Holdings:	26.70%	
Number of Institutions:	3227	
Primary Market:	Nasdaq NMS	
Component of:	DJIA, S&P 500	

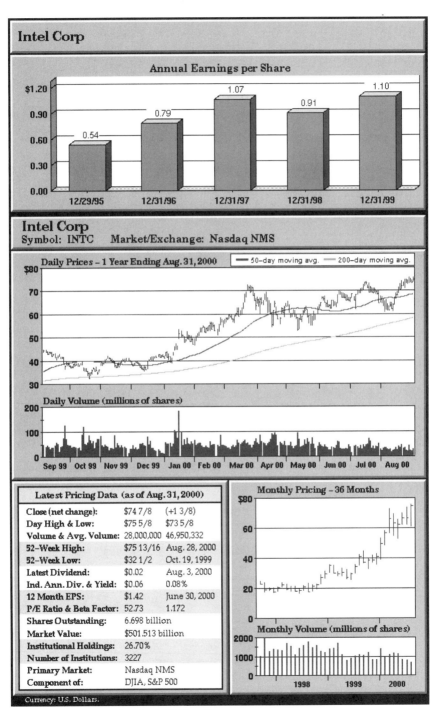

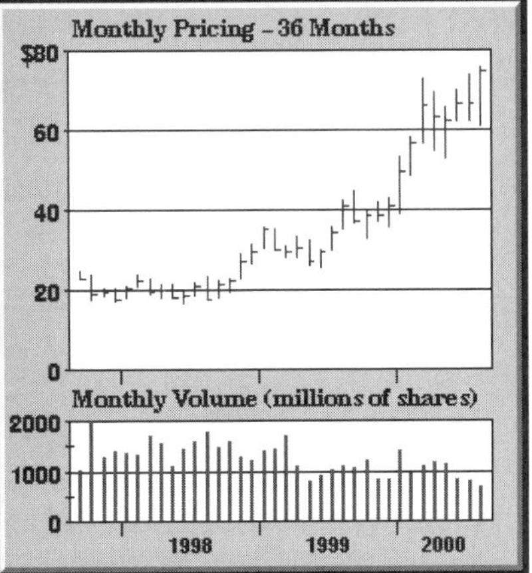

Currency: U.S. Dollars.

Source: Tradeline.Com, a Platinum Equity Holdings Company

Intel Corp

Symbol : INTC Market/Exchange : Nasdaq NMS

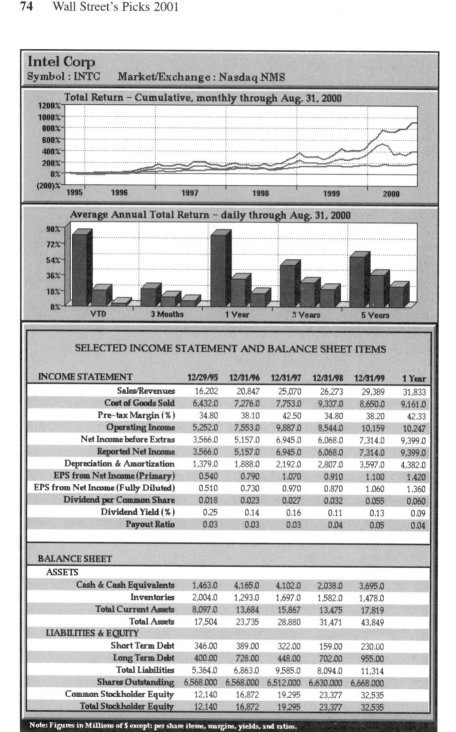

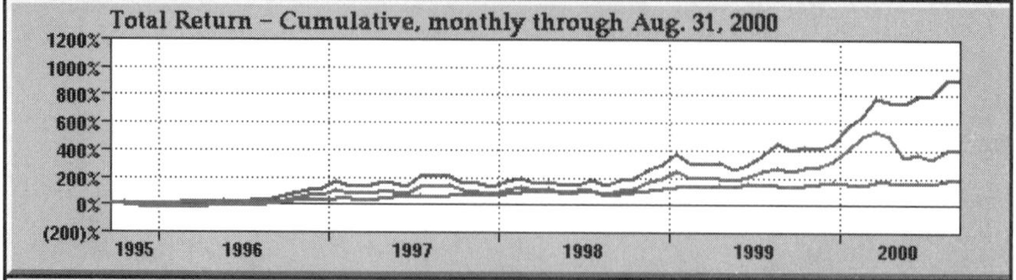

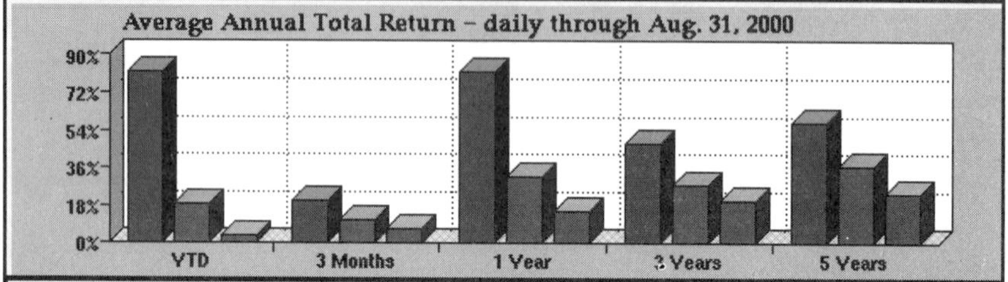

SELECTED INCOME STATEMENT AND BALANCE SHEET ITEMS

INCOME STATEMENT	12/29/95	12/31/96	12/31/97	12/31/98	12/31/99	1 Year
Sales/Revenues	16,202	20,847	25,070	26,273	29,389	31,833
Cost of Goods Sold	6,432.0	7,276.0	7,753.0	9,337.0	8,650.0	9,161.0
Pre-tax Margin (%)	34.80	38.10	42.50	34.80	38.20	42.33
Operating Income	5,252.0	7,553.0	9,887.0	8,544.0	10,159	10,247
Net Income before Extras	3,566.0	5,157.0	6,945.0	6,068.0	7,314.0	9,399.0
Reported Net Income	3,566.0	5,157.0	6,945.0	6,068.0	7,314.0	9,399.0
Depreciation & Amortization	1,379.0	1,888.0	2,192.0	2,807.0	3,597.0	4,382.0
EPS from Net Income (Primary)	0.540	0.790	1.070	0.910	1.100	1.420
EPS from Net Income (Fully Diluted)	0.510	0.730	0.970	0.870	1.060	1.360
Dividend per Common Share	0.018	0.023	0.027	0.032	0.055	0.060
Dividend Yield (%)	0.25	0.14	0.16	0.11	0.13	0.09
Payout Ratio	0.03	0.03	0.03	0.04	0.05	0.04

BALANCE SHEET					
ASSETS					
Cash & Cash Equivalents	1,463.0	4,165.0	4,102.0	2,038.0	3,695.0
Inventories	2,004.0	1,293.0	1,697.0	1,582.0	1,478.0
Total Current Assets	8,097.0	13,684	15,867	13,475	17,819
Total Assets	17,504	23,735	28,880	31,471	43,849
LIABILITIES & EQUITY					
Short Term Debt	346.00	389.00	322.00	159.00	230.00
Long Term Debt	400.00	728.00	448.00	702.00	955.00
Total Liabilities	5,364.0	6,863.0	9,585.0	8,094.0	11,314
Shares Outstanding	6,568.000	6,568.000	6,512.000	6,630.000	6,668.000
Common Stockholder Equity	12,140	16,872	19,295	23,377	32,535
Total Stockholder Equity	12,140	16,872	19,295	23,377	32,535

Note: Figures in Millions of $ except: per share items, margins, yields, and ratios.

Source: Tradeline.Com, a Platinum Equity Holdings Company

I-STAT

Michael DiCarlo
DFS Advisors

Company Background

I-STAT is a razor blade story of the medical industry. It manufactures a device the size of two cellular phones that is used in point-of-care blood testing. The kicker is it makes a cartridge that must be used in the device. At the same time, this device makes life easier for you and me. It used to be that you'd go to the doctor and he'd draw three or four vials of blood for analysis. These vials would be sent to a lab, which would give your doctor the results in 24 to 48 hours. The I-STAT device does a complete blood test in about 90 seconds. Instead of drawing several vials, it takes three or four drops from your fingertip. This blood is inserted into a cartridge, which is put into the device for analysis. In less than two minutes, you have your complete results. The tests are also cheaper for the patient and insurance companies.

Reason for Recommendation

This is a company that has been around for a long time. The technology has always been there, but it's been difficult getting the hospitals to accept it. For one thing, hospitals used to get paid based on the number of tests done in the lab. So if you're trying to sell a simple device like this to a lab administrator, he's not going to be very interested. A while back, Hewlett-Packard bought 12.5 percent of the company, but never did much to help with marketing. About one year ago, Abbott Labs purchased 12.5 percent of I-STAT, and now uses its sales force to sell the device both domestically and abroad. The obstacles the company once faced are disappearing. Abbott Labs is starting to open numerous doors for the company, which was the whole idea behind the alliance in the first place. I-STAT should sell around 11.5 million cartridges in 2000, more in 2001. And while it's not profitable yet, I expect the company to start making money in 2001.

Biggest Risks

The biggest risk is one of execution. For instance, the company could fall behind in manufacturing the cartridges. Other than that, I don't see much on the downside. I-STAT would welcome competition, because competition generally lends credence to the entire category. So while the company's market share might slip a bit, the pie would get significantly bigger.

Bottom Line

I-STAT is growing very fast, and I expect the growth to pick up even more in 2001. I look for the stock to hit at least $30 a share by the end of 2001.

Contact Information: I-STAT Corporation
104 Windsor Center Drive
East Windsor, NJ 08520
609-443-9300
<www.i-stat.com>

BONUS PICK FOR 2001

HOTJOBS.COM

Symbol: HOTJ
Exchange: Nasdaq

HotJobs.com operates a job recruitment site on the Internet. The company offers a phenomenal solution for both job seekers and companies looking to hire new talent. I believe this is one of the biggest marketplaces online. Companies are finding it is easier and more cost-effective to conduct their recruitment efforts on the Internet, as opposed to classified advertising in newspapers. By logging on to the HotJobs.com site at absolutely no charge, candidates can easily search for jobs and gain access to the company's entire database. HotJobs.com isn't profitable yet, although it should be within two years. It's the number-two player in the industry, behind TMP Worldwide's Monster.com, but gaining ground fast.

I-Stat Corp

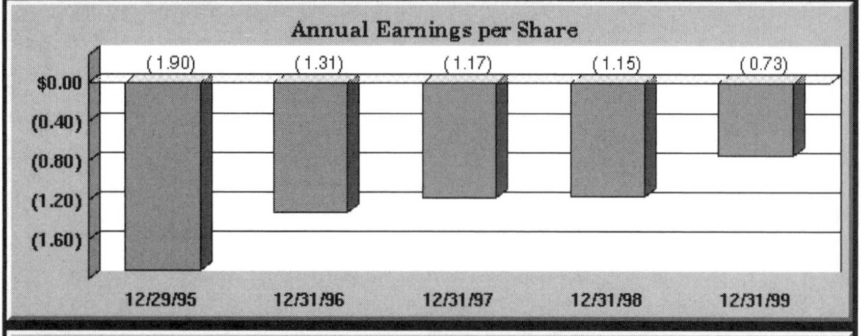

I-Stat Corp

Symbol: STAT Market/Exchange: Nasdaq NMS

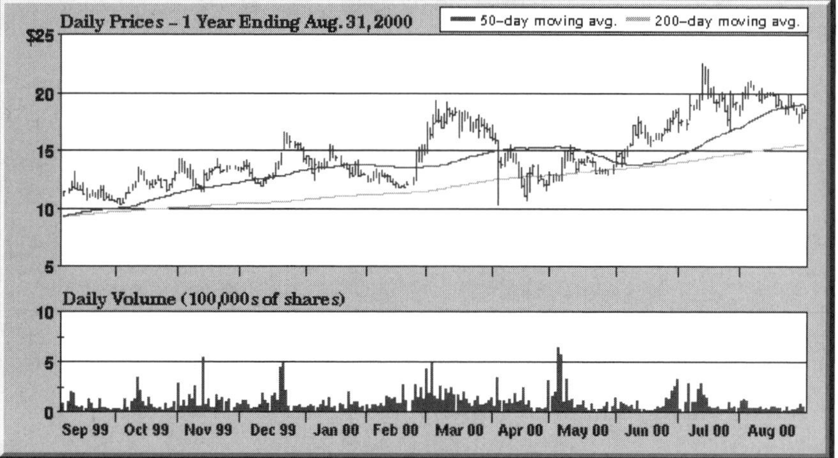

Latest Pricing Data (as of Aug. 31, 2000)		
Close (net change):	$18 9/16	(+3/16)
Day High & Low:	$18 15/16	$18 1/4
Volume & Avg. Volume:	62,800	108,332
52-Week High:	$22 1/2	July 12, 2000
52-Week Low:	$10 1/8	Apr. 4, 2000
Latest Dividend:	$0.00	
Ind. Ann. Div. & Yield:	$0.00	N.A.
12 Month EPS:	($0.66)	June 30, 2000
P/E Ratio & Beta Factor:	N.A.	0.787
Shares Outstanding:	18.234 million	
Market Value:	$338 million	
Institutional Holdings:	41.94%	
Number of Institutions:	60	
Primary Market:	Nasdaq NMS	

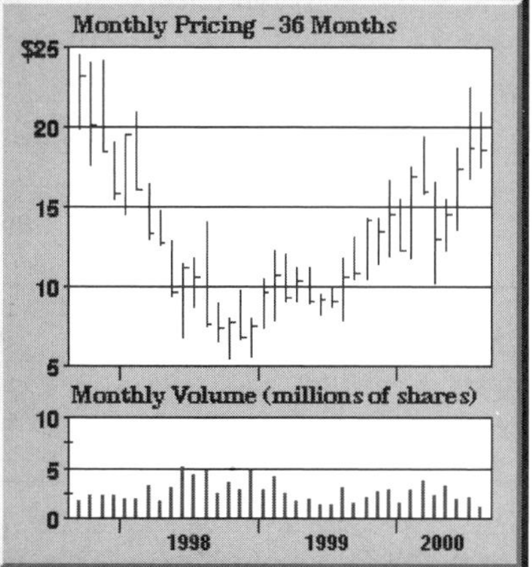

Currency: U.S. Dollars.

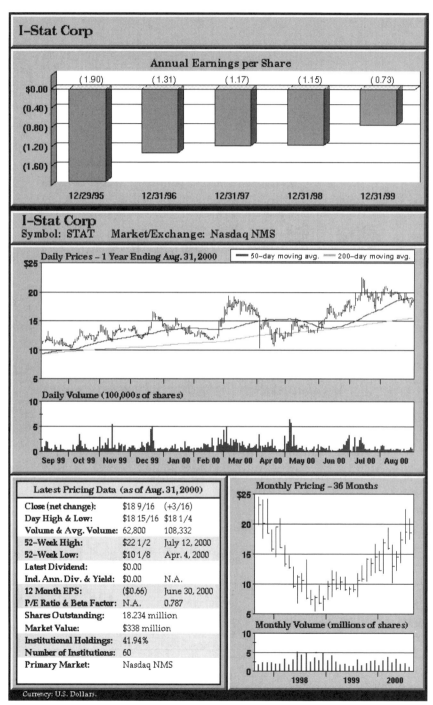

Source: Tradeline.Com, a Platinum Equity Holdings Company

I-Stat Corp
Symbol : STAT Market/Exchange : Nasdaq NMS

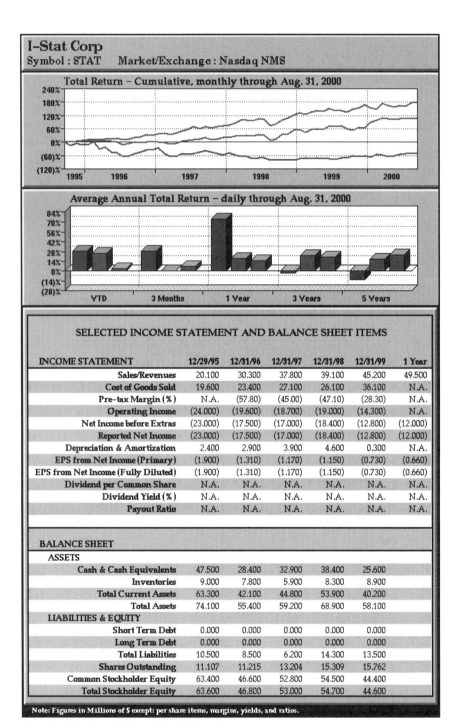

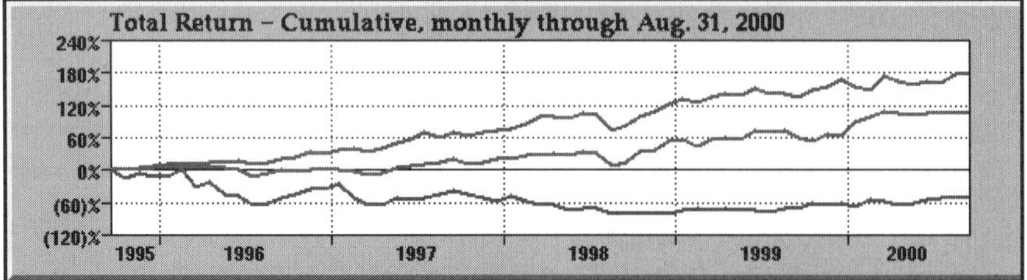

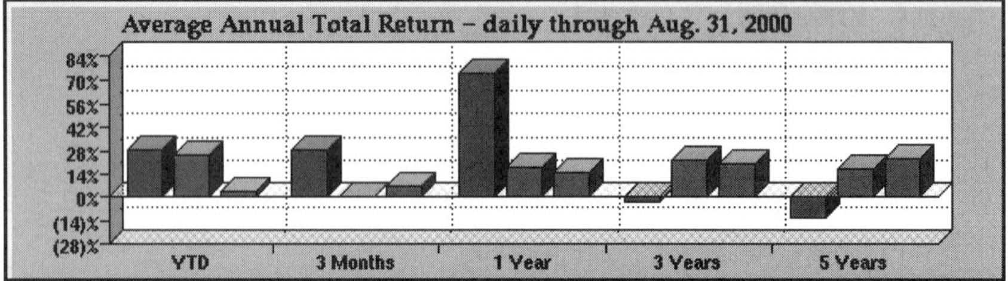

SELECTED INCOME STATEMENT AND BALANCE SHEET ITEMS

INCOME STATEMENT	12/29/95	12/31/96	12/31/97	12/31/98	12/31/99	1 Year
Sales/Revenues	20.100	30.300	37.800	39.100	45.200	49.500
Cost of Goods Sold	19.600	23.400	27.100	26.100	36.100	N.A.
Pre-tax Margin (%)	N.A.	(57.80)	(45.00)	(47.10)	(28.30)	N.A.
Operating Income	(24.000)	(19.600)	(18.700)	(19.000)	(14.300)	N.A.
Net Income before Extras	(23.000)	(17.500)	(17.000)	(18.400)	(12.800)	(12.000)
Reported Net Income	(23.000)	(17.500)	(17.000)	(18.400)	(12.800)	(12.000)
Depreciation & Amortization	2.400	2.900	3.900	4.600	0.300	N.A.
EPS from Net Income (Primary)	(1.900)	(1.310)	(1.170)	(1.150)	(0.730)	(0.660)
EPS from Net Income (Fully Diluted)	(1.900)	(1.310)	(1.170)	(1.150)	(0.730)	(0.660)
Dividend per Common Share	N.A.	N.A.	N.A.	N.A.	N.A.	N.A.
Dividend Yield (%)	N.A.	N.A.	N.A.	N.A.	N.A.	N.A.
Payout Ratio	N.A.	N.A.	N.A.	N.A.	N.A.	N.A.

BALANCE SHEET					
ASSETS					
Cash & Cash Equivalents	47.500	28.400	32.900	38.400	25.600
Inventories	9.000	7.800	5.900	8.300	8.900
Total Current Assets	63.300	42.100	44.800	53.900	40.200
Total Assets	74.100	55.400	59.200	68.900	58.100
LIABILITIES & EQUITY					
Short Term Debt	0.000	0.000	0.000	0.000	0.000
Long Term Debt	0.000	0.000	0.000	0.000	0.000
Total Liabilities	10.500	8.500	6.200	14.300	13.500
Shares Outstanding	11.107	11.215	13.204	15.309	15.762
Common Stockholder Equity	63.400	46.600	52.800	54.500	44.400
Total Stockholder Equity	63.600	46.800	53.000	54.700	44.600

Note: Figures in Millions of $ except: per share items, margins, yields, and ratios.

Source: Tradeline.Com, a Platinum Equity Holdings Company

LITTELFUSE

John Rogers
Ariel Capital Management

Company Background

For a long time, Littelfuse has been the largest manufacturer of fuses for the auto industry. As cars become more technologically proficient, they need really sophisticated fuses. Littelfuse has about a 90 percent market share. But there is more to the story: Littelfuse is a primary manufacturer of small fuses and circuit protection products for the telecommunications industry, the personal computer industry, and a lot of the sophisticated new technology equipment that people use on a regular basis. Palm Pilots, for example, have Littelfuse products in them. So do Nokia cell phones. Business is so terrific, they're short of supplies in certain products.

I first started looking at this company about three years ago. It has grown rapidly since then. The auto fuse industry is still a major part of what Littelfuse does, especially because cars are like portable offices these days. But you can see in this short time how the company's business model has changed. The company also has superb management. I'm very impressed with CEO Howard Witt. Despite all this, the stock price is fairly reasonable. I think much of that has to do with the fact that the company never completely recovered from some of the international economic turmoil in 1998. That really impacted its business.

Reason for Recommendation

I like Littelfuse for a combination of reasons. To begin with, it trades for a PE multiple that's about half relative to the competition. Witt told me he thinks that's because the company has always been followed by old-fashioned auto industry analysts, who don't view it as a technology stock. Second, business is great. The company has been able to take its technological expertise to build fuses that are so small you can shake them out of a pepper shaker. This sophisticated technology is now being expanded into a broadly wider universe, so it's the best of all worlds. Littelfuse has this super niche in the auto industry, and it has now moved right in to the fastest growing part of the overall economy. It's a wonderful story.

Biggest Risks

What should you watch out for? Perhaps the technology could advance to the point where you wouldn't need to use these fuses any more. I can't imagine that happening any time soon, but it's always a risk that a company's product will become obsolete.

Bottom Line

I think the company currently has a private market value of at least $45 per share. It has been growing rapidly. In fact, it's the fastest-growing stock in my portfolio. I expect it to continue to grow in the 20 percent range in the foreseeable future. It's a wonderful little company.

Contact Information: Littelfuse, Inc.
800 East Northwest Highway
Des Plaines, IL 60016
(847) 824-1188
<www.littelfuse.com>

BONUS PICK FOR 2001

LEE ENTERPRISES

Symbol: LEE
Exchange: NYSE

The newspaper industry is definitely out of favor right now. Lee Enterprises is one company in this sector that I have a lot of faith in. Lee owns 21 daily newspapers and 80 other publications, primarily in small to mid-sized cities. I think newspaper companies have been beaten up because of fear the Internet will hurt them and concerns about newsprint prices. But I feel both of those risks are minimal. What's more, the Internet just isn't that influential in the markets in which Lee has a monopoly. Until mid-2000, Lee also owned a number of broadcasting outlets. It sold these operations to enhance shareholder value and now is solely focused on the newspaper business. This is a company sitting on a lot of cash and selling at a significant discount to what I think it's worth. I suspect this stock could reach $47 or more per share by the end of 2001.

Littelfuse Inc

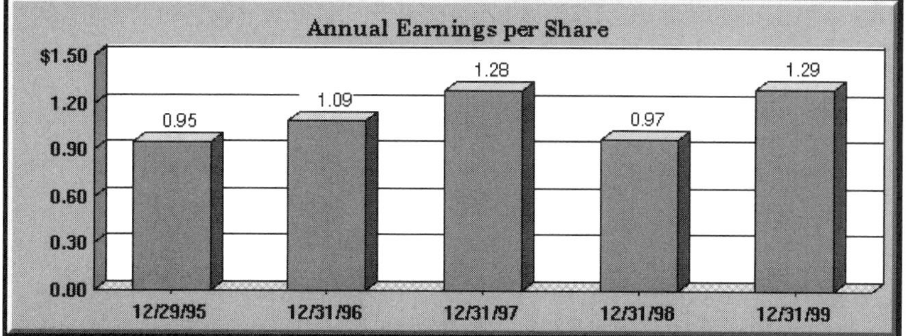

Littelfuse Inc

Symbol: LFUS Market/Exchange: Nasdaq NMS

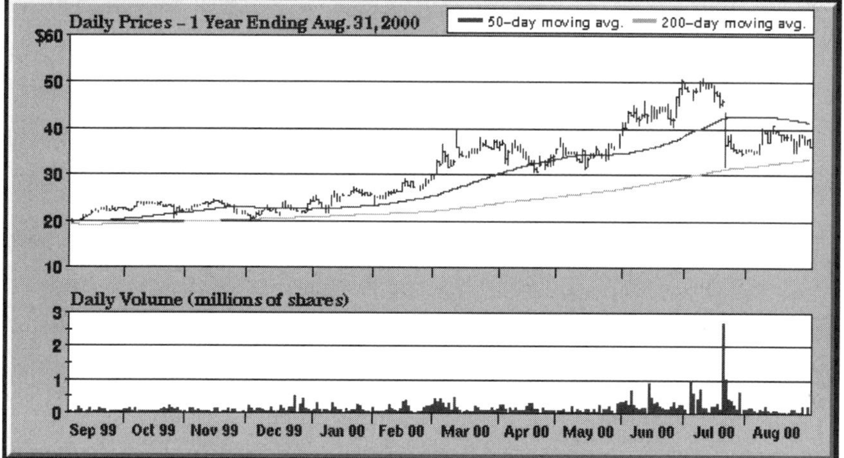

Latest Pricing Data (as of Aug. 31, 2000)

Close (net change):	$36 5/16	(–1 7/16)
Day High & Low:	$38	$36 5/16
Volume & Avg. Volume:	229,300	162,043
52-Week High:	$51 1/8	July 10, 2000
52-Week Low:	$19 3/4	Sep. 8, 1999
Latest Dividend:	$0.00	
Ind. Ann. Div. & Yield:	$0.00	N.A.
12 Month EPS:	$1.79	June 30, 2000
P/E Ratio & Beta Factor:	20.29	0.749
Shares Outstanding:	19.579 million	
Market Value:	$711 million	
Institutional Holdings:	93.83%	
Number of Institutions:	212	
Primary Market:	Nasdaq NMS	

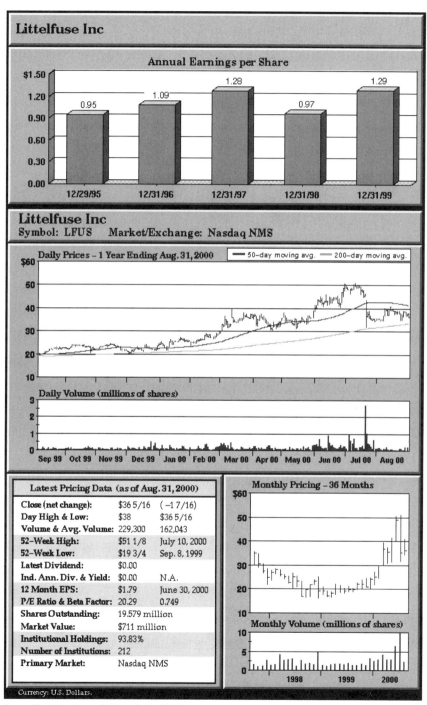

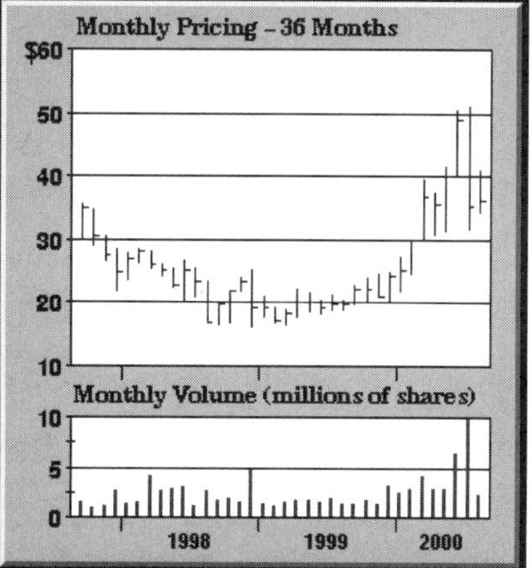

Currency: U.S. Dollars.

Source: Tradeline.Com, a Platinum Equity Holdings Company

Littelfuse Inc

Symbol : LFUS   Market/Exchange : Nasdaq NMS

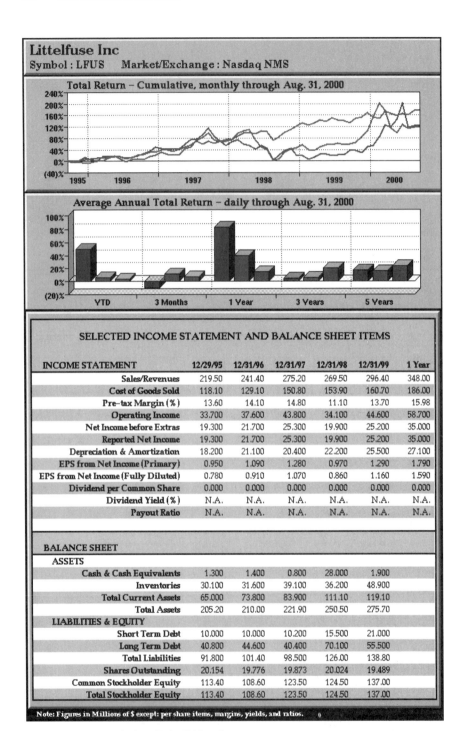

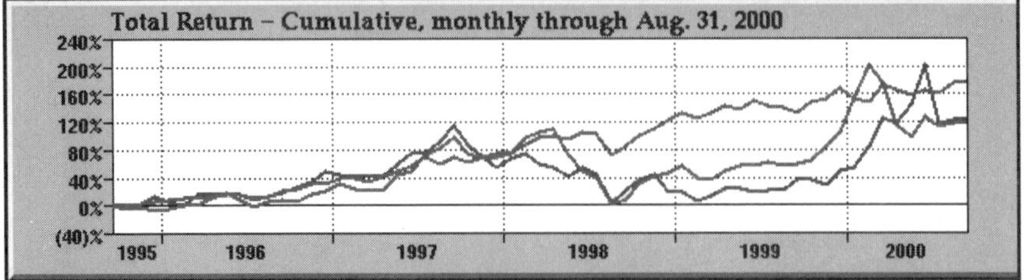

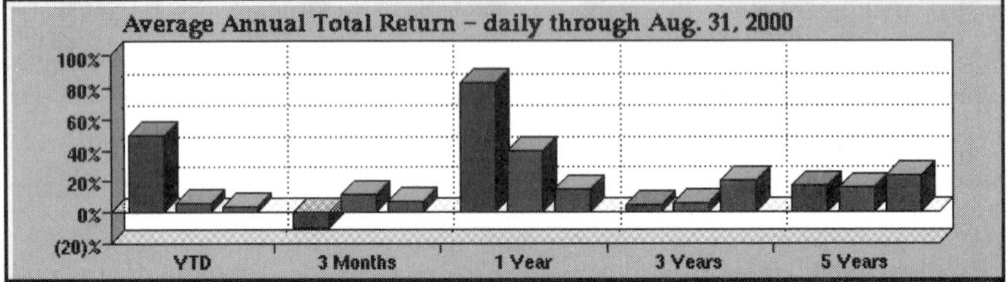

SELECTED INCOME STATEMENT AND BALANCE SHEET ITEMS

INCOME STATEMENT	12/29/95	12/31/96	12/31/97	12/31/98	12/31/99	1 Year
Sales/Revenues	219.50	241.40	275.20	269.50	296.40	348.00
Cost of Goods Sold	118.10	129.10	150.80	153.90	160.70	186.00
Pre-tax Margin (%)	13.60	14.10	14.80	11.10	13.70	15.98
Operating Income	33.700	37.600	43.800	34.100	44.600	58.700
Net Income before Extras	19.300	21.700	25.300	19.900	25.200	35.000
Reported Net Income	19.300	21.700	25.300	19.900	25.200	35.000
Depreciation & Amortization	18.200	21.100	20.400	22.200	25.500	27.100
EPS from Net Income (Primary)	0.950	1.090	1.280	0.970	1.290	1.790
EPS from Net Income (Fully Diluted)	0.780	0.910	1.070	0.860	1.160	1.590
Dividend per Common Share	0.000	0.000	0.000	0.000	0.000	0.000
Dividend Yield (%)	N.A.	N.A.	N.A.	N.A.	N.A.	N.A.
Payout Ratio	N.A.	N.A.	N.A.	N.A.	N.A.	N.A.

BALANCE SHEET					
ASSETS					
Cash & Cash Equivalents	1.300	1.400	0.800	28.000	1.900
Inventories	30.100	31.600	39.100	36.200	48.900
Total Current Assets	65.000	73.800	83.900	111.10	119.10
Total Assets	205.20	210.00	221.90	250.50	275.70
LIABILITIES & EQUITY					
Short Term Debt	10.000	10.000	10.200	15.500	21.000
Long Term Debt	40.800	44.600	40.400	70.100	55.500
Total Liabilities	91.800	101.40	98.500	126.00	138.80
Shares Outstanding	20.154	19.776	19.873	20.024	19.489
Common Stockholder Equity	113.40	108.60	123.50	124.50	137.00
Total Stockholder Equity	113.40	108.60	123.50	124.50	137.00

Note: Figures in Millions of $ except: per share items, margins, yields, and ratios.

Source: Tradeline.Com, a Platinum Equity Holdings Company

NOBEL LEARNING COMMUNITIES

Marcus Robins
RedChip.com

Company Background

Nobel Learning Communities began in 1984 as Rocking Horse, an operator of childcare centers. In 1992, the current management took over and changed the strategic direction into the field of education for profit. Since then, the company has grown to 149 schools and is the largest for-profit operator of private schools in the nation. Today, education is the number-one priority in the U.S. and education spending (approximately $700 billion) is second only to defense in total governmental budgeted dollars. Politicians, both Republicans and Democrats, are talking about education reform and giving parents the ability to send their kids to a school of their choice, including private schools. Nobel seems to be in the right spot at the right time.

Reason for Recommendation

Nobel's estimated revenues in 2000/2001 are approximately $150 million and the company's operations are very profitable. In addition to private schools, the company has broadened its scope by entering the specialty school market, such as schools for learning disabled children, high schools for underachieving children, and charter schools. Nobel schools are relatively unique in that they are available 12 hours per day, 12 months per year; schools and class sizes are small; and they are very safe.

In addition to the fact that education is the hottest political item, alternative schools seem to be the up-and-coming approach for education in the public arena. Nobel is in an ideal position to take advantage of the situation being the largest for-profit operator of schools in the country. Nobel's existing infrastructure gives it a competitive advantage in expanding the charter school business. Charter schools are essentially set up and run by parents and local community groups, but are funded out of public school annual budgets. Nobel has established itself as a management company of choice for charter schools. It opened a charter school in Philadelphia for 624 children, for which it had more than 4,000 applicants. The school was essentially profitable from day one.

Biggest Risks

Because the company has a long operating history, profitability isn't a risk. Service and management are not risks either, because Nobel is strong in both of those areas. Probably the biggest risk is that the stock won't go from trading at 10 times earnings to 35 times earnings because the market doesn't get excited about education.

Bottom Line

My analysis of the competition leads me to believe that Nobel should be trading for about three to five times as much as it is right now. This is a company that works on teaching and producing educational results, and does a great job at it. Once the market realizes this, I would expect the stock to rise accordingly.

Contact Information: Nobel Learning Communities, Inc.
1400 North Providence Road, Suite 3055
Media, PA 19063
610-891-8200
<www.nobeleducation.com>

BONUS PICK FOR 2001

BEI TECHNOLOGIES

Symbol: BEIQ
Exchange: Nasdaq

BEI Technologies produces a sonic gyroscope. This sensor device is used to control the braking system in automobiles. The sensor is being put in Cadillacs and several other General Motors products. It is gaining acceptance by other carmakers as well, including BMW, Mercedes, Volvo, and Audi. This growing acceptance is one of the main reasons I like the stock. There is competition, but the prime competitors' products are much more expensive. I expect BEI Technologies products to really pervade the auto industry. I think you can see earnings per share in the range of $1.30 to $1.40 in 2001, and would expect the stock to make it up to around $30 per share by the end of the year.

Nobel Learning Communities

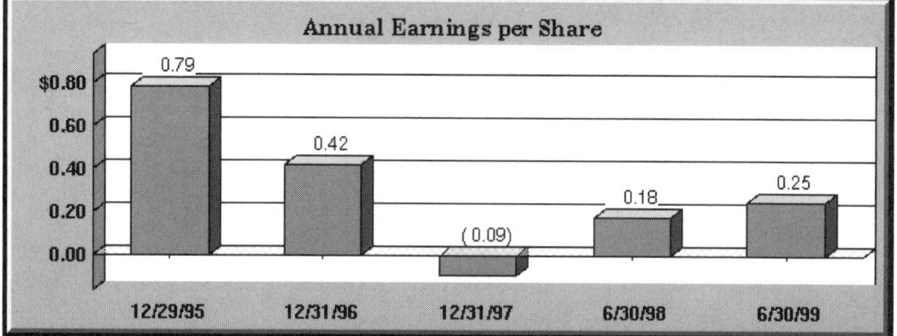

Nobel Learning Communities

Symbol: NLCI Market/Exchange: Nasdaq NMS

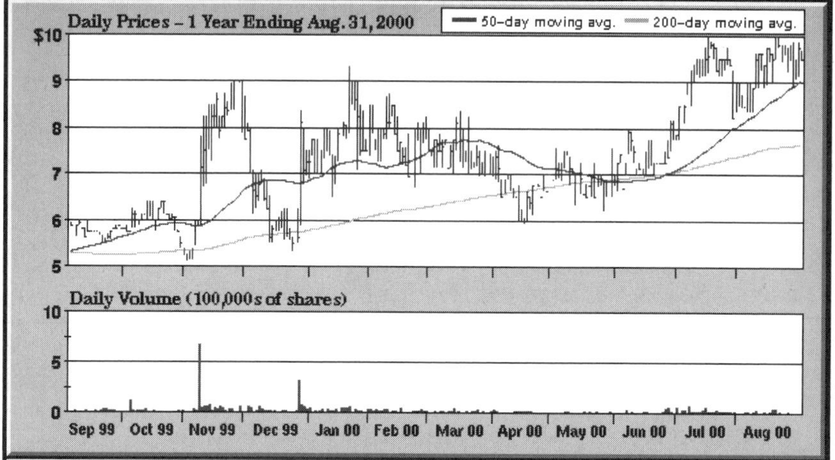

Latest Pricing Data (as of Aug. 31, 2000)		
Close (net change):	$9 1/2	(–1/4)
Day High & Low:	$9 11/16	$9 1/2
Volume & Avg. Volume:	1,300	18,937
52-Week High:	$10	Aug. 21, 2000
52-Week Low:	$5 1/8	Nov. 3, 1999
Latest Dividend:	$0.00	
Ind. Ann. Div. & Yield:	$0.00	N.A.
12 Month EPS:	$0.35	June 30, 2000
P/E Ratio & Beta Factor:	27.14	0.518
Shares Outstanding:	5.925 million	
Market Value:	$56.3 million	
Institutional Holdings:	12.25%	
Number of Institutions:	19	
Primary Market:	Nasdaq NMS	

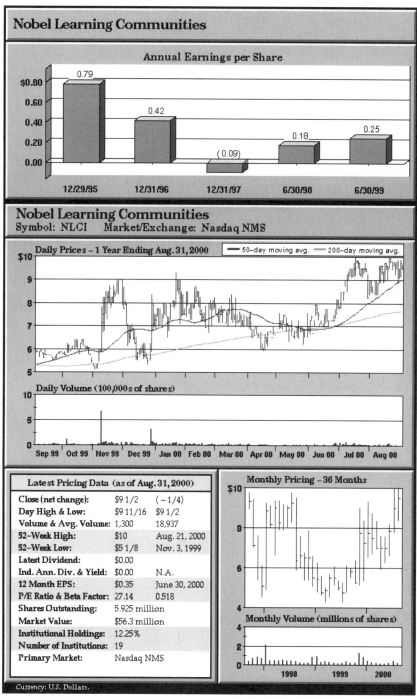

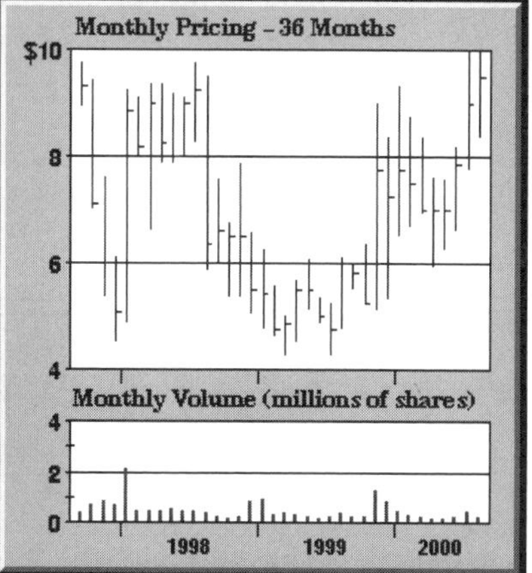

Currency: U.S. Dollars.

Source: Tradeline.Com, a Platinum Equity Holdings Company

Nobel Learning Communities

Symbol : NLCI Market/Exchange : Nasdaq NMS

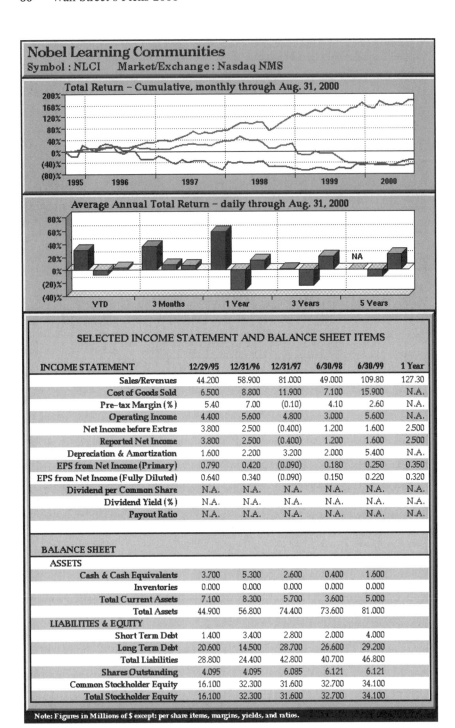

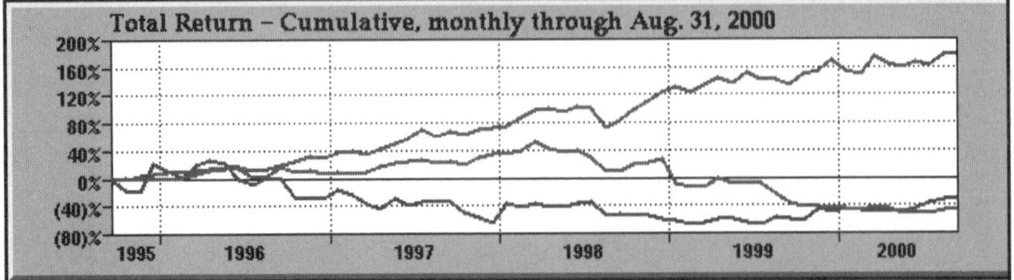

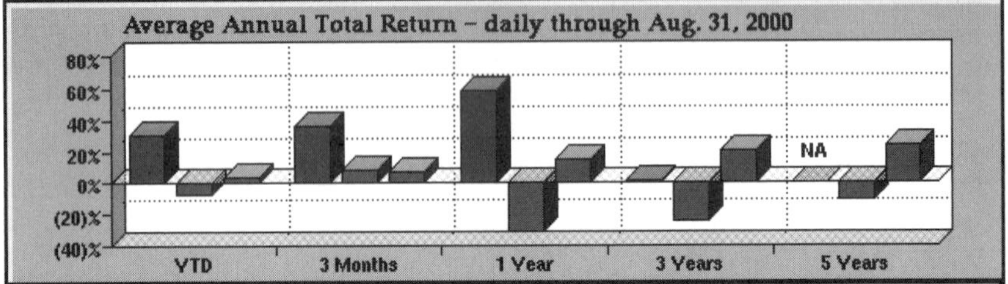

SELECTED INCOME STATEMENT AND BALANCE SHEET ITEMS

INCOME STATEMENT	12/29/95	12/31/96	12/31/97	6/30/98	6/30/99	1 Year
Sales/Revenues	44.200	58.900	81.000	49.000	109.80	127.30
Cost of Goods Sold	6.500	8.800	11.900	7.100	15.900	N.A.
Pre-tax Margin (%)	5.40	7.00	(0.10)	4.10	2.60	N.A.
Operating Income	4.400	5.600	4.800	3.000	5.600	N.A.
Net Income before Extras	3.800	2.500	(0.400)	1.200	1.600	2.500
Reported Net Income	3.800	2.500	(0.400)	1.200	1.600	2.500
Depreciation & Amortization	1.600	2.200	3.200	2.000	5.400	N.A.
EPS from Net Income (Primary)	0.790	0.420	(0.090)	0.180	0.250	0.350
EPS from Net Income (Fully Diluted)	0.640	0.340	(0.090)	0.150	0.220	0.320
Dividend per Common Share	N.A.	N.A.	N.A.	N.A.	N.A.	N.A.
Dividend Yield (%)	N.A.	N.A.	N.A.	N.A.	N.A.	N.A.
Payout Ratio	N.A.	N.A.	N.A.	N.A.	N.A.	N.A.

BALANCE SHEET					
ASSETS					
Cash & Cash Equivalents	3.700	5.300	2.600	0.400	1.600
Inventories	0.000	0.000	0.000	0.000	0.000
Total Current Assets	7.100	8.300	5.700	3.600	5.000
Total Assets	44.900	56.800	74.400	73.600	81.000
LIABILITIES & EQUITY					
Short Term Debt	1.400	3.400	2.800	2.000	4.000
Long Term Debt	20.600	14.500	28.700	26.600	29.200
Total Liabilities	28.800	24.400	42.800	40.700	46.800
Shares Outstanding	4.095	4.095	6.085	6.121	6.121
Common Stockholder Equity	16.100	32.300	31.600	32.700	34.100
Total Stockholder Equity	16.100	32.300	31.600	32.700	34.100

Note: Figures in Millions of $ except: per share items, margins, yields, and ratios.

Source: Tradeline.Com, a Platinum Equity Holdings Company

ORACLE CORPORATION

Michael Murphy

California Technology Stock Letter

Company Background

Oracle is a company that I consider to be a core holding in every technology portfolio. It is a dominant industry leader that I suspect no one will ever be able to catch up with. Oracle is the largest supplier of relational databases. These are databases that hold information in a way that makes it easy to add new data, write reports, get data out, and so forth. For transactional data, such as airline reservations, relational databases are the way to go.

Oracle has taken this a step further by giving people access to these databases over any device—a Palm Pilot, cell phone, high-end computer, whatever—using the Internet. It's incredibly expensive to have software in dozens of different machines. Oracle has replaced this by putting everything into one huge server that people can access anywhere in the world, using any simple device. By applying Internet computing to all corporate functions—from human resources to accounting—companies can save billions of dollars a year. Oracle alone saves $2 billion a year by using its own technology. The company is now going out to other Fortune 500 companies and showing them what they can do using Oracle technology.

Reason for Recommendation

You've heard a lot about how B2B (business-to-business) e-commerce is going to be huge in the future. Oracle is the ultimate B2B player. It provides the technology large corporations will need to conduct commerce over the Internet. Oracle is also spinning off related companies, creating additional value for shareholders.

Biggest Risks

The biggest risk is the actual functioning of the application software, because the company's database is pretty much bulletproof. The company also has to get out and sell its systems. Each time it does so, it faces competition from other providers known as "point competitors." Point competitors are companies that develop systems for one particular product area. Oracle, on the other hand, is a generalist, developing a generic system that can be used in any industry. It is therefore essential that the company maintain the quality of its application software.

Bottom Line

I believe Oracle can continue to compound earnings, and therefore its share price, at about 25 percent annually for the next five to ten years. That's why I began by saying it is a dominant core holding for every technology investor.

Contact Information: Oracle Corporation
500 Oracle Parkway
Redwood City, CA 94065
650-506-7000
<www.oracle.com>

BONUS PICK FOR 2001

GENE LOGIC

Symbol: GLGC
Exchange: Nasdaq

Gene Logic has the biggest database of gene expression data. Many companies are making headlines for sequencing and discovering genes. But once you find a gene, you must figure out what it does. The discovery creates many additional issues. Gene Logic has a huge library of tissue, and literally compares gene-by-gene what each one turns on and off. It then documents this information and makes it available to researchers. In other words, while the company doesn't make drugs, it helps pharmaceutical companies do so through the analysis of these genes. The company licenses this gene expression information and gets paid a royalty on any drug developed as a result. The company isn't profitable yet, but isn't far away from breakeven. I expect Gene Logic to be profitable in 2002. The stock has come down significantly in price, yet it is of high quality and far ahead of anyone else in this area.

Oracle Corp

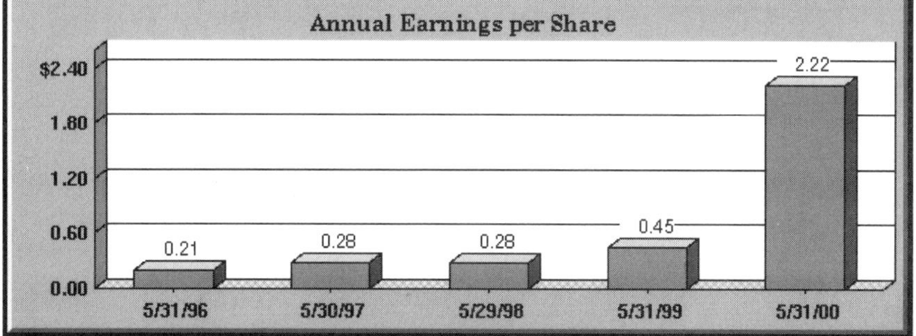

Oracle Corp

Symbol: ORCL Market/Exchange: Nasdaq NMS

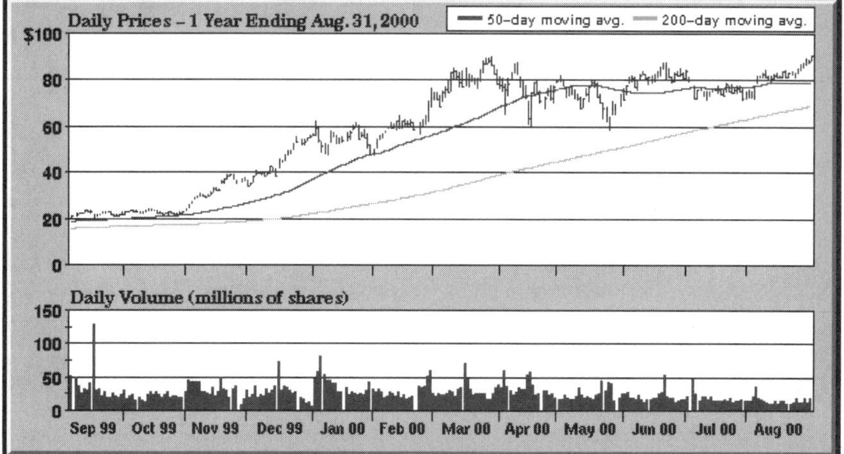

Latest Pricing Data (as of Aug. 31, 2000)		
Close (net change):	$90 15/16	(+2 11/16)
Day High & Low:	$91	$88 7/16
Volume & Avg. Volume:	19,513,000	26,750,084
52-Week High:	$91	Aug. 31, 2000
52-Week Low:	$19 7/16	Sep. 3, 1999
Latest Dividend:	$0.00	
Ind. Ann. Div. & Yield:	$0.00	N.A.
12 Month EPS:	$2.22	May 31, 2000
P/E Ratio & Beta Factor:	40.96	1.732
Shares Outstanding:	2.838 billion	
Market Value:	$258.118 billion	
Institutional Holdings:	44.29%	
Number of Institutions:	2022	
Primary Market:	Nasdaq NMS	
Component of:	S&P 500	

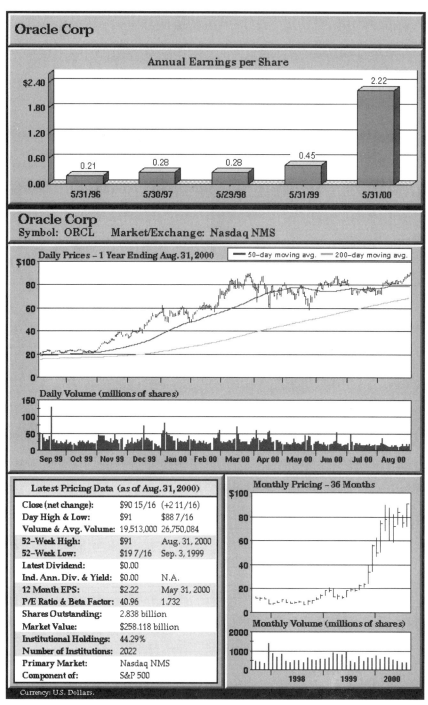

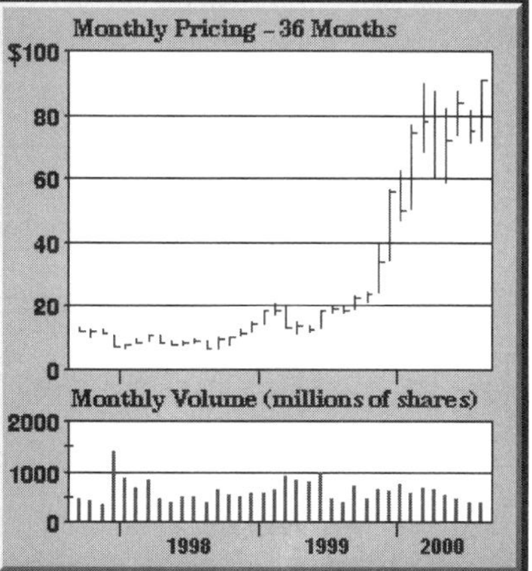

Currency: U.S. Dollars.

Source: Tradeline.Com, a Platinum Equity Holdings Company

Oracle Corp

Symbol : ORCL Market/Exchange : Nasdaq NMS

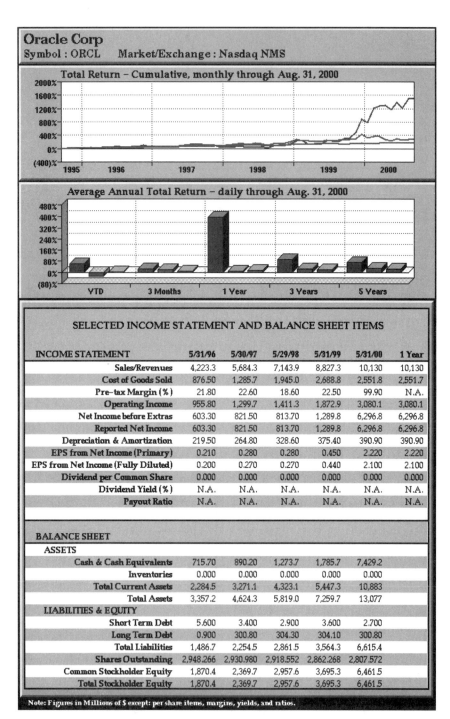

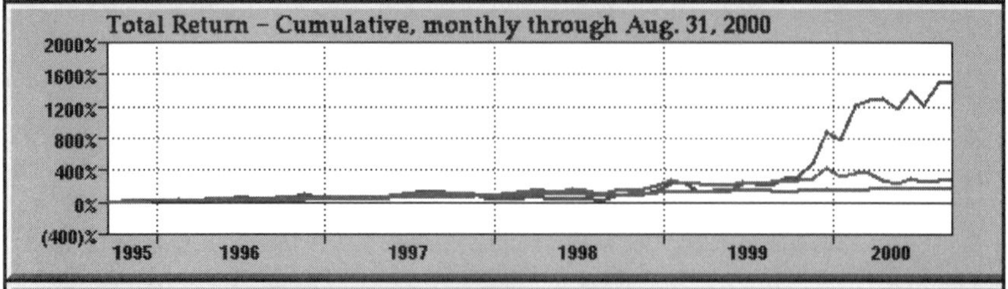

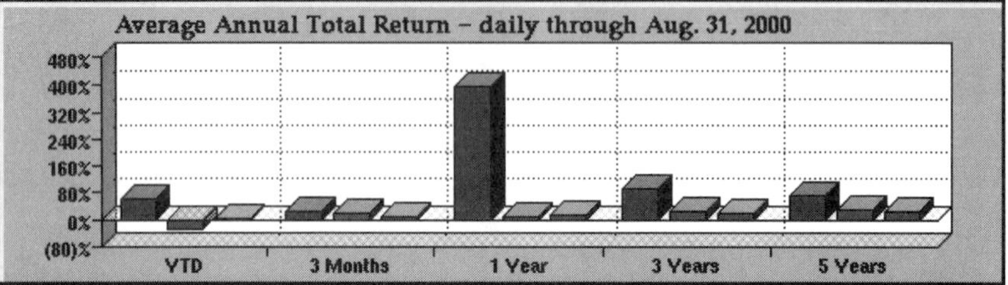

SELECTED INCOME STATEMENT AND BALANCE SHEET ITEMS

INCOME STATEMENT	5/31/96	5/30/97	5/29/98	5/31/99	5/31/00	1 Year
Sales/Revenues	4,223.3	5,684.3	7,143.9	8,827.3	10,130	10,130
Cost of Goods Sold	876.50	1,285.7	1,945.0	2,688.8	2,551.8	2,551.7
Pre-tax Margin (%)	21.80	22.60	18.60	22.50	99.90	N.A.
Operating Income	955.80	1,299.7	1,411.3	1,872.9	3,080.1	3,080.1
Net Income before Extras	603.30	821.50	813.70	1,289.8	6,296.8	6,296.8
Reported Net Income	603.30	821.50	813.70	1,289.8	6,296.8	6,296.8
Depreciation & Amortization	219.50	264.80	328.60	375.40	390.90	390.90
EPS from Net Income (Primary)	0.210	0.280	0.280	0.450	2.220	2.220
EPS from Net Income (Fully Diluted)	0.200	0.270	0.270	0.440	2.100	2.100
Dividend per Common Share	0.000	0.000	0.000	0.000	0.000	0.000
Dividend Yield (%)	N.A.	N.A.	N.A.	N.A.	N.A.	N.A.
Payout Ratio	N.A.	N.A.	N.A.	N.A.	N.A.	N.A.

BALANCE SHEET					
ASSETS					
Cash & Cash Equivalents	715.70	890.20	1,273.7	1,785.7	7,429.2
Inventories	0.000	0.000	0.000	0.000	0.000
Total Current Assets	2,284.5	3,271.1	4,323.1	5,447.3	10,883
Total Assets	3,357.2	4,624.3	5,819.0	7,259.7	13,077
LIABILITIES & EQUITY					
Short Term Debt	5.600	3.400	2.900	3.600	2.700
Long Term Debt	0.900	300.80	304.30	304.10	300.80
Total Liabilities	1,486.7	2,254.5	2,861.5	3,564.3	6,615.4
Shares Outstanding	2,948.266	2,930.980	2,918.552	2,862.268	2,807.572
Common Stockholder Equity	1,870.4	2,369.7	2,957.6	3,695.3	6,461.5
Total Stockholder Equity	1,870.4	2,369.7	2,957.6	3,695.3	6,461.5

Note: Figures in Millions of $ except: per share items, margins, yields, and ratios.

Source: Tradeline.Com, a Platinum Equity Holdings Company

SARA LEE

Vita Nelson
The Moneypaper

Company Background

Sara Lee is a diversified food and apparel company, known for its famous slogan, "Nobody doesn't like Sara Lee." It is a global manufacturer of brand-name food, coffee, tea, household, body care, foodservice, and branded apparel products. I must admit one of the main reasons I like this stock is because I love the company's cheesecake and Coach leather products. Coach makes some beautiful handbags. They are good, solid products that cost about one-third of what you would pay for fancy designer Italian goods, yet they look exactly the same. I also buy the company's Hanes and L'eggs stockings products. Yes, as you might have gathered, I'm a big believer in investing in companies you are familiar with. I'm very familiar with the products made by Sara Lee, and bet you are, too.

But before buying any stock, you should dig deeper to make sure it's also a good investment. I believe Sara Lee is. Earnings have consistently been growing, although not as fast as one might hope for. That's largely because the company has made several strategic acquisitions in recent years. In the branded apparel division, Sara Lee has seen strong growth in its knit products, legware, and Coach leatherware operations. It also completed its $3 billion stock repurchase plan in early 2000, and launched a bid for British lingerie maker Courtaulds Textiles. Before that, the company acquired Chock Full o' Nuts.

Reason for Recommendation

This stock is down considerably from the high it reached in 1998, yet earnings continue to grow. It sells for a reasonable PE ratio that is low by historical standards, and the stock has a yield of around 3 percent. The company has really restructured itself to get rid of some of its manufacturing elements, and that should help it to produce even better earnings in subsequent years.

Biggest Risks

Perhaps the biggest risk is that this is considered to be a so-called old economy stock. Such investments aren't very sexy these days on Wall Street. But I have a lot of confidence in Sare Lee. It's not always easy to explain why a stock like this doesn't do well, or why it can fall 50 percent (as Sara Lee did) for no good reason. Still, one concern is that investors might be slow to bid this stock up because its businesses are so boring.

Bottom Line

Sara Lee is, in my opinion, making all the right moves to streamline its business, and its products are better than ever. I also like the company's dividend reinvestment program, which allows you to buy additional shares of stock and reinvest your dividends directly through the company without paying any fees or brokerage commissions.

Contact Information: Sara Lee Corp.
Three First National Plaza, Suite 4600
Chicago, IL 60602
312-726-2600
<www.saralee.com>

BONUS PICK FOR 2001

H.J. HENIZ

Symbol: HNZ
Exchange: NYSE

Here's another stock I like because I'm a fan of its products. I love Heinz ketchup. I hate to be so simplistic, but in a market environment like the one we're in now, I think you should stick with quality companies with proven records, and Heinz definitely fits the bill. The company was founded in 1876 and has a top rating from Standard & Poors. It manufactures and markets an extensive line of processed food products around the world, including ketchup and other condiments, pet food, baby food, frozen potatoes, and low-calorie items. Some of the more popular product lines from Heinz include Star-Kist tuna, Nine Lives cat food, and, of course, the ketchup. The stock now trades at the low end of its historical PE range. My only complaint is that sometimes the company's ketchup takes too long to get out of the bottle!

Sara Lee Corp

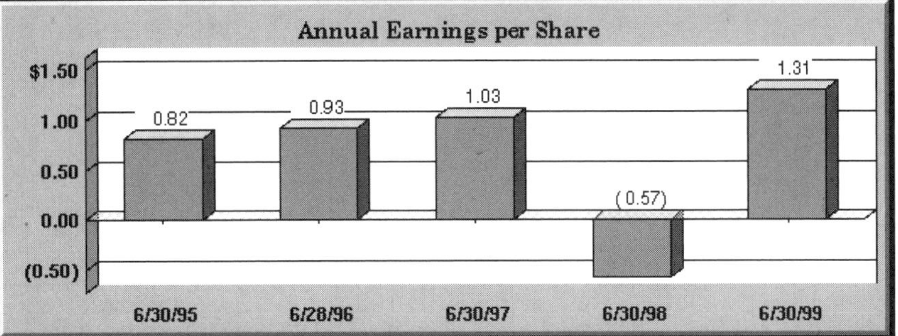

Sara Lee Corp

Symbol: SLE Market/Exchange: NYSE

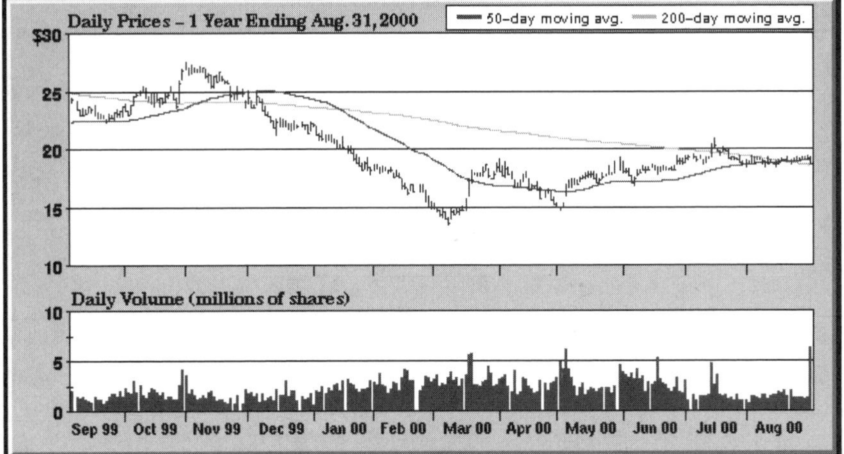

Latest Pricing Data (as of Aug. 31, 2000)		
Close (net change):	$18 41/64	(–35/64)
Day High & Low:	$19 1/4	$18 9/16
Volume & Avg. Volume:	6,293,000	2,215,935
52-Week High:	$27 1/2	Oct. 29, 1999
52-Week Low:	$13 3/8	Mar. 7, 2000
Latest Dividend:	$0.14	Aug. 30, 2000
Ind. Ann. Div. & Yield:	$0.54	2.90%
12 Month EPS:	$1.39	June 30, 2000
P/E Ratio & Beta Factor:	13.41	0.298
Shares Outstanding:	869.567 million	
Market Value:	$16.209 billion	
Institutional Holdings:	54.82%	
Number of Institutions:	1153	
Primary Market:	NYSE	
Component of:	S&P 500	

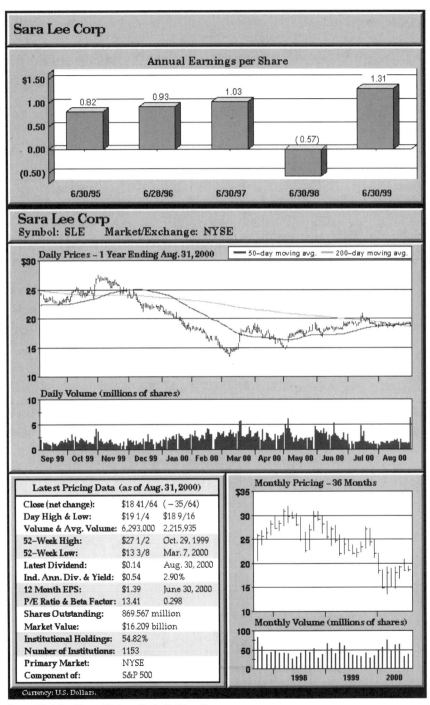

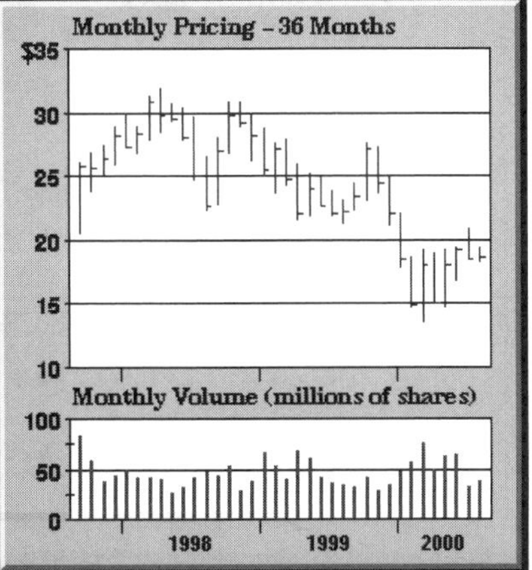

Currency: U.S. Dollars.

Source: Tradeline.Com, a Platinum Equity Holdings Company

Sara Lee Corp

Symbol : SLE Market/Exchange : NYSE

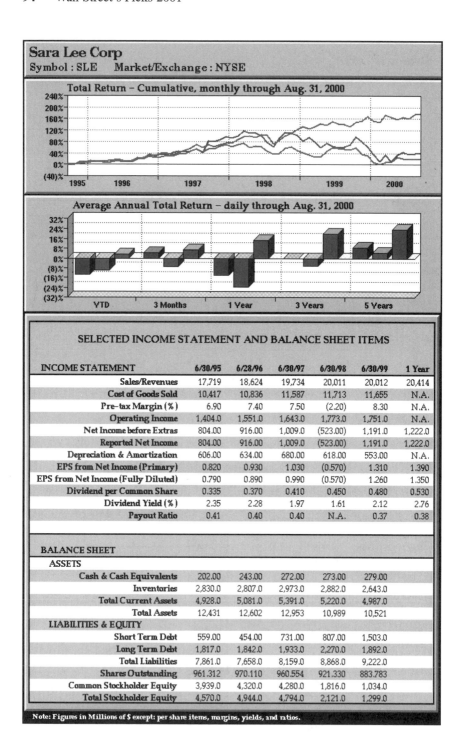

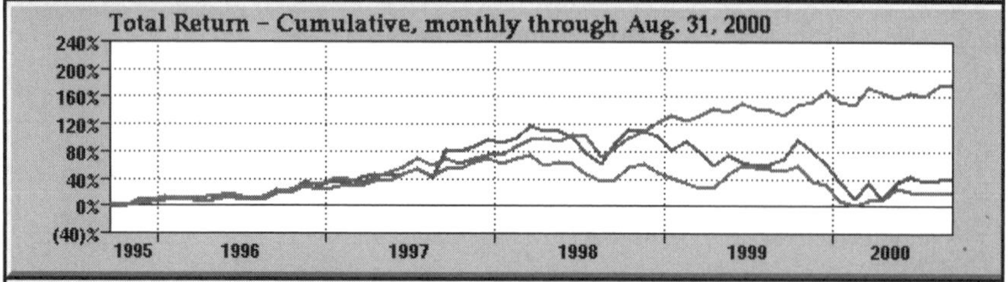

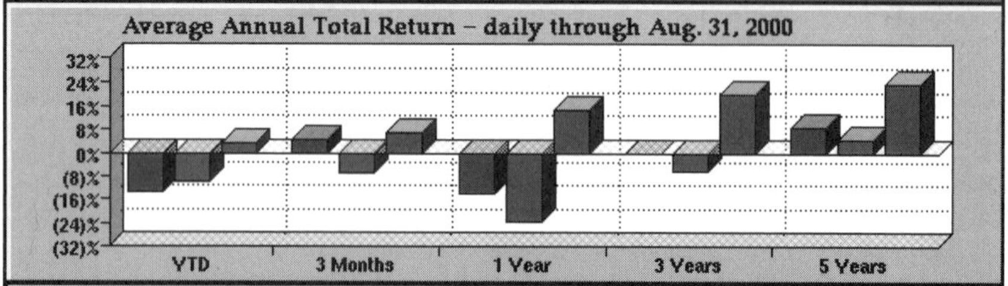

SELECTED INCOME STATEMENT AND BALANCE SHEET ITEMS

INCOME STATEMENT	6/30/95	6/28/96	6/30/97	6/30/98	6/30/99	1 Year
Sales/Revenues	17,719	18,624	19,734	20,011	20,012	20,414
Cost of Goods Sold	10,417	10,836	11,587	11,713	11,655	N.A.
Pre-tax Margin (%)	6.90	7.40	7.50	(2.20)	8.30	N.A.
Operating Income	1,404.0	1,551.0	1,643.0	1,773.0	1,751.0	N.A.
Net Income before Extras	804.00	916.00	1,009.0	(523.00)	1,191.0	1,222.0
Reported Net Income	804.00	916.00	1,009.0	(523.00)	1,191.0	1,222.0
Depreciation & Amortization	606.00	634.00	680.00	618.00	553.00	N.A.
EPS from Net Income (Primary)	0.820	0.930	1.030	(0.570)	1.310	1.390
EPS from Net Income (Fully Diluted)	0.790	0.890	0.990	(0.570)	1.260	1.350
Dividend per Common Share	0.335	0.370	0.410	0.450	0.480	0.530
Dividend Yield (%)	2.35	2.28	1.97	1.61	2.12	2.76
Payout Ratio	0.41	0.40	0.40	N.A.	0.37	0.38

BALANCE SHEET					
ASSETS					
Cash & Cash Equivalents	202.00	243.00	272.00	273.00	279.00
Inventories	2,830.0	2,807.0	2,973.0	2,882.0	2,643.0
Total Current Assets	4,928.0	5,081.0	5,391.0	5,220.0	4,987.0
Total Assets	12,431	12,602	12,953	10,989	10,521
LIABILITIES & EQUITY					
Short Term Debt	559.00	454.00	731.00	807.00	1,503.0
Long Term Debt	1,817.0	1,842.0	1,933.0	2,270.0	1,892.0
Total Liabilities	7,861.0	7,658.0	8,159.0	8,868.0	9,222.0
Shares Outstanding	961.312	970.110	960.554	921.330	883.783
Common Stockholder Equity	3,939.0	4,320.0	4,280.0	1,816.0	1,034.0
Total Stockholder Equity	4,570.0	4,944.0	4,794.0	2,121.0	1,299.0

Note: Figures in Millions of $ except: per share items, margins, yields, and ratios.

Source: Tradeline.Com, a Platinum Equity Holdings Company

SILICONIX

Al Frank
Al Frank Asset Management

Company Background

Siliconix is a leading manufacturer of power MOSFETs, power integrated circuits, and analog signal processing devices for computers, cell phones, fixed communication networks, automobiles, and other electronic systems. (MOSFETs are integrated circuits used in a variety of applications.) Many semiconductor-related companies are doing extremely well these days, and Siliconix is no exception.

My research director, John Buckingham, follows this company rather closely. We always focus on a company's fundamentals, and Siliconix seems to be hitting on all cylinders. I must tell you that this stock has shot up more than 700 percent since we first bought it in April 1998. How can a value investor recommend a stock that has gone up so much? For that matter, how can a value investor recommend a semiconductor company in the first place? Because I believe growth is a component of value. When you look at what the overall stock market is paying for growth companies of Siliconix's magnitude, you can quickly see that the stock is still a good value.

Reason for Recommendation

What's impressive is how Siliconix was able to grow its earnings well before the other major semiconductor companies began to benefit from this recent upcycle. In fact, year-over-year growth at Siliconix has been in the 200 percent range. The big question is how long that can continue. One indication is to look at what is coming out of New York Stock Exchange–traded Vishay, which owns 80 percent of Siliconix. So far, Vishay keeps telling analysts it will exceed earnings expectations. I believe that's largely due to the growth of Siliconix. Cell phone technology, in particular, is booming, and Siliconix should continue to deliver phenomenal earnings for the next few quarters.

Biggest Risks

Nevertheless, the semiconductor industry has always been cyclical. The market seems to have forgotten that, but this could quickly change. It's sexy to own semiconductor stocks right now. The risk is it won't be next year. The stock has also risen considerably, so valuation is a concern. But I would argue that comparable semiconductor stocks are much more pricey than Siliconix.

Bottom Line

Shares of Siliconix are thinly traded on the Nasdaq, but I believe they are worth a close look. My three-to-five-year target for this stock is $167 per share.

Contact Information: Siliconix Incorporated
2201 Laurelwood Road
Santa Clara, CA 95054
408-988-8000
<www.siliconix.com>

BONUS PICK FOR 2001

FEDERAL MOGUL

Symbol: FMO
Exchange: NYSE

Auto parts maker Federal Mogul is a former momentum stock that has basically crashed. It traded up to around $70 per share on expectations of earning $5 per share in 1999. When earnings came in at only $4, the stock fell all the way down to $14. This is a company that is involved in a variety of areas and manufactures a number of innovative solutions to global customers in the automotive, light truck, heavy-duty farm, and industrial markets. Anco wiper blades and Champion spark plugs are two of the company's most popular lines. This company does have a lot of debt, along with some potential asbestos liability, but I think it's fair to say that's more than factored into the stock. I think what has happened is that Wall Street is focused solely on hyper growth. Federal Mogul is growing, but at a more reasonable rate. As a result, you can get this quality, profitable company at a PE of less than 4. I don't know what catalyst will drive the stock higher, but value is almost always eventually rewarded. My three-to-five-year target for Federal Mogul is $60 per share.

Siliconix Inc New De

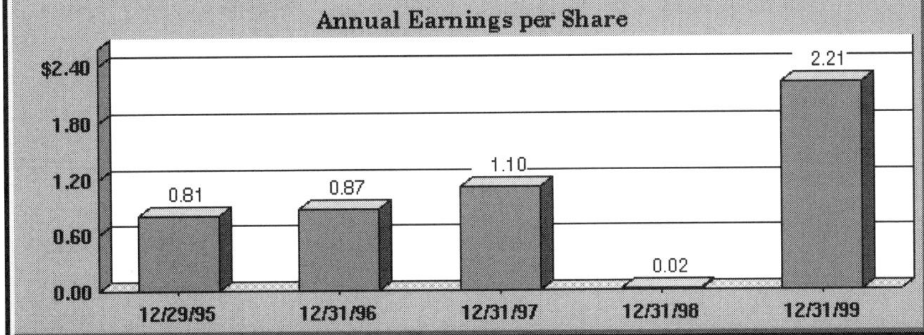

Siliconix Inc New De

Symbol: SILI **Market/Exchange: Nasdaq NMS**

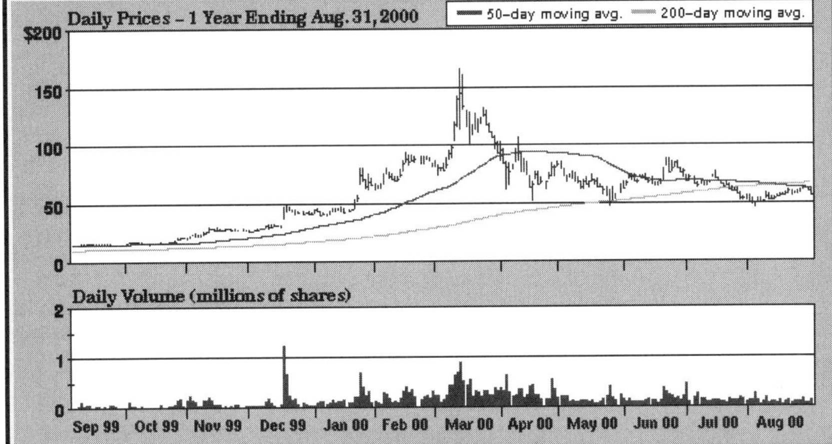

Latest Pricing Data (as of Aug. 31, 2000)		
Close (net change):	$55 7/8	(–3 5/8)
Day High & Low:	$61 15/32	$55 7/8
Volume & Avg. Volume:	107,200	155,013
52-Week High:	$165	Mar. 13, 2000
52-Week Low:	$13 21/64	Sep. 23, 1999
Latest Dividend:	$0.00	Nov. 3, 1980
Ind. Ann. Div. & Yield:	$0.00	N.A.
12 Month EPS:	$3.27	June 30, 2000
P/E Ratio & Beta Factor:	17.09	1.062
Shares Outstanding:	29.879 million	
Market Value:	$1.669 billion	
Institutional Holdings:	8.51%	
Number of Institutions:	106	
Primary Market:	Nasdaq NMS	

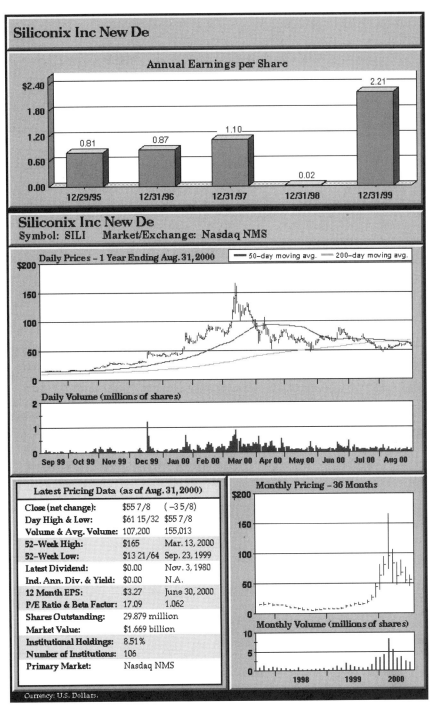

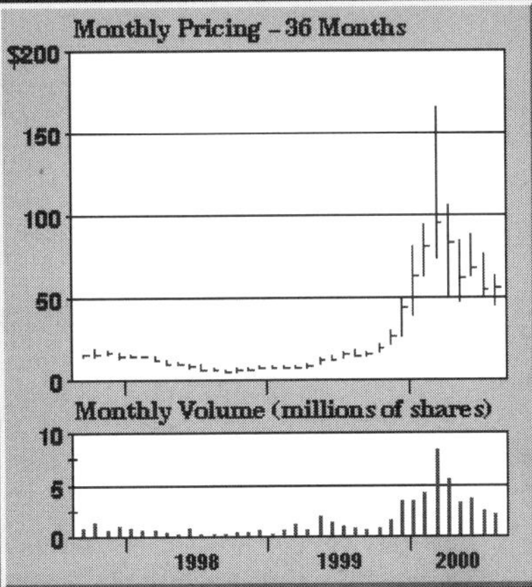

Currency: U.S. Dollars.

Source: Tradeline.Com, a Platinum Equity Holdings Company

Siliconix Inc New De

Symbol : SILI Market/Exchange : Nasdaq NMS

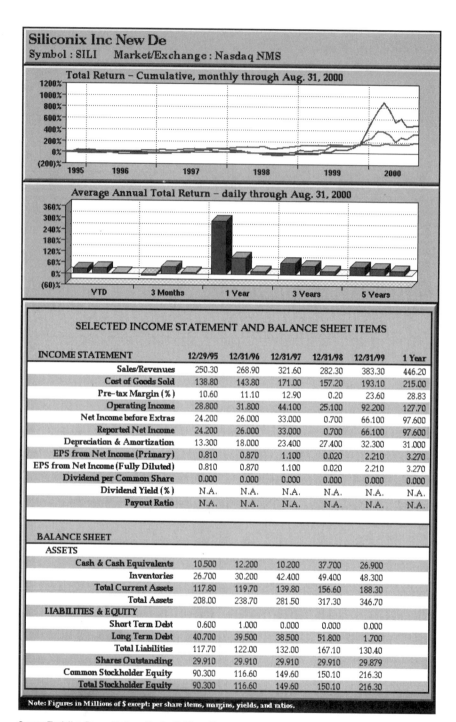

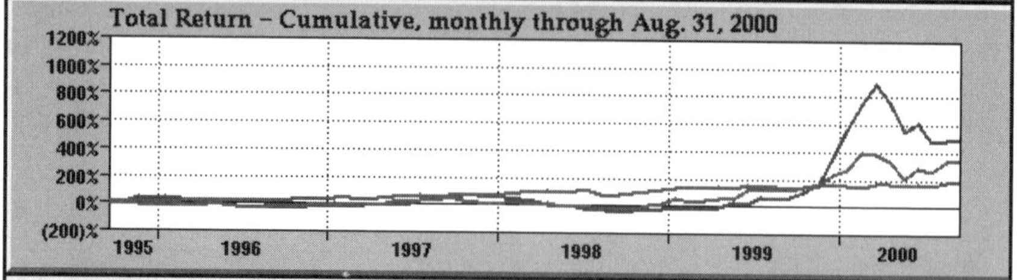

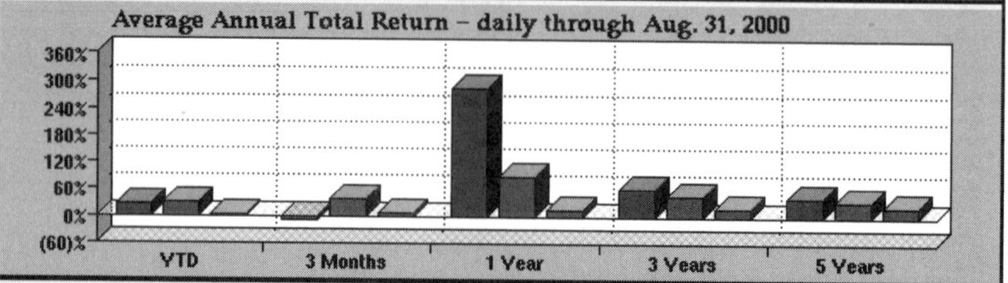

SELECTED INCOME STATEMENT AND BALANCE SHEET ITEMS

INCOME STATEMENT	12/29/95	12/31/96	12/31/97	12/31/98	12/31/99	1 Year
Sales/Revenues	250.30	268.90	321.60	282.30	383.30	446.20
Cost of Goods Sold	138.80	143.80	171.00	157.20	193.10	215.00
Pre-tax Margin (%)	10.60	11.10	12.90	0.20	23.60	28.83
Operating Income	28.800	31.800	44.100	25.100	92.200	127.70
Net Income before Extras	24.200	26.000	33.000	0.700	66.100	97.600
Reported Net Income	24.200	26.000	33.000	0.700	66.100	97.600
Depreciation & Amortization	13.300	18.000	23.400	27.400	32.300	31.000
EPS from Net Income (Primary)	0.810	0.870	1.100	0.020	2.210	3.270
EPS from Net Income (Fully Diluted)	0.810	0.870	1.100	0.020	2.210	3.270
Dividend per Common Share	0.000	0.000	0.000	0.000	0.000	0.000
Dividend Yield (%)	N.A.	N.A.	N.A.	N.A.	N.A.	N.A.
Payout Ratio	N.A.	N.A.	N.A.	N.A.	N.A.	N.A.

BALANCE SHEET					
ASSETS					
Cash & Cash Equivalents	10.500	12.200	10.200	37.700	26.900
Inventories	26.700	30.200	42.400	49.400	48.300
Total Current Assets	117.80	119.70	139.80	156.60	188.30
Total Assets	208.00	238.70	281.50	317.30	346.70
LIABILITIES & EQUITY					
Short Term Debt	0.600	1.000	0.000	0.000	0.000
Long Term Debt	40.700	39.500	38.500	51.800	1.700
Total Liabilities	117.70	122.00	132.00	167.10	130.40
Shares Outstanding	29.910	29.910	29.910	29.910	29.879
Common Stockholder Equity	90.300	116.60	149.60	150.10	216.30
Total Stockholder Equity	90.300	116.60	149.60	150.10	216.30

Note: Figures in Millions of $ except: per share items, margins, yields, and ratios.

Source: Tradeline.Com, a Platinum Equity Holdings Company

STANLEY FURNITURE

Ronald Muhlenkamp
Muhlenkamp & Company

Company Background

Stanley Furniture makes three lines of wood furniture for the upper-medium price range. The first is youth furniture, which accounts for about one-third of the company's total business. Stanley's chairman tells me that youth furniture is not price sensitive. If the parents don't buy it, the grandparents will. That's good, especially in the event the economy slows down. The second line, which accounts for another third of overall business, is home office furniture. If you believe people will buy computers, they'll probably also buy new furniture for their home offices. The final third is comprised of bedroom and dining room furniture.

Stanley Furniture has a historic return on equity of well over 20 percent, and revenues have been growing in excess of 10 percent annually. The company just added more capacity, to keep up with demand, and I expect that going forward earnings will grow by more than 15 percent. The company should earn around $3.10 per share in 2001.

Several years ago, the company tried to get into the upholstered furniture business, but found it wasn't very good at it. That business was quickly shut down. This shows you management doesn't spend its cash flow on dumb things that don't make money for shareholders.

Reason for Recommendation

There are a few reasons I like this stock. First, I believe the economy is in good shape, and the consumer knows it. People won't keep buying cell phones and computers without buying cars and furniture. They're either confident or they're not. But the market is pricing this company as if we've gone through a recession. Three years ago, Stanley Furniture traded for 15 to 20 times earnings. Today it's down to around 8 times earnings. So even though the company has done nicely over the past couple of years, the stock hasn't. I think you're getting a chance to buy this stock at very attractive levels. I've known management for around ten years and like them very much. They've always done what they've said they would do and they own a sizeable chunk of stock.

Biggest Risks

The biggest risk is that the Federal Reserve raises rates so high that people stop buying furniture. I think if that were going to happen, it would have already happened by now. The funny thing is that we've had a great excuse for a recession for about two years now, yet we haven't had one. The other risk is that this isn't a tech stock, so you have to believe investors will show a renewed interest in non-sexy stocks. In some ways, that's already starting to happen.

Bottom Line

This is a company that's been around for a long time with a good record of profitability, a quality product, and great prospects for the coming year.

Contact Information: Stanley Furniture Company
1641 Fairystone Park Highway
Stanleytown, VA 24168
540-627-2000
<www.stanleyfurniture.com>

BONUS PICK FOR 2001

CONSECO

Symbol: CSC
Exchange: Nasdaq

I consider Conseco to be a second-level financial stock. The company is a source for insurance, investing, and lending products. Unfortunately, Conseco has been forced to make several recent changes to satisfy Wall Street. For one thing, there were complaints about how the company was accounting for various items. Then management was forced to sell off its acquisition of Green Tree Financial, which I think is a very nice franchise. A big investor out of Boston recently bought $500 million of Conseco stock for $19 per share. This guy is smart. For him to put that much money in this company shows me he agrees with my assessment that Conseco has a promising future and is trading at a cheap price.

Stanley Furniture Inc New

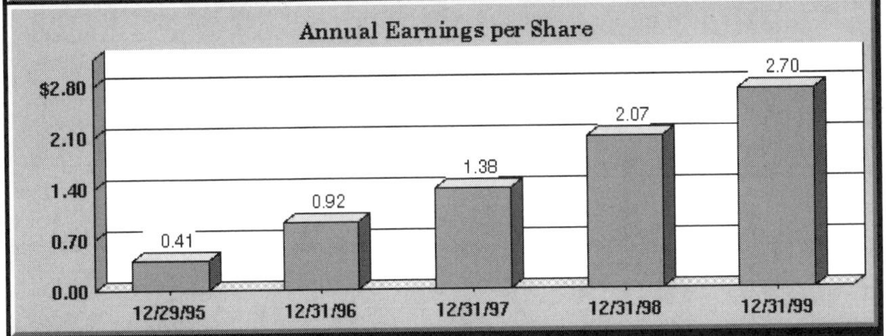

Stanley Furniture Inc New

Symbol: STLY Market/Exchange: Nasdaq NMS

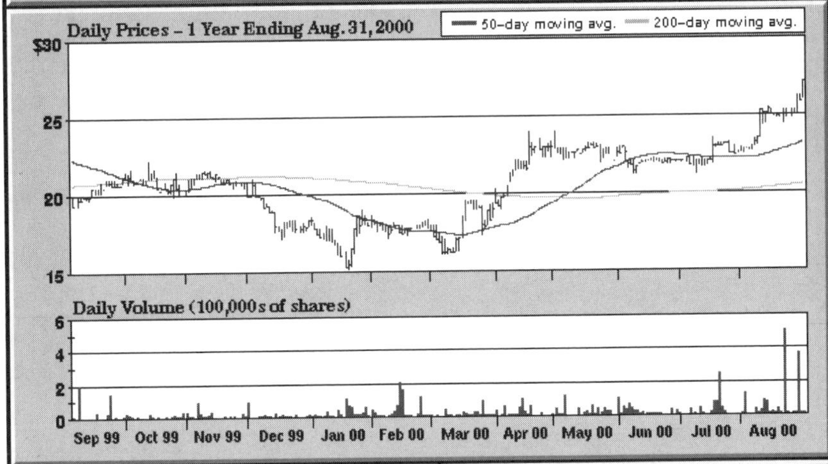

Latest Pricing Data (as of Aug. 31, 2000)

Close (net change):	$27 1/8	(+1 1/4)
Day High & Low:	$27 1/8	$25 15/16
Volume & Avg. Volume:	11,400	24,716
52-Week High:	$27 1/8	Aug. 31, 2000
52-Week Low:	$15 1/8	Jan. 19, 2000
Latest Dividend:	$0.00	
Ind. Ann. Div. & Yield:	$0.00	N.A.
12 Month EPS:	$2.90	June 30, 2000
P/E Ratio & Beta Factor:	9.35	0.555
Shares Outstanding:	7.347 million	
Market Value:	$199 million	
Institutional Holdings:	86.35%	
Number of Institutions:	66	
Primary Market:	Nasdaq NMS	

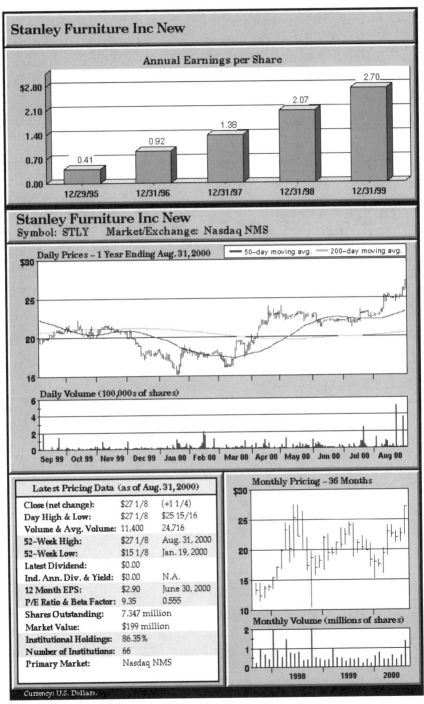

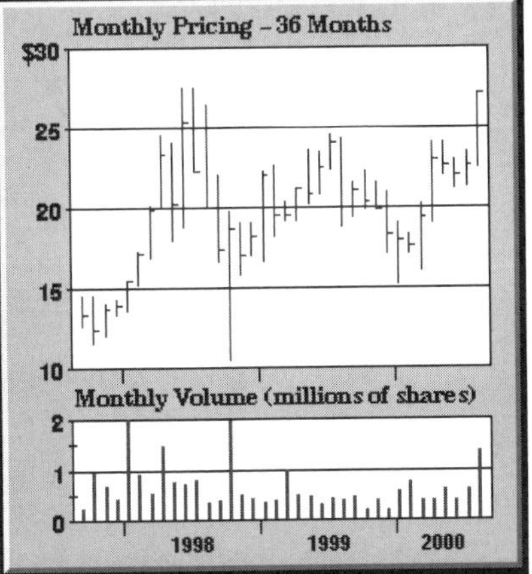

Currency: U.S. Dollars.

Source: Tradeline.Com, a Platinum Equity Holdings Company

Stanley Furniture Inc New

Symbol : STLY Market/Exchange : Nasdaq NMS

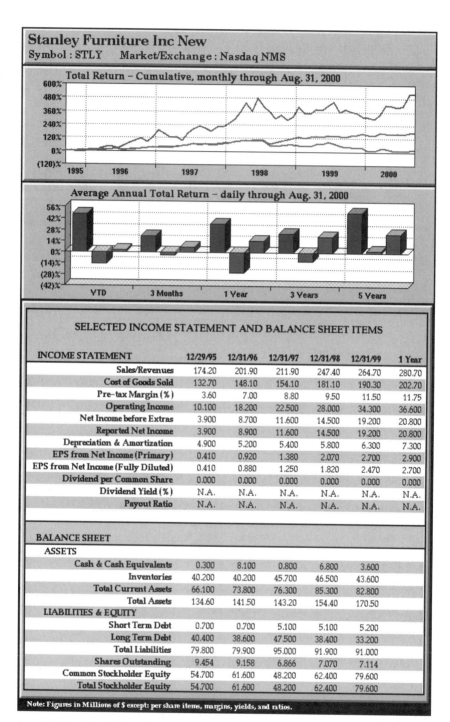

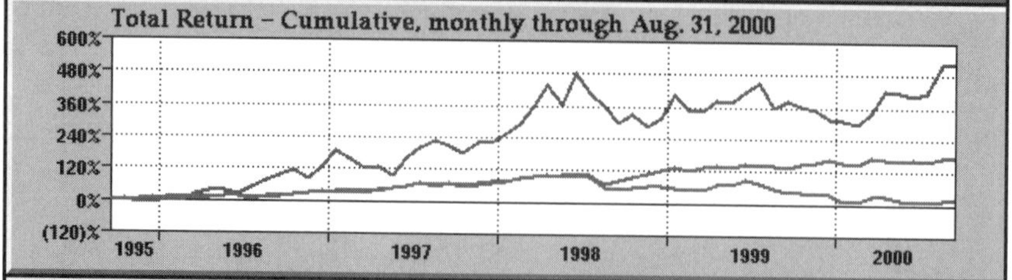

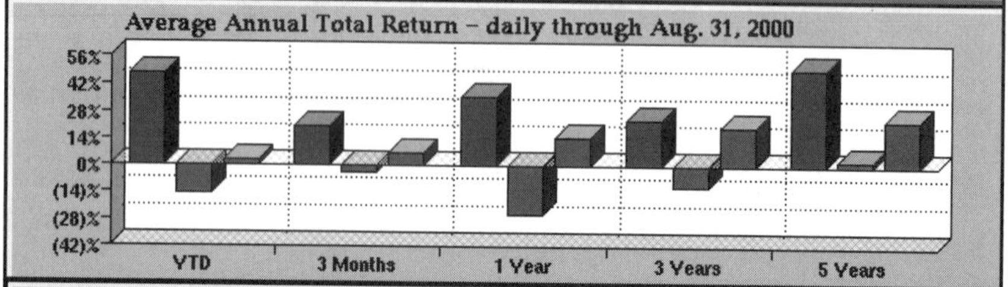

SELECTED INCOME STATEMENT AND BALANCE SHEET ITEMS

INCOME STATEMENT	12/29/95	12/31/96	12/31/97	12/31/98	12/31/99	1 Year
Sales/Revenues	174.20	201.90	211.90	247.40	264.70	280.70
Cost of Goods Sold	132.70	148.10	154.10	181.10	190.30	202.70
Pre-tax Margin (%)	3.60	7.00	8.80	9.50	11.50	11.75
Operating Income	10.100	18.200	22.500	28.000	34.300	36.600
Net Income before Extras	3.900	8.700	11.600	14.500	19.200	20.800
Reported Net Income	3.900	8.900	11.600	14.500	19.200	20.800
Depreciation & Amortization	4.900	5.200	5.400	5.800	6.300	7.300
EPS from Net Income (Primary)	0.410	0.920	1.380	2.070	2.700	2.900
EPS from Net Income (Fully Diluted)	0.410	0.880	1.250	1.820	2.470	2.700
Dividend per Common Share	0.000	0.000	0.000	0.000	0.000	0.000
Dividend Yield (%)	N.A.	N.A.	N.A.	N.A.	N.A.	N.A.
Payout Ratio	N.A.	N.A.	N.A.	N.A.	N.A.	N.A.

BALANCE SHEET					
ASSETS					
Cash & Cash Equivalents	0.300	8.100	0.800	6.800	3.600
Inventories	40.200	40.200	45.700	46.500	43.600
Total Current Assets	66.100	73.800	76.300	85.300	82.800
Total Assets	134.60	141.50	143.20	154.40	170.50
LIABILITIES & EQUITY					
Short Term Debt	0.700	0.700	5.100	5.100	5.200
Long Term Debt	40.400	38.600	47.500	38.400	33.200
Total Liabilities	79.800	79.900	95.000	91.900	91.000
Shares Outstanding	9.454	9.158	6.866	7.070	7.114
Common Stockholder Equity	54.700	61.600	48.200	62.400	79.600
Total Stockholder Equity	54.700	61.600	48.200	62.400	79.600

Note: Figures in Millions of $ except: per share items, margins, yields, and ratios.

Source: Tradeline.Com, a Platinum Equity Holdings Company

STARTEC GLOBAL COMMUNICATIONS

John Wallace
RS Investment Management

Company Background

Startec Global Communications is an international long distance company that owns its own global network. It has a unique focus, in that it gears its marketing primarily toward ethnic communities in the U.S., including the Hispanic, Latin, Chinese, Middle Eastern, and Eastern European markets. Wall Street tends to look at small long distance companies like this and yawn, largely because their revenue mix tends to be more low-margin wholesale than retail. Startec is no exception. About 70 percent of the company's revenue comes from low-margin wholesale operations. But Startec is slowly changing this, and within the next couple of years, it intends to have retail operations account for up to 70 percent of revenues.

More importantly, Startec owns its own network. Plus, the company's strategic expansion plans tie it right into the Internet. The company will be able to expand its reach by bundling long distance services with voice and data transport, as well as being an Internet service provider. This bundling should lead to higher revenues, less customer churn, better margins, and a greater stock price valuation. Startec is already headed in this direction. It owns five foreign Internet portals, including sites for both the Chinese and Middle Eastern communities, and more are on the way. Competing portals have astronomical valuations.

Reason for Recommendation

Startec's North American operations are already profitable from an EBITDA point of view. The company has a market capitalization of less than $200 million and owns five Internet portals. By comparison, as this book goes to press, China.com has a market capitalization of $1.6 billion. Startec also has the ability to offer a technology called VoIP, which stands for voice over the Internet, in 44 different countries. Competitors offering this technology also have much higher market capitalizations. What's more, Startec is a leading Internet service provider in a number of foreign markets. It will be able to bundle all of its many services to consumers around the world.

Biggest Risks

The company has enough cash on hand and debt borrowing facilities to fund capital spending needs well into 2001, but after that it will have to raise more money to fund its growth plans. If the stock markets remain unfriendly to Internet-related companies, that could be a problem. In addition, this is an illiquid, underowned, and underfollowed company. But that is also an opportunity.

Bottom Line

This is a company with revenues, a growing business, and solid financing through mid-2001. It is a full-service telecommunications and Internet company building a global network, with agreements already in place in 44 different countries. I could see Startec being a $60 to $70 per share stock in a couple of years.

Contact Information: Startec Global Communications Corporation
10411 Motor City Drive
Bethesda, MD 20817
301-365-8959
<www.startec.com>

BONUS PICK FOR 2001

EL PASO ENERGY

Symbol: EPG
Exchange: NYSE

El Paso Energy is a much larger company than Startec. It recently merged with Coastal Corporation, becoming the largest natural gas transmission company in North America. It is also the second-largest gatherer and third-largest producer of gas. I think El Paso will be among the prime beneficiaries of what I see as good demand for natural gas growth in North America. The company has more than 40,000 miles of pipeline across the U.S. El Paso plans to expand into the communications business by putting fiber-optic cables along the pipelines. I believe the company could see earnings growth above 20 percent for the next couple of years. The stock is relatively priced and should have very low risk from here.

Startee Global Communications Corp

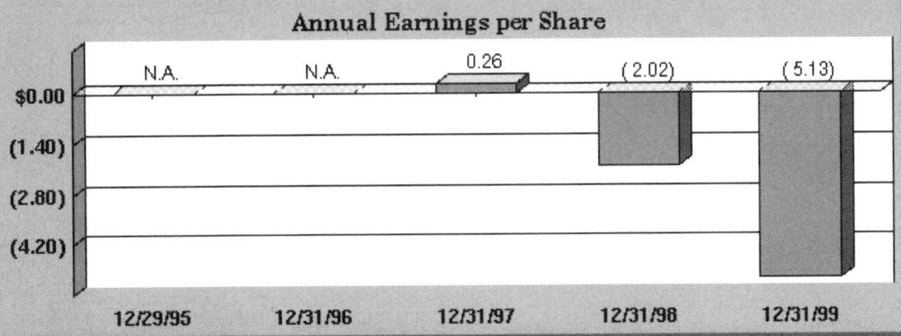

Startee Global Communications Corp

Symbol: STGC Market/Exchange: Nasdaq NMS

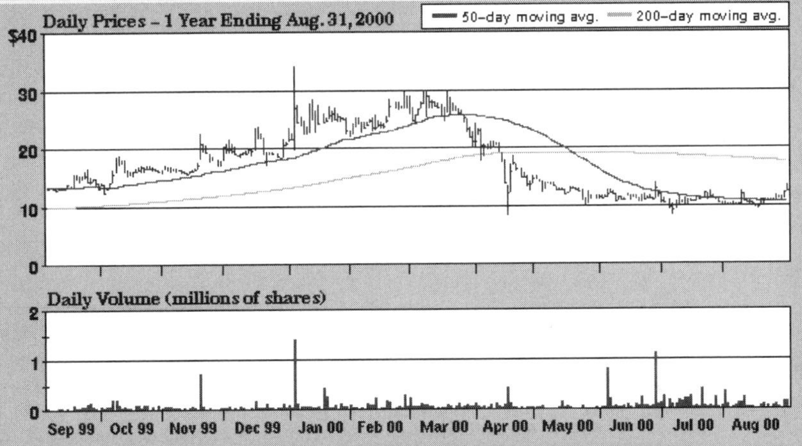

Latest Pricing Data (as of Aug. 31, 2000)		
Close (net change):	$12 3/8	(+5/16)
Day High & Low:	$13 1/4	$12 1/8
Volume & Avg. Volume:	131,800	77,971
52-Week High:	$34 1/8	Jan. 4, 2000
52-Week Low:	$8 1/8	July 6, 2000
Latest Dividend:	$0.00	
Ind. Ann. Div. & Yield:	$0.00	N.A.
12 Month EPS:	($4.48)	Jun. 30, 2000
P/E Ratio & Beta Factor:	N.A.	1.248
Shares Outstanding:	14.268 million	
Market Value:	$177 million	
Institutional Holdings:	31.85%	
Number of Institutions:	51	
Primary Market:	Nasdaq NMS	

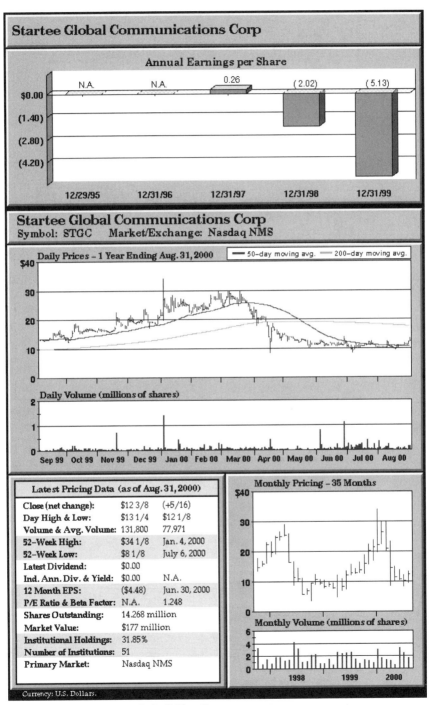

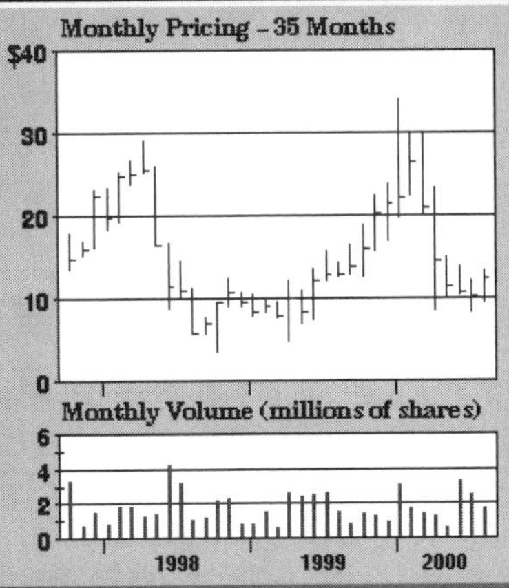

Currency: U.S. Dollars.

Source: Tradeline.Com, a Platinum Equity Holdings Company

Startec Global Communications Corp
Symbol : STGC Market/Exchange : Nasdaq NMS

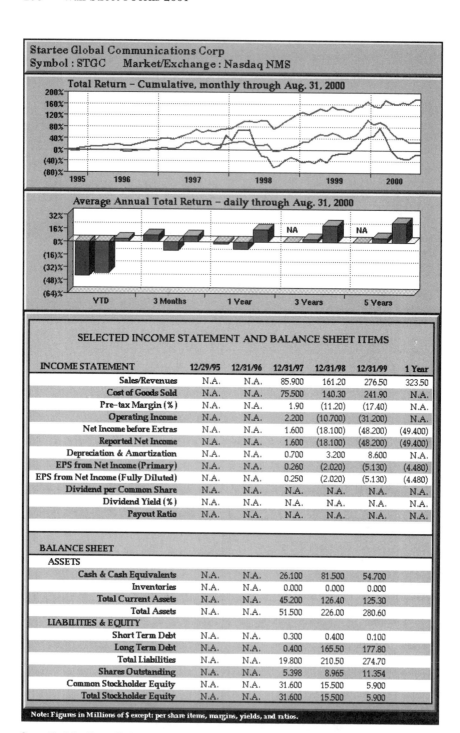

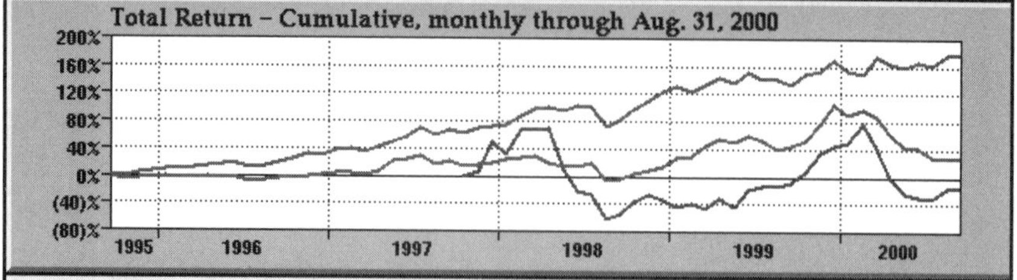

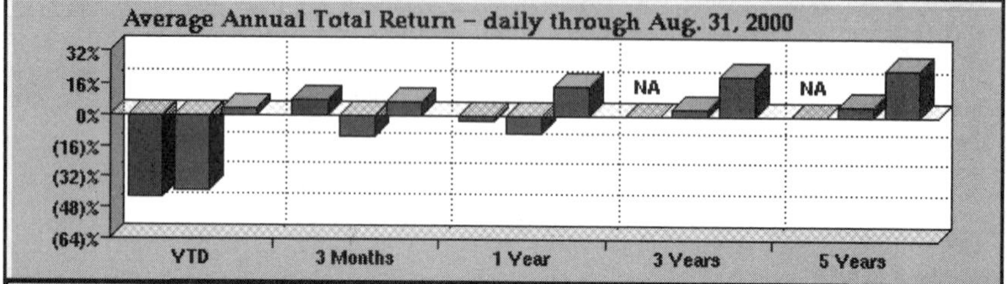

SELECTED INCOME STATEMENT AND BALANCE SHEET ITEMS

INCOME STATEMENT	12/29/95	12/31/96	12/31/97	12/31/98	12/31/99	1 Year
Sales/Revenues	N.A.	N.A.	85.900	161.20	276.50	323.50
Cost of Goods Sold	N.A.	N.A.	75.500	140.30	241.90	N.A.
Pre-tax Margin (%)	N.A.	N.A.	1.90	(11.20)	(17.40)	N.A.
Operating Income	N.A.	N.A.	2.200	(10.700)	(31.200)	N.A.
Net Income before Extras	N.A.	N.A.	1.600	(18.100)	(48.200)	(49.400)
Reported Net Income	N.A.	N.A.	1.600	(18.100)	(48.200)	(49.400)
Depreciation & Amortization	N.A.	N.A.	0.700	3.200	8.600	N.A.
EPS from Net Income (Primary)	N.A.	N.A.	0.260	(2.020)	(5.130)	(4.480)
EPS from Net Income (Fully Diluted)	N.A.	N.A.	0.250	(2.020)	(5.130)	(4.480)
Dividend per Common Share	N.A.	N.A.	N.A.	N.A.	N.A.	N.A.
Dividend Yield (%)	N.A.	N.A.	N.A.	N.A.	N.A.	N.A.
Payout Ratio	N.A.	N.A.	N.A.	N.A.	N.A.	N.A.

BALANCE SHEET					
ASSETS					
Cash & Cash Equivalents	N.A.	N.A.	26.100	81.500	54.700
Inventories	N.A.	N.A.	0.000	0.000	0.000
Total Current Assets	N.A.	N.A.	45.200	126.40	125.30
Total Assets	N.A.	N.A.	51.500	226.00	280.60
LIABILITIES & EQUITY					
Short Term Debt	N.A.	N.A.	0.300	0.400	0.100
Long Term Debt	N.A.	N.A.	0.400	165.50	177.80
Total Liabilities	N.A.	N.A.	19.800	210.50	274.70
Shares Outstanding	N.A.	N.A.	5.398	8.965	11.354
Common Stockholder Equity	N.A.	N.A.	31.600	15.500	5.900
Total Stockholder Equity	N.A.	N.A.	31.600	15.500	5.900

Note: Figures in Millions of $ except: per share items, margins, yields, and ratios.

Source: Tradeline.Com, a Platinum Equity Holdings Company

USG CORPORATION

Seth Glickenhaus
Glickenhaus & Co.

Company Background

USG is by far the cheapest stock I follow. At this time, the stock sells for just five times earnings. USG is one of the largest manufacturers and distributors of building materials. It owns about 30 percent of the market in manufacturing gypsum board, which is used in construction. New home building accounts for 40 percent of the company's business, with another 40 percent going to the reconstruction of new homes, and 20 percent to industrial and office buildings. USG has around 200 offices around the U.S. and is a very fine, low-cost producer.

To show you how powerful this company is, five years ago USG, Georgia Pacific, and National Gypsum had about 50 percent of the building materials market. Today they collectively have close to 80 percent. It's a semi-oligopoly. The price of these materials has been going up steadily. In fact, not long ago, builders were unable to get gypsum board, because the demand was so great. USG is a very low-cost producer, which gives it an extra advantage.

Reason for Recommendation

The company has around 50 million shares of stock outstanding. Management has bought back about 5 million shares, and has authorized a second buyback of another 5 million shares. This will artificially increase USG's earnings going forward, because earnings will be apportioned against 40 million instead of 50 million shares. The company is buying back stock with its free cash flow. Management obviously agrees with me that the stock is cheap.

Given all of the positives, why hasn't the stock gone higher? Because the stock market is a market of fashion. If you're not in technology these days, it seems people aren't interested in your company. But eventually everything comes back to value. Plus, housing starts and reconstruction are very strong right now, which should propel earnings even higher.

Biggest Risks

There are some negatives to this stock. The first is that if interest rates continue to rise, it will eventually arrest the growth of construction. The second risk is an asbestos risk. For five years, the company has been hit with asbestos claims. USG has always set up reserves, which have been more than adequate. But about two years ago, the Supreme Court threw out a class action case where both sides had agreed on a settlement to end the lawsuits. So this issue is still up in the air. Again, the company has set aside a reserve, and is also covered by insurance. But it's still bad for investor psychology.

Bottom Line

This is a chance to buy a great company at an absurdly inexpensive price. USG has huge future earnings potential, is an established company with good management, and manufactures a product that is always in demand.

Contact Information: USG Corporation
125 South Franklin Street
Chicago, IL 60606
312-606-4000
<www.usg.com>

BONUS PICK FOR 2001

COUNTRYWIDE CREDIT

Symbol: CCR
Exchange: NYSE

Countrywide is a mortgage company that services $253 billion in loans. This amount is growing at the rate of 16 percent annually. The company gets a fee for doing this. It's really a riskless business, because Countrywide doesn't own the mortgages. With interest rates moving higher, the company is getting very few internal refinancings. Countrywide also makes money from buying and selling mortgages. In addition, it recently bought an insurance company to guarantee mortgages, which is a second source of income. This is a solid, high-quality, growth company in an attractive market that you can get right now at a reasonable price.

USG Corporation New

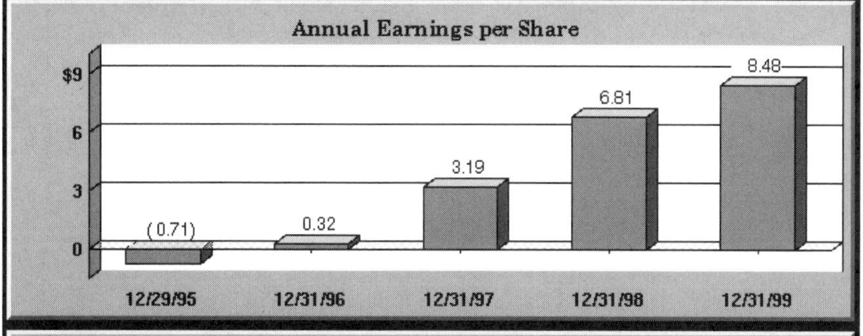

USG Corporation New

Symbol: USG Market/Exchange: NYSE

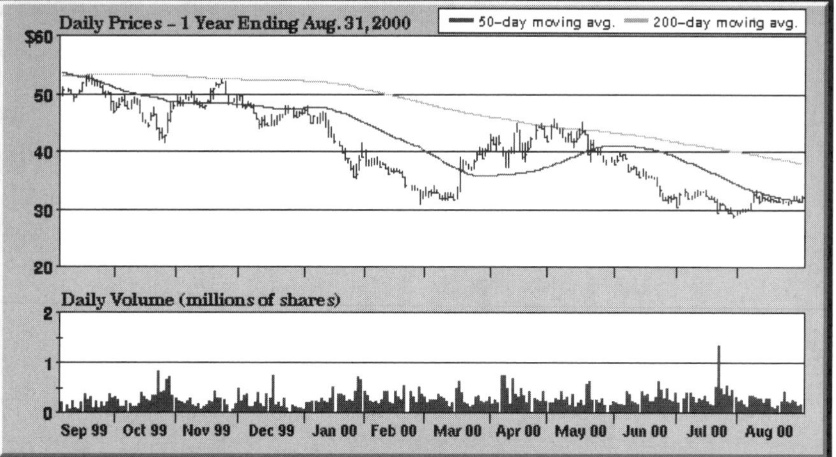

Latest Pricing Data (as of Aug. 31, 2000)		
Close (net change):	$32 3/16	(+15/16)
Day High & Low:	$32 7/16	$31
Volume & Avg. Volume:	182,100	284,376
52-Week High:	$53 1/8	Sep. 15, 1999
52-Week Low:	$28 3/8	July 28, 2000
Latest Dividend:	$0.15	Aug. 23, 2000
Ind. Ann. Div. & Yield:	$0.60	1.86%
12 Month EPS:	$8.91	June 30, 2000
P/E Ratio & Beta Factor:	3.61	0.831
Shares Outstanding:	44.443 million	
Market Value:	$1.431 billion	
Institutional Holdings:	70.67%	
Number of Institutions:	374	
Primary Market:	NYSE	

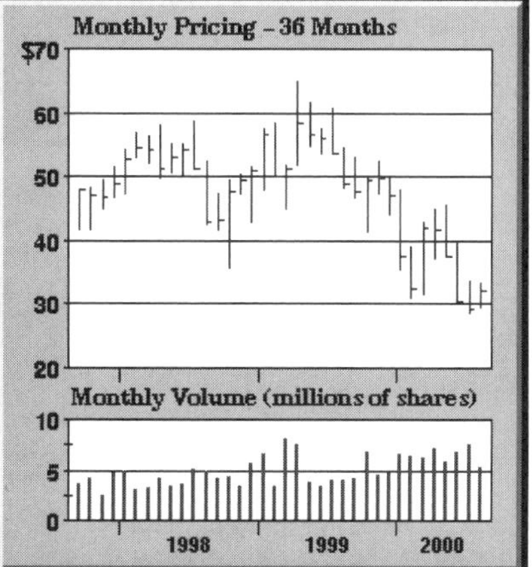

Currency: U.S. Dollars.

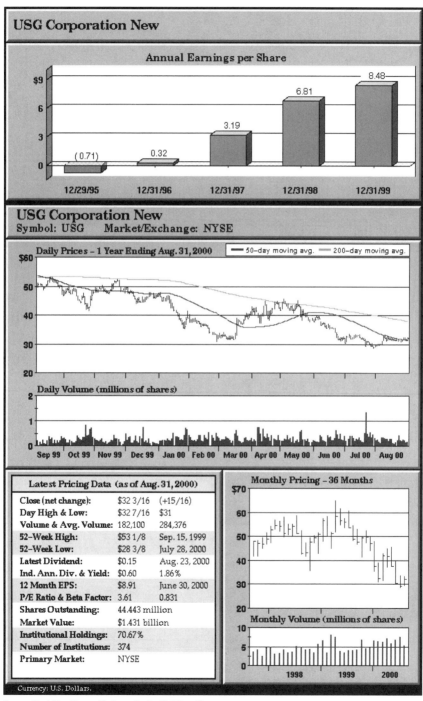

Source: Tradeline.Com, a Platinum Equity Holdings Company

USG Corporation New

Symbol : USG Market/Exchange : NYSE

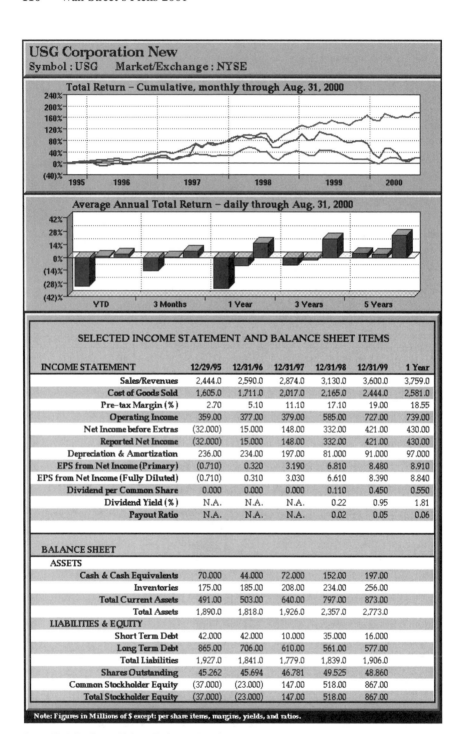

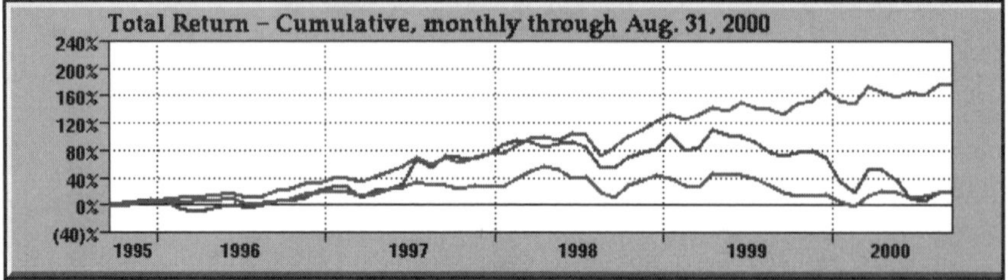

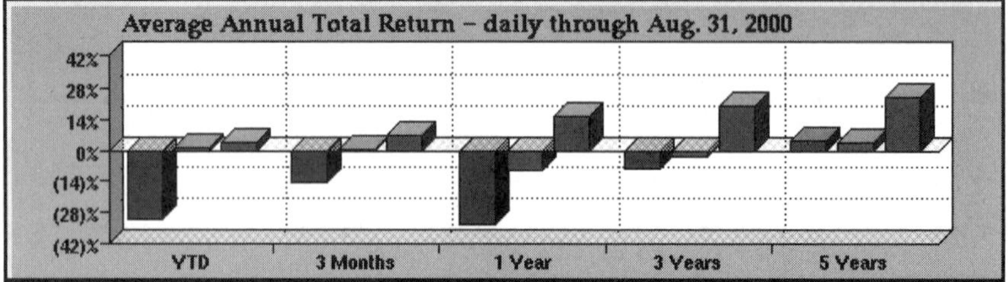

SELECTED INCOME STATEMENT AND BALANCE SHEET ITEMS

INCOME STATEMENT	12/29/95	12/31/96	12/31/97	12/31/98	12/31/99	1 Year
Sales/Revenues	2,444.0	2,590.0	2,874.0	3,130.0	3,600.0	3,759.0
Cost of Goods Sold	1,605.0	1,711.0	2,017.0	2,165.0	2,444.0	2,581.0
Pre-tax Margin (%)	2.70	5.10	11.10	17.10	19.00	18.55
Operating Income	359.00	377.00	379.00	585.00	727.00	739.00
Net Income before Extras	(32.000)	15.000	148.00	332.00	421.00	430.00
Reported Net Income	(32.000)	15.000	148.00	332.00	421.00	430.00
Depreciation & Amortization	236.00	234.00	197.00	81.000	91.000	97.000
EPS from Net Income (Primary)	(0.710)	0.320	3.190	6.810	8.480	8.910
EPS from Net Income (Fully Diluted)	(0.710)	0.310	3.030	6.610	8.390	8.840
Dividend per Common Share	0.000	0.000	0.000	0.110	0.450	0.550
Dividend Yield (%)	N.A.	N.A.	N.A.	0.22	0.95	1.81
Payout Ratio	N.A.	N.A.	N.A.	0.02	0.05	0.06

BALANCE SHEET					
ASSETS					
Cash & Cash Equivalents	70.000	44.000	72.000	152.00	197.00
Inventories	175.00	185.00	208.00	234.00	256.00
Total Current Assets	491.00	503.00	640.00	797.00	873.00
Total Assets	1,890.0	1,818.0	1,926.0	2,357.0	2,773.0
LIABILITIES & EQUITY					
Short Term Debt	42.000	42.000	10.000	35.000	16.000
Long Term Debt	865.00	706.00	610.00	561.00	577.00
Total Liabilities	1,927.0	1,841.0	1,779.0	1,839.0	1,906.0
Shares Outstanding	45.262	45.694	46.781	49.525	48.860
Common Stockholder Equity	(37.000)	(23.000)	147.00	518.00	867.00
Total Stockholder Equity	(37.000)	(23.000)	147.00	518.00	867.00

Note: Figures in Millions of $ except: per share items, margins, yields, and ratios.

Source: Tradeline.Com, a Platinum Equity Holdings Company

part

2

THE TOP MUTUAL FUNDS FOR 2001

A FEW WORDS ABOUT MUTUAL FUNDS

Although mutual funds have been around for more than seven decades, they experienced a plethora of popularity in the 1990s. There are now some 12,000 funds on the market, which is roughly twice the number of issues on the New York and American Stock Exchanges combined.

You can literally find funds of every flavor, from conservative money market instruments to more aggressive funds investing in small-capitalization stocks (small-caps). It's easy to put money to work in a specific sector (like health care or technology), or diversify among a wide range of industries. It's even possible to take advantage of growth in exotic international markets, from Argentina to Zimbabwe, through funds.

The explosion of this industry is nothing short of phenomenal. Total fund assets stood at $500 million in 1940, skyrocketed to $500 billion in 1985, and exceed $6.5 trillion today. Assets continue to flow in at a rapid pace. Furthermore, you can buy funds practically everywhere, from the local bank to your nearby discount broker. There's even a multilevel marketing company offering folks a chance to peddle these investment pools door-to-door.

The Appeal of Mutual Funds

What led to this sudden popularity? To begin with, people are more concerned than ever about savings. Baby boomers realize that without a carefully crafted investment plan they could fall short when it comes time to retire.

In addition, many businesses, both large and small, use mutual funds to manage employee benefit and profit-sharing plans—a major growth area for the fund families that will continue to flourish for years to come.

Perhaps the number-one reason for the public's insatiable appetite for funds rests with the overwhelming amount of publicity they have received in recent years. More than a dozen personal finance magazines are currently available, all of which devote a lot of space to mutual fund investing. Moreover, virtually every major newspaper carries a regular column on funds, and financial commentators on radio and television continue to sing their praises.

Aside from all this free editorial space, the mutual fund companies themselves have spent millions educating and enticing the public to send in their hard-earned cash. The message is obviously getting through. New money is still coming into funds at a rapid rate.

Using Funds

There's no question that mutual funds make a great deal of sense regardless of how much you have to invest. Many of the experts featured in this book invest in funds themselves. Funds are most useful for equities. After all, the first rule of successful investing is diversification. You certainly don't want to put all your eggs in one basket when dealing with stocks.

When you buy a stock mutual fund, you automatically achieve instant diversification. Smaller funds, in terms of asset size, spread their money over dozens of companies, while larger ones may take positions in hundreds. Either way, your overall exposure is significantly reduced, though not entirely eliminated.

Funds make the process of investing a breeze. You simply send in a check and, for a small fee, hire a professional manager to make all investment decisions for you. What could be easier? It's even possible, as well as advisable, to accumulate wealth in funds over time through dollar cost averaging, a method in which you invest on a regular basis regardless of market conditions, enabling you to buy more shares when prices are down and less when they're up.

Just remember that not every fund is created equal. Roughly 75 percent of all stock funds actually underperform the unmanaged S&P 500 over time—rising to over 90 percent in the past few years. These underperformers are funds supposedly spearheaded by top-notch investment professionals. With so many choices, picking a fund is about as complicated as sorting through individual stocks. Therefore, the key to success rests with proper selection, which is the focus of Part 2.

The Downside of Funds

There are disadvantages to owning funds. To begin with, you have little control over exactly how your money is invested. Sure, you can buy a fund full of stocks, but you're not allowed to choose the companies. The fund manager is free to purchase anything he or she wants within the guidelines of the prospectus, without regard to your preferences.

In addition, fund companies can be extremely impersonal. Many are huge organizations that hire scantily trained representatives to answer shareholder questions. That's no problem if you just want to know your account balance or the fund's total return for a given year. However, should you have specific questions about what investments the fund is making or which stocks it recently purchased, you'll probably be out of luck. And you can forget about talking directly with the fund manager. That kind of access is almost unheard of.

Another problem is that good funds tend to grow quite large, which can hamper returns. A fund with $1 billion or more in assets is usually forced to diversify over dozens, if not hundreds, of companies. That makes it difficult to outperform the market because each stock probably only makes up a small percentage of the total assets. Therefore, when one or two issues double or triple in value, they have little impact on overall results. It's a case of being overdiversified.

Furthermore, funds are required to pay out any realized capital gains to shareholders each year, meaning you could have a tax liability even if you sit tight with your shares. Some of these gains will likely be short-term and taxed at higher than ordinary income rates. Conversely, when you buy stocks, you don't experience a gain until you liquidate your holdings. If that's more than 12 months after making your initial purchase, your tax rate is capped at 20 percent under current law.

Finally, funds can take some of the fun out of investing. Many people find the process of hunting down stocks and then watching them (hopefully) rise to be quite exciting. It's thrilling to match wits with the market in pursuit of profits. Because fund managers do everything for you, that pleasure is gone.

More on Asset Allocation

Still, mutual funds have a place in most portfolios, particularly for those more eager to spend time on the golf course or at the beach than reading through stock reports and monitoring price movements. If that describes you, simply choose from the following recommendations and relax.

We've divided the funds into three categories: aggressive growth, growth, and international. Aggressive growth funds typically invest in the stocks of smaller companies, making them susceptible to dramatic short-term price swings but also potentially more rewarding. Growth funds these days generally hold a combination of small, midsize, and large companies, though the selections in this book tend to stick with the bigger names that are global powerhouses. International funds, as you might guess, invest primarily (and sometimes exclusively) in foreign-based securities of all sizes. Although foreign funds are inherently risky because of such factors as currency fluctuations and political turmoil, they can actually help to reduce your portfolio's overall volatility as overseas markets don't necessarily move in tandem with U.S. markets.

Which types of funds should you buy? As a general rule, younger investors and those not requiring immediate income would be wise to focus on the aggressive growth selections, while older and more conservative investors may want to pay close attention to the growth offerings.

Bond funds weren't included among the top picks for a couple of reasons. First of all, you can often do better by purchasing bonds, like Treasuries, directly from the government or through a discount broker. Furthermore, when you look at the evidence, one thing is clear: Over time, stocks provide the highest returns. Since 1926, the S&P 500 has compounded at an average annual rate of 11.2 percent compared with 5.3 percent for long-term government bonds and 3.8 percent for money market funds. That means it's impossible for your capital to grow significantly without putting a large portion of it into equities.

Unfortunately, the stock market doesn't always go up, and losses in any given period can be dramatic. Luckily, so can the rewards, as we've seen in recent years. That's why it makes sense for younger investors to be more heavily and aggressively invested in equities than older investors, although almost everyone should have a respectable exposure to stocks.

A rule of thumb states that a person should subtract his or her age from 100 and put that percentage in equities and the rest in bonds. So under this theory, if you're 40, you would have 60 percent of your assets in the stock market. Nevertheless, the late Philip Carret, the renowned investment legend who in 1928 launched what is now called the Pioneer Fund, called that philosophy "nonsense." As he said in a previous edition of *Wall Street's Picks,* "What difference does age make? That has nothing to do with it. Why, just because I'm [over 100], should I sell all my stocks and sit on bonds? I still have 75 to 80 percent of my money in stocks." (Carret died at the age of 101 in May 1998. At the time of his passing, most of his portfolio was invested in equities.)

Even if you need a monthly check to live on, stock funds remain a good choice. You can always redeem a set number of shares each month to produce the required amount of income (it's called a systematic withdrawal plan) while your principal continues to grow.

Though there are no magic formulas, here are some general stock and bond asset allocation guidelines for each age group that might even be considered somewhat conservative. In fact, several panelists argue that you should avoid bonds entirely.

Age	Suggested Weighting
Under 40	80% to 100% stocks, 0% to 20% bonds
40–50	75% stocks, 25% bonds
50–60	65% stocks, 35% bonds
60–70	60% stocks, 40% bonds
70+	50% stocks, 50% bonds

Selecting Your Funds

The next question: How many funds do you need? The answers vary widely; if you have less than $10,000 to invest, however, one or two funds are probably enough. When you get up to $50,000, it makes sense to buy up to three. If your investment capital exceeds $100,000, it's possible to own four to six different funds. However, each fund should have a slightly different focus or investment objective. Otherwise, you could end up owning a bunch of funds holding the exact same companies.

A well-rounded collection of stock funds might include one with each of the following objectives: large company growth, large company value, small-cap growth, small-cap value, and diversified international. The market tends to favor various groups at different times. By investing in numerous areas, your chances of always making money increase greatly. Our experts offer more advice on this subject in Part 3.

Load versus No-Load

Fortunately, most of the funds listed in this book are offered on a no-load basis, meaning you won't pay any sales fees to get in or out, so every cent of your investment goes to work for you. You might ask, "How do the fund companies make any money then?" The answer is by charging an annual management fee, which is reflected in the fund's expense ratio. This fee is usually under 1 percent for bond funds, 2 percent for those invested in equities. You are never actually billed for this fee. Instead, it is taken directly out of the fund's daily net asset value (NAV), which is listed in the business section of most major newspapers.

It's important to note that both load and no-load funds carry management fees. The only difference is that load funds cost you up to 8 percent more. The load is simply a commission that comes off the top and goes directly into the pocket of the person who sells it to you, usually a broker or commission-based financial planner. The fund companies generally don't get a penny. Therefore, if you do your homework and read books like this one, there's no reason to ever pay a load to buy a fund. In fact, several studies have shown that, as a group, no-loads actually perform better than their load counterparts, which means they not only save you money, but also are more profitable in the long run.

Buying Your Funds

After you figure out how many and which types of funds you want, it's time to decide where you should buy them. One option is to simply call the fund company directly to request a prospectus and application. You then merely fill in the blanks, send in a check for the required opening investment, and you're in business. Each confirmation slip comes with a coupon, enabling you to easily mail off additional contributions as often as you like, which is helpful for dollar cost averaging.

The latest and perhaps most convenient way to purchase funds is through the many national discount brokers, especially the big three—Charles Schwab, Fidelity Investments, and Waterhouse Securities. All offer no-transaction-fee programs, enabling you to buy hundreds of no-load funds from many different families without ever paying a commission. The brokers make their money through a service charge paid by the mutual fund companies. It doesn't cost you a penny more than if you were to buy the funds directly.

These no-transaction-fee programs are definitely worth investigating. They have two major advantages. The first is that all of your funds are consolidated on one easy-to-read monthly statement, which is very convenient. What's more, you can purchase shares and make trades on a specific day through your broker with a simple phone call. This saves you the hassle of writing out and mailing in a check, and it enables you to direct exactly when you want the trade to take place. With the U.S. Postal Service, it could take up to two weeks for your check to arrive.

Funds that can be purchased through any or all of the programs described above without paying a fee are noted in italics at the end of each profile in the following pages. For more information on opening an account, just call the discount broker of your choice. All are accessible through the following toll-free numbers and Internet addresses:

Charles Schwab & Co.	800-845-1714	<www.schwab.com>
Fidelity Investments	800-544-9697	<www.fidelity.com>
Muriel Siebert	800-872-0711	<www.msiebert.com>
TD Waterhouse	800-934-4410	<www.waterhouse.com>

I have also included the Internet address for each featured fund that has one. And, as with the stock experts, each fund analyst has also selected a second bonus pick, giving you 22 fund selections in all.

By the way, if you are a serious fund investor, we suggest you check out the *Mutual Fund Investor's Guide 2001* (Prentice-Hall) by Kirk Kazanjian. This book goes into greater depth on how to construct a winning fund program, contains several model portfolios, and includes performance data on more than 8,000 funds from the respected rating service Value Line. You should be able to find it at your local bookstore.

About the Recommendations

What follows are some specific picks for 2001 from some of the world's leading mutual fund authorities. There are four aggressive growth, four growth, and three international selections. Each description lists the fund's primary objective and investment focus (to help you construct a diversified portfolio) along with its past performance record, expense ratio, top holdings, management profile, and contact information. As you read, remember that past performance is no guarantee of future results. There are a lot of dogs in the mutual fund world, so stick with these gems and savor the rewards.

MAS MID-CAP VALUE

Louis Stanasolovich
Legend Financial Advisors

Fund Profile

I should first point out that this fund is made available primarily to institutional investors and financial advisors, like me. However, individuals can purchase it through most of the discount brokers, including Schwab, Fidelity, and TD Waterhouse, in some cases without paying any transaction fees.

MAS Mid-Cap Value is really a growth-at-a-price fund. The team-managed fund, led by Gary Schlarbaum and Bradley Daniels, is not looking for what I call traditional value by any means. They look to buy beaten up growth stocks. They're not searching for the real high flyers, but traditional growth companies that they can buy at cheap prices. They invest in almost every sector. At last check, service had the highest allocation, at around 21 percent. It's highly diversified, with most sector weightings in the single to low double digits. They also keep about 15 percent in technology, with a little foreign exposure thrown in for good measure. The fund's median market capitalization is $2.6 billion, which lands it squarely in mid-cap territory.

About the Managers

MAS, the firm that runs this fund, is now a part of Morgan Stanley, having been bought out by the company a few years ago. They are based in West Conshohocken, Pennsylvania, and are known as a top-flight investment group with a bent on value. This is really a first-class organization.

Reason for Recommendation

Mid-cap stocks are much more attractively valued than large-caps right now, in my opinion. Also, it has been shown that mid-caps offer the best overall returns on a risk-adjusted basis over long periods of time. This is a great fund for gaining exposure to that market segment. The returns provided by MAS Mid-Cap Value have been very consistent.

Bottom Line

If you could only own one fund, this would be a top contender. It should perform well in all types of markets because of its blended approach, which looks for stocks combining the best attributes of both growth and value. I would add that because the fund tends to have higher-than-average annual distributions, it would be best suited for a tax-deferred account.

Minimum Initial Investment: $2,500 ($500 for IRAs) through most discount brokers. [$5 million through MAS directly]

(Available without a transaction fee through Fidelity, Schwab, and TD Waterhouse.)

Contact Information: MAS Mid-Cap Value Institutional Shares
One Tower Bridge #1150, P.O. Box 868
West Conshohocken, PA 19428-0868
800-354-8185
<www.mas.com>

BONUS PICK FOR 2001

ICM/ISABELLE SMALL CAP VALUE

Symbol: IZZYX

This fund had the disadvantage of starting up in mid-1998, right before the market for small-cap stocks sank. That's good news for new investors, because the fund has losses that it can apply to future gains, making the fund more tax-efficient. I also like this fund because it has a tiny asset base and is run by a proven manager. Warren Isabelle ran several small-cap value offerings for the Pioneer Funds. He left because it was difficult for him to be effective with all of the assets Pioneer was gathering for him to manage. He went out and started his own fund and has done very well with it. Isabelle is a balance sheet guy, who looks at cash flow statements and buys what he sees as being underpriced. Because of his small asset base, he's able to be nimble and quickly get in and out of companies, which I think is extremely important. Isabelle is committed to closing the fund once it reaches $500 million in assets. Moreover, this fund should be relatively tax-efficient. (For more information on this fund, call 800-472-6114, or visit the fund's Web site at <www.icmfunds.com>.)

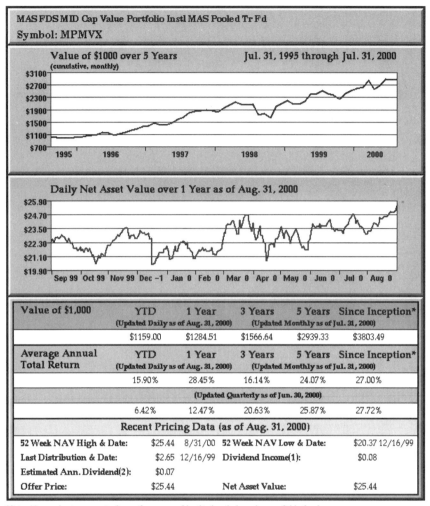

MAS FDS MID Cap Value Portfolio Instl MAS Pooled Tr Fd
Symbol: MPMVX

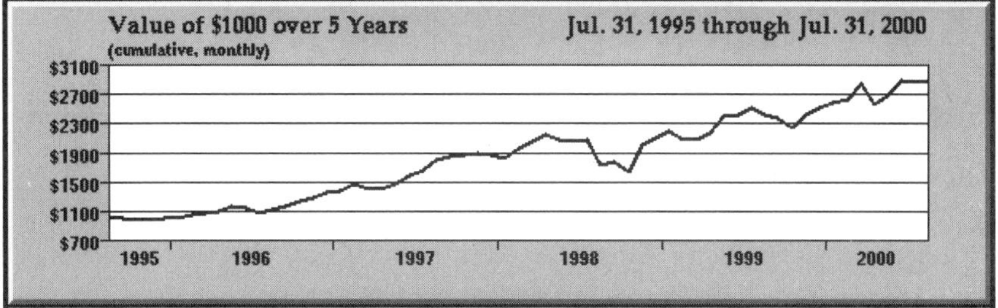

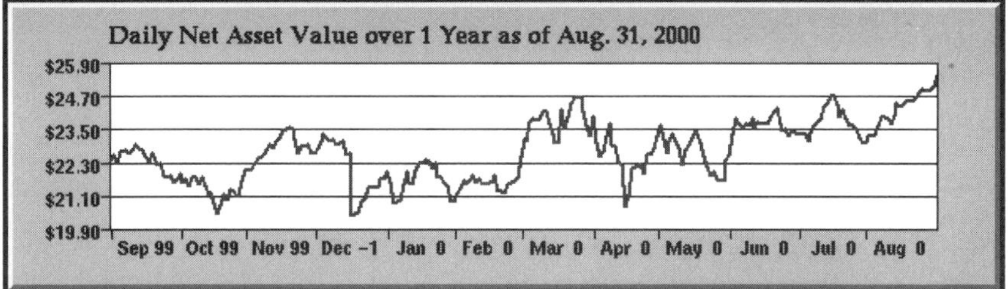

Value of $1,000	YTD	1 Year	3 Years	5 Years	Since Inception*
	(Updated Daily as of Aug. 31, 2000)		(Updated Monthly as of Jul. 31, 2000)		
	$1159.00	$1284.51	$1566.64	$2939.33	$3803.49
Average Annual Total Return	**YTD**	**1 Year**	**3 Years**	**5 Years**	**Since Inception***
	(Updated Daily as of Aug. 31, 2000)		(Updated Monthly as of Jul. 31, 2000)		
	15.90%	28.45%	16.14%	24.07%	27.00%
	(Updated Quarterly as of Jun. 30, 2000)				
	6.42%	12.47%	20.63%	25.87%	27.72%

Recent Pricing Data (as of Aug. 31, 2000)

52 Week NAV High & Date:	$25.44	8/31/00	**52 Week NAV Low & Date:**	$20.37	12/16/99
Last Distribution & Date:	$2.65	12/16/99	**Dividend Income(1):**	$0.08	
Estimated Ann. Dividend(2):	$0.07				
Offer Price:	$25.44		**Net Asset Value:**	$25.44	

Note: Above chart represents the performance of institutional class shares of this fund.
Source: Tradeline.Com, a Platinum Equity Holdings Company

Top 10 Holdings	Key Statistics	
Valassis Comms.	Sales Load (max)	0.00%
SanDisk	Redemption Charge (max)	0.00%
Nabors Industries	Expense Ratio	1.12%
Natl. Semiconductor	Management Fee	0.75%
Fairchild Semi.	12b-1 Marketing Fees	0.25%
Calpine	PE Ratio	30.70
Sybron Intl.	Dividend Yield	0.15%
Dover	Turnover Ratio	244.00%
Digital Microwave	Beta Factor	N/A
Global Marine	Total Assets	$78.00 mil.

MERIDIAN VALUE

Michael Stolper
Stolper & Company

Fund Profile

Meridian Value is a small-cap value fund that is based on a simple notion: If a so-called small-cap growth stock makes a mistake, such as missing an earnings estimate, Wall Street will purge it from the portfolio. Everybody sells and brokerage coverage disappears. At that point, the stock is resigned to Wall Street's equivalent of a leper colony. But the managers of Meridian Value have noted that when a company crashes, it usually goes on to have two consecutive quarters of positive results. That's when Meridian Value tends to buy. The managers talk to the company after these two positive quarters to try and determine whether, in fact, the fortunes have changed. If so, they'll buy, even though the stock might look brain dead until you get another quarter or two on that positive trajectory before Wall Street interest and coverage returns. In other words, they're looking to buy small-cap growth stocks when they turn into value stocks and before they turn into growth stocks again. They hold a concentrated portfolio and don't rely heavily on technology, like so many others in this category.

About the Managers

Meridian Value is managed by Richard Aster and Kevin O'Boyle. O'Boyle is young and smart. He's the one who dreamed up this technique. It's an approach that will have efficacy and perpetuity because it represents trafficking in what appears to be problem companies. There is never a shortage of problem companies. This technique plays, in my opinion, to the dynamic between Wall Street's perception of a business and how a business really operates.

Reason for Recommendation

Even though I'm singling out this idea for 2001, the fund really follows an evergreen philosophy. I think it's a fund you can buy and hold for a long time. The most dangerous part of the overall strategy is the re-entry point, because you must have conviction that the company is back on trend. But O'Boyle has a great record of being right.

Bottom Line

For investors looking to add exposure to the small-cap market to their portfolio, I highly recommend Meridian Value.

Minimum Initial Investment: $1,000

Contact Information: Meridian Value
60 East Sir Francis Drake Boulevard, #306
Larkspur, CA 94939
800-446-6662

(Available without a transaction fee through TD Waterhouse.)

BONUS PICK FOR 2001

SIT MID CAP GROWTH *Symbol:* NBNGX

Sit Mid Cap Growth is run by a great organization in Minneapolis. Founder Eugene Sit is a Chinese immigrant who came to the U.S. penniless in the late 1940s. He ended up at IDS (now American Express) and eventually started his own firm. He runs this fund with Erik Anderson. Unlike Meridian Value, this fund is very interested in growth and does have a heavy weighting in technology. This is a fine, aggressive addition to any portfolio. It's also a relatively undiscovered fund, because Sit does little advertising to promote its offerings. The fund is available without a transaction fee through most of the major brokerage supermarkets, including Fidelity, Schwab, and TD Waterhouse. (For more information on the fund, call 800-332-5580, or visit the fund's Web site at <www.sitfunds.com>.)

Meridian Fd Inc Value Fd

Symbol: MVALX

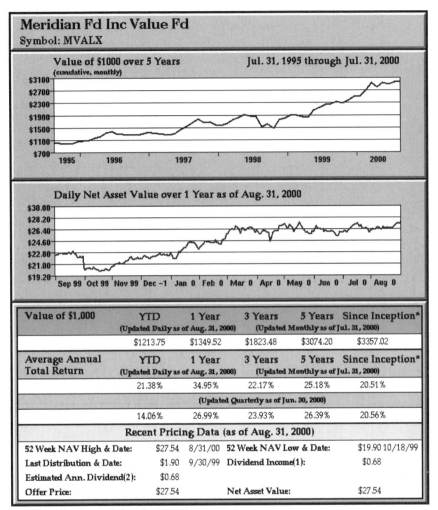

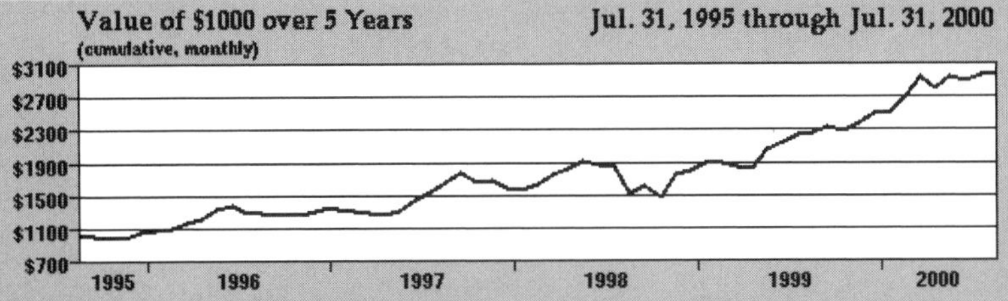

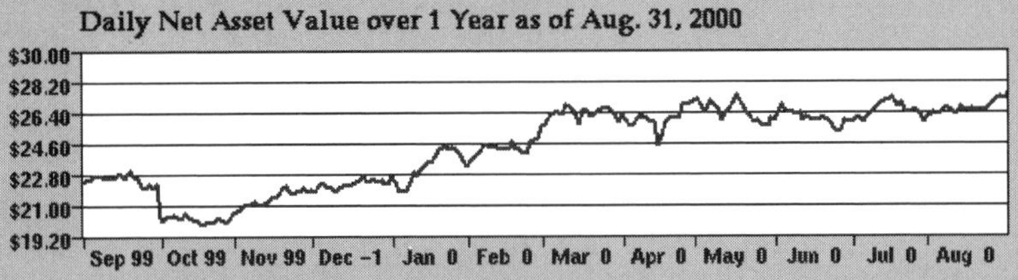

Value of $1,000	YTD	1 Year	3 Years	5 Years	Since Inception*
	(Updated Daily as of Aug. 31, 2000)		(Updated Monthly as of Jul. 31, 2000)		
	$1213.75	$1349.52	$1823.48	$3074.20	$3357.02
Average Annual Total Return	**YTD**	**1 Year**	**3 Years**	**5 Years**	**Since Inception***
	(Updated Daily as of Aug. 31, 2000)		(Updated Monthly as of Jul. 31, 2000)		
	21.38%	34.95%	22.17%	25.18%	20.51%
	(Updated Quarterly as of Jun. 30, 2000)				
	14.06%	26.99%	23.93%	26.39%	20.56%

Recent Pricing Data (as of Aug. 31, 2000)

52 Week NAV High & Date:	$27.54	8/31/00	**52 Week NAV Low & Date:**	$19.90 10/18/99
Last Distribution & Date:	$1.90	9/30/99	**Dividend Income(1):**	$0.68
Estimated Ann. Dividend(2):	$0.68			
Offer Price:	$27.54		**Net Asset Value:**	$27.54

Source: Tradeline.Com, a Platinum Equity Holdings Company

Top 10 Holdings	Key Statistics	
Hyperion Solutions	Sales Load (max)	0.00%
Burlington Resources	Redemption Charge (max)	0.00%
Omnicare	Expense Ratio	1.63%
SLM Hldg.	Management Fee	1.00%
Haemonetics	12b-1 Marketing Fees	0.00%
Buffets	PE Ratio	22.30
Federal Signal	Dividend Yield	2.45%
Lakehead Pipe Line	Turnover Ratio	124.00%
PartnerRe	Beta Factor	0.64
Tom Brown	Total Assets	$99.00 mil.

RYDEX OTC

Bob Markman
Markman Capital Management

Fund Profile

Rydex OTC is a fund that tries to mirror the performance of the Nasdaq 100, which is comprised of the 100 largest nonfinancial stocks on the Nasdaq. That means it's mostly a technology fund, because about 70 percent of all assets are invested in that sector. The top holdings are really the 800-pound gorillas of tech. You'll find big household names such as Microsoft, Qualcomm, Cisco Systems, Intel, Oracle Systems, Yahoo!, Sun Microsystems, and Dell. These are successful companies with visible and strong earnings. They form the establishment of the tech world. We don't know which of these companies will do best over time, but we do know we own a basket of the biggest, best, and most successful technology companies in the world. You don't have to worry about dot-com blow-ups, companies with no earnings, or companies with business plans that may or may not pan out.

I call the Nasdaq 100 "the success index," because it is capitalization weighted. As companies grow bigger and more successful, they become a larger and larger part of the index. Less successful companies are superceded by other companies, and automatically become a smaller part of the index. As a result, you are always on the cutting edge of where tech is going.

About the Manager

Rydex OTC is run by Michael Byrum, although he doesn't add to the equation like your typical fund manager. Operating the portfolio is more of a mechanical effort, in which Byrum tries to replicate the index as best as possible. He buys both stocks and options. In addition, Rydex OTC is incredibly tax-efficient, particularly relative to the gains it has achieved. I'm willing to go on record that relative to the gains, this has been the most tax-efficient fund in America.

Reason for Recommendation

While some feel the stocks in the Nasdaq 100 are overpriced, I disagree. The critics miss that these companies are growing at an incredible rate. Yes, some individual stocks may not justify current valuations. That's why you want to own a big basket like the Nasdaq 100.

Bottom Line

By investing in the Rydex OTC, you're betting that our world is becoming more technologically based, and that these companies are going to make fortunes. I believe that buy owning the whole basket, you will prosper in the growth of the world to come.

Minimum Initial Investment: $25,000

Contact Information: Rydex OTC Fund
6116 Executive Boulevard, Suite 400
Rockville, MD 20852
800-820-0888
<www.rydexfunds.com>

BONUS PICK FOR 2001

FIRSTHAND COMMUNICATIONS *Symbol:* TCFQX

Continuing with the technology theme, Firsthand Communications is a fund that invests in the areas that are at the core of building out the communications network of the twenty-first century. If you agree that we're going to keep living in a house of technology (as I do), this fund invests in the people who are like the plumbers and electricians of the house. Manager Kevin Landis buys companies that allow the Internet to be the Internet. He's a manager who really adds value and who understands the technology. (For more information on the fund, you can call 888-884-2675, or visit the fund's Web site at <www.firsthandfunds.com>.)

Rydex OTC Fund
Symbol: RYOCX

Value of $1000 over 5 Years (cumulative, monthly) — **Jul. 31, 1995 through Jul. 31, 2000**

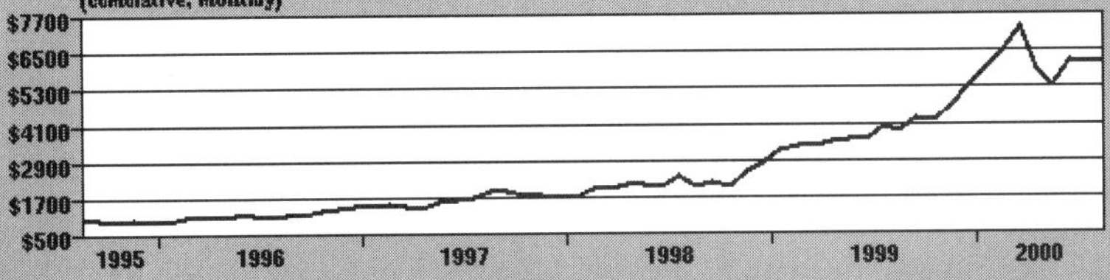

Daily Net Asset Value over 1 Year as of Aug. 31, 2000

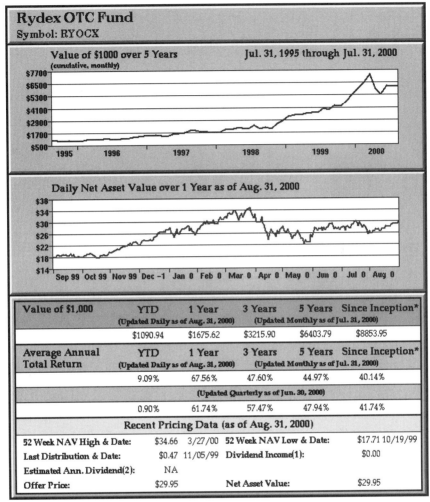

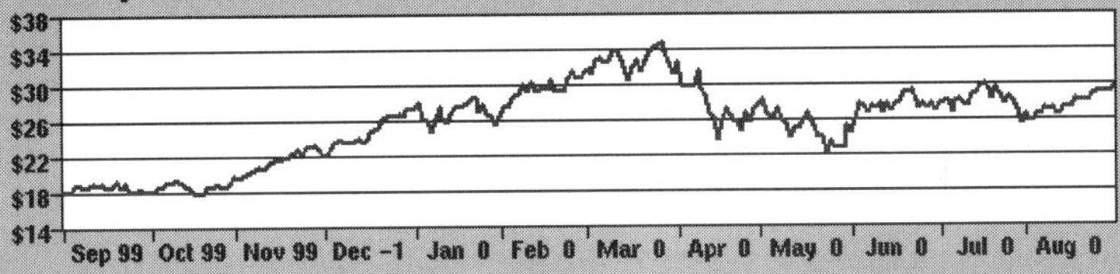

Value of $1,000	YTD	1 Year	3 Years	5 Years	Since Inception*
	(Updated Daily as of Aug. 31, 2000)		(Updated Monthly as of Jul. 31, 2000)		
	$1090.94	$1675.62	$3215.90	$6403.79	$8853.95

Average Annual Total Return	YTD	1 Year	3 Years	5 Years	Since Inception*
	(Updated Daily as of Aug. 31, 2000)		(Updated Monthly as of Jul. 31, 2000)		
	9.09%	67.56%	47.60%	44.97%	40.14%
	(Updated Quarterly as of Jun. 30, 2000)				
	0.90%	61.74%	57.47%	47.94%	41.74%

Recent Pricing Data (as of Aug. 31, 2000)

52 Week NAV High & Date:	$34.66	3/27/00	**52 Week NAV Low & Date:**	$17.71 10/19/99
Last Distribution & Date:	$0.47	11/05/99	**Dividend Income(1):**	$0.00
Estimated Ann. Dividend(2):	NA			
Offer Price:	$29.95		**Net Asset Value:**	$29.95

Source: Tradeline.Com, a Platinum Equity Holdings Company

Top 10 Holdings	Key Statistics	
Cisco Systems	Sales Load (max)	0.00%
Intel	Redemption Charge (max)	0.00%
Microsoft	Expense Ratio	1.61%
Oracle	Management Fee	0.75%
JDS Uniphase	12b-1 Marketing Fees	0.25%
Sun Microsystems	PE Ratio	50.10
Nextel Comms.	Dividend Yield	0.00%
Qualcomm	Turnover Ratio	385.00%
WorldCom	Beta Factor	1.33
Dell Computer	Total Assets	$3.21 bil.

TCW GALILEO SELECT EQUITY

Thurman Smith
Equity Fund Research

Fund Profile

TCW Galileo Select Equity has a very flexible charter. It's clearly a large-cap growth fund, but manager Glen Bickerstaff can basically buy anything he wants, including foreign companies, derivatives, and forward contracts. He's not doing any of that at the moment, but has the option. Bickerstaff holds a concentrated portfolio, and keeps 5 to 7 percent in each of his top ideas.

I rank funds according to their risk-reward profile. TCW Galileo Select Equity clearly has a higher risk exposure than the broad market. It will probably go down about 25 percent more than the S&P 500 in falling markets. However, it more than makes up for that on the upside. As a result, the combined reward-risk profile is extremely attractive.

The fund is well diversified, in terms of market sectors, with about 40 percent in technology. The other two sectors with the most representation include financials and health services. At last check, Bickerstaff owned 31 different issues, which means he can get to know and follow each of the companies closely.

About the Manager

Bickerstaff has about 19 years of investment experience. Before joining Trust Company of the West, which runs the TCW Galileo Funds, he managed pension money for Transamerica and the Transamerica Premier Equity fund. He has outperformed the market almost every single year. He just always seems to know where to move with the market. Also, given that so few funds today are managed by people with only a few years on the job, it's nice to have an experienced pro at the helm.

Reason for Recommendation

Another positive is that this fund has a relatively small asset base, especially for a large-cap portfolio. That means Bickerstaff has plenty of room to grow, and the flexibility to do whatever he wants for several years to come. It's also tax efficient, available on a no-load basis, and easy to buy through one of the discount brokers.

Bottom Line

This would make a fine choice for investors looking to own a more aggressive large-cap holding in either a taxable or tax-deferred account.

Minimum Initial Investment: $2,000 ($500 for IRAs)
(Available without a transaction fee through Fidelity, Schwab, and TD Waterhouse.)

Contact Information: TCW Galileo Select Equity
865 South Figueroa, 18th Floor
Los Angeles, CA 90017
800-386-3829
<www.tcwgroup.com>

BONUS PICK FOR 2001

GABELLI GROWTH *Symbol:* GABGX

Gabelli Growth has a lower risk profile than TCW Galileo Select Equity and places more emphasis on mid-cap names. Manager Howard Ward follows a blended approach to stock picking, meaning he combines elements of value and growth. He really has his act together. This fund has held up well in periods of market weakness. Ward has a habit of not buying overpriced securities, and will trim his holdings when prices get out of hand. For instance, in late 1999 he shifted some money out of the high-priced tech stocks and into financial and drug companies. Ward holds a more diversified portfolio than Bickerstaff in terms of the number of issues he owns. This is a perfect fund for a more conservative investor looking to invest in growth stocks without taking an unreasonable amount of risk. And it's run by a manager who won't pay just any price for a stock. (For more information on this fund, call 800-422-3554, or visit the fund's Web site at <www.gabelli.com>.)

TCW Galileo Funds Incorporated
Symbol: TGCEX

Value of $1000 Since Inception* (cumulative, monthly) **Dec. 31, 1998 through Jul. 31, 2000**

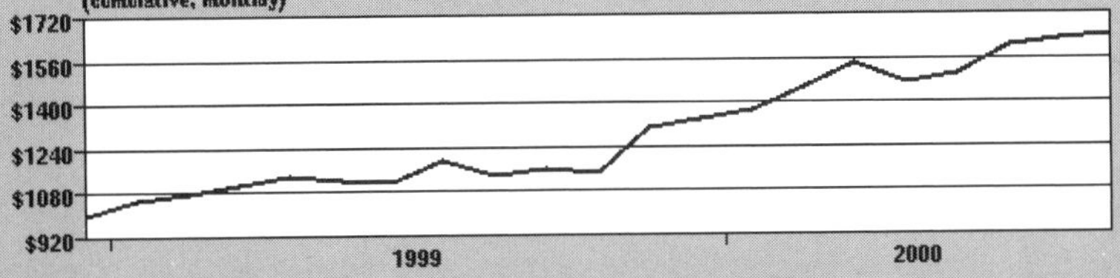

Daily Net Asset Value over 1 Year as of Aug. 31, 2000

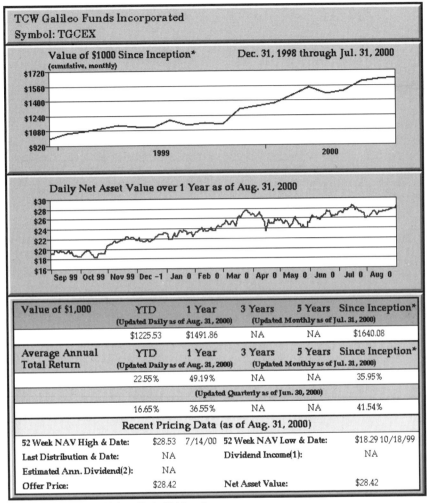

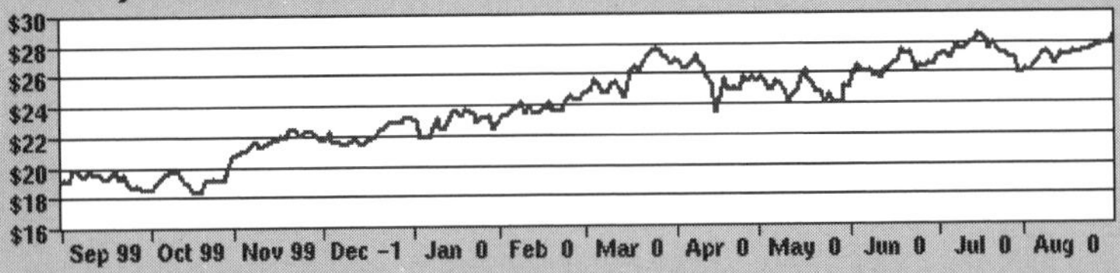

Value of $1,000	YTD	1 Year	3 Years	5 Years	Since Inception*
	(Updated Daily as of Aug. 31, 2000)		(Updated Monthly as of Jul. 31, 2000)		
	$1225.53	$1491.86	NA	NA	$1640.08
Average Annual Total Return	**YTD**	**1 Year**	**3 Years**	**5 Years**	**Since Inception***
	(Updated Daily as of Aug. 31, 2000)		(Updated Monthly as of Jul. 31, 2000)		
	22.55%	49.19%	NA	NA	35.95%
		(Updated Quarterly as of Jun. 30, 2000)			
	16.65%	36.55%	NA	NA	41.54%

Recent Pricing Data (as of Aug. 31, 2000)

52 Week NAV High & Date:	$28.53 7/14/00	52 Week NAV Low & Date:	$18.29 10/18/99
Last Distribution & Date:	NA	Dividend Income(1):	NA
Estimated Ann. Dividend(2):	NA		
Offer Price:	$28.42	Net Asset Value:	$28.42

Source: Tradeline.Com, a Platinum Equity Holdings Company

Top 10 Holdings	Key Statistics	
Dell Computer	Sales Load (max)	0.00%
Siebel Systems	Redemption Charge (max)	0.00%
Progressive	Expense Ratio	1.46%
Kansas City Southern	Management Fee	0.75%
Maxim Integrated Prods.	12b-1 Marketing Fees	0.25%
Pfizer	PE Ratio	45.70
Intel	Dividend Yield	0.00%
Cisco Systems	Turnover Ratio	48.00%
Biogen	Beta Factor	N/A
Paychex	Total Assets	$77.00 mil.

COHEN & STEERS REALTY

Reuben Gregg Brewer
Value Line

Fund Profile

I'm quite fond of real estate investment trusts (REITs) going into 2001. They are reasonably priced compared to the overall market and offer very good dividend yields. As you may know, REITs are companies that own and operate real estate. Some specialize in commercial property, others residential. In all cases, they pass through most of the rental income from properties to shareholders in the form of a dividend. You can think of a REIT as sort of a mutual fund of properties. My favorite REIT fund is Cohen & Steers Realty. I like it because the managers have been around for a long time and they know the industry.

About the Managers

Managers Martin Cohen and Robert Steers claim to have started one of the first real estate funds in the 1980s. They've watched the landscape for REITs change and evolve, and they follow a very company-specific approach. They mostly stick with blue chip names and stay diversified across the various subsectors.

Reason for Recommendation

REITs have been beaten down, even though as a group they continue to turn in strong numbers. One reason for this is that a few years ago investors were fascinated with REITs because they posted such great returns. Well, they weren't growth vehicles then, and they aren't really aggressive growth vehicles now. They are steady investments that you can expect to provide a steady dividend stream and a slight amount of growth. People were so disappointed that these abnormally high double-digit returns didn't continue that they categorically got rid of the stocks. Many of them now sell below the actual value of the property they own, while paying out dividends of 8 to 10 percent. They are financially sound companies and give you exposure to an industry that I expect to see a pop to the upside soon.

Bottom Line

Most equity investors should also own REITs because of the diversification they provide. REITs tend to zig when the market zags. If the market continues to be volatile going forward, which most experts feel it will, having some exposure to REITs should add an element of stability to your portfolio. The managers of Cohen & Steers Realty know how to pick REITs. They've proven themselves in this area over many years. The biggest downside may be the fund's high minimum investment of $10,000.

Minimum Initial Investment: $10,000

Contact Information: Cohen & Steers Realty
757 Third Avenue
New York, NY 10017
800-437-9912
<www.cohenandsteers.com>

(Available without a transaction fee through Fidelity, Schwab, and TD Waterhouse.)

BONUS PICK FOR 2001

VANGUARD HEALTH CARE

Symbol: VGHCX

The Vanguard Health Care Fund has been around since 1984, and managed by Edward Owens since inception. It has been a strong performer over this time. More recently, because Owens hasn't had a high weighting in biotechnology, his returns have been hindered a bit. But health care is going to be an important area going forward. I definitely think it's a sector to have exposure to in your portfolio, but you want an experienced manager doing the investing for you. Owens invests across the gambit, from large pharmaceuticals to hospital chains and HMOs. I could see an investor keeping around 5 percent in a sector-specific fund like this. (For more information on this fund, call 800-662-7447, or visit the fund's Web site at <www.vanguard.com>.)

Cohen & Steers Realty Shs
Symbol: CSRSX

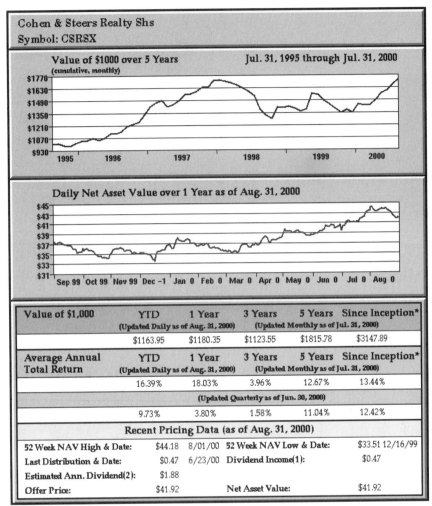

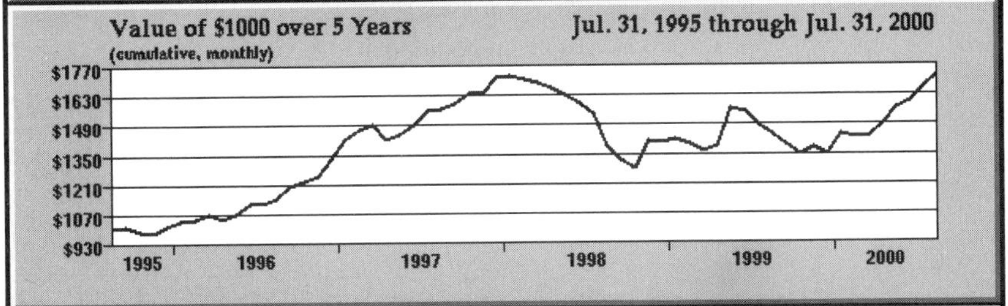

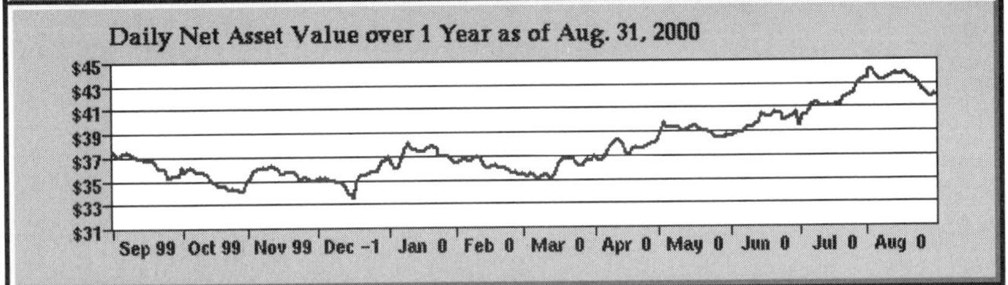

Value of $1,000	YTD	1 Year	3 Years	5 Years	Since Inception*
	(Updated Daily as of Aug. 31, 2000)		(Updated Monthly as of Jul. 31, 2000)		
	$1163.95	$1180.35	$1123.55	$1815.78	$3147.89
Average Annual Total Return	**YTD**	**1 Year**	**3 Years**	**5 Years**	**Since Inception***
	(Updated Daily as of Aug. 31, 2000)		(Updated Monthly as of Jul. 31, 2000)		
	16.39%	18.03%	3.96%	12.67%	13.44%
	(Updated Quarterly as of Jun. 30, 2000)				
	9.73%	3.80%	1.58%	11.04%	12.42%

Recent Pricing Data (as of Aug. 31, 2000)

52 Week NAV High & Date:	$44.18	8/01/00	**52 Week NAV Low & Date:**	$33.51 12/16/99
Last Distribution & Date:	$0.47	6/23/00	**Dividend Income(1):**	$0.47
Estimated Ann. Dividend(2):	$1.88			
Offer Price:	$41.92		**Net Asset Value:**	$41.92

Source: Tradeline.Com, a Platinum Equity Holdings Company

Top 10 Holdings	Key Statistics	
Vornado Realty Tr.	Sales Load (max)	0.00%
Apartment Inv. & Mgt.	Redemption Charge (max)	0.00%
Avalon Bay Comms.	Expense Ratio	1.03%
Reckson Svc. Inds.	Management Fee	0.83%
Mack-Cali Realty	12b-1 Marketing Fees	0.00%
Starwood Hotels & Resorts	PE Ratio	21.80
Spieker Properties	Dividend Yield	4.57%
Reckson Assoc. Realty	Turnover Ratio	30.00%
Arden Realty Grp.	Beta Factor	0.40
AMB Ppty.	Total Assets	$1.19 bil.

LONGLEAF PARTNERS

Stephen Savage

The No-Load Fund Analyst

Fund Profile

Longleaf Partners is a fine fund that recently reopened to new investors. The fund is run by Mason Hawkins and Staley Cates and is a concentrated portfolio of solid companies that have been beaten up for one reason or another. Hawkins and Cates do traditional value analysis when selecting stocks. They look for companies trading at at least a 40 percent discount to what they judge the company to be worth. This means doing a lot of fundamental number crunching to uncover the economic value of a company's assets.

The fund has been somewhat of a laggard in the recent past, mostly because the managers made a big bet on Waste Management that blew up on them. At last check, this position alone accounted for some 16 percent of total assets. But they're confident that this investment will pay off in the end. I'm not concerned about the fund's short streak of underperformance. They have a very successful long-term record and I view this as an aberration.

About the Managers

Hawkins and Cates are really focused and driven. When researching stocks, they look for those companies where the interests of management are aligned with shareholders. They feel that's crucial to investment success. They also carry this same philosophy through to their own firm, by aligning their interests with those of the shareholders of their funds. For example, the employees who work for Longleaf have to keep all of their investment assets in Longleaf funds. I like that. I'm also impressed that they hold such concentrated positions. After all, you're hiring fund managers to invest in their best ideas. I don't think managers with 300 picks can honestly tell you they feel strongly about all of those names.

Reason for Recommendation

Because of the fund's value approach, I believe the portfolio is positioned well for a period when the broad market cools down, which we're already seeing. I have concerns about the overall valuations of growth and technology stocks. There's a huge disparity that's arisen between traditional value and growth stocks, or what we often hear as the "new economy" versus the "old economy." This current trend has been carried to an unsustainable excess and stock prices have a tendency over time to gravitate back to intrinsic value.

Bottom Line

Hawkins and Cates believe in staying within their core competencies of evaluating what companies are worth. They look not only at the numbers, but also closely assess management, future prospects, and what's happening in the given industry to make sure they're not putting their money in a sinking boat. They're investing in companies where they see a catalyst that should restore the stock's valuation to a more realistic level. As value funds go, this one is at the top of the heap.

Minimum Initial Investment: $10,000

Contact Information: Longleaf Partners
6410 Poplar Avenue, Suite 900
Memphis, TN 38119
800-445-9469
<www.longleafpartners.com>

BONUS PICK FOR 2001

DEUTSCHE INTERNATIONAL

Symbol: BTEQX

This is an international fund run by a very competent team. They have an open management system where each team member specializes in a specific area, although there is a strong cross-disciplinary focus. In other words, they don't want any analyst locked into one specific area or region that might preclude them from being aware of or considering broader global trends that might impact the companies they're following. They've been keeping a majority of the portfolio in Europe, with most of that in England and France. They like Europe because of the overall restructuring taking place and because there are a lot of good opportunities there. In my model portfolios right now, I recommend that investors keep about 20 percent invested in an overseas fund like Deutsche International. (For more information on this fund, call 800-730-1313, or visit the fund's Web site at <www.usfunds.db.com>.)

Longleaf Partners FDS Tr Sh Ben Int
Symbol: LLPFX

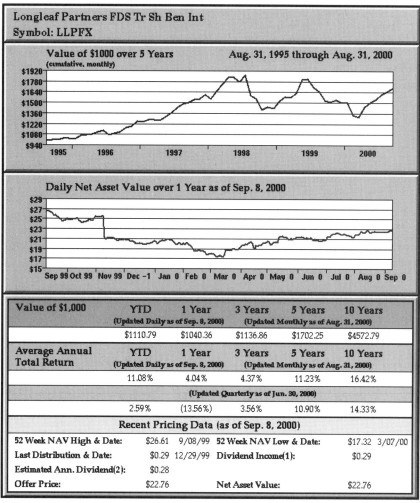

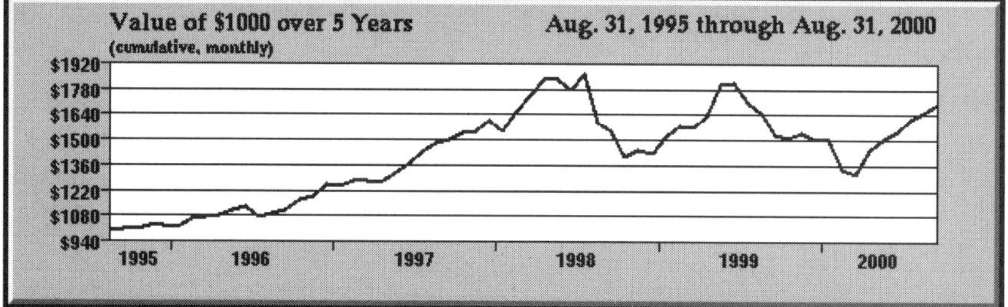

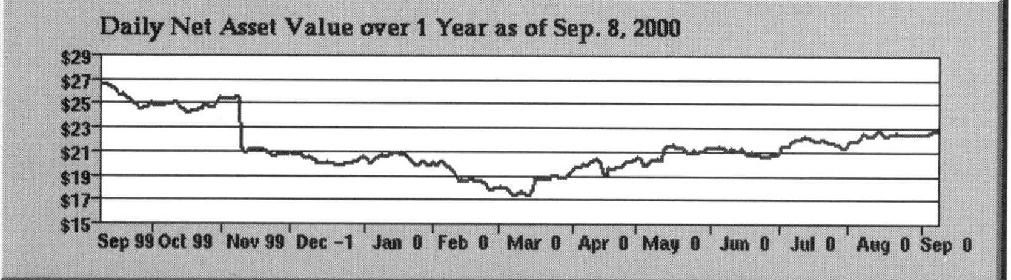

Value of $1,000	YTD	1 Year	3 Years	5 Years	10 Years
	(Updated Daily as of Sep. 8, 2000)		(Updated Monthly as of Aug. 31, 2000)		
	$1110.79	$1040.36	$1136.86	$1702.25	$4572.79
Average Annual Total Return	**YTD**	**1 Year**	**3 Years**	**5 Years**	**10 Years**
	(Updated Daily as of Sep. 8, 2000)		(Updated Monthly as of Aug. 31, 2000)		
	11.08%	4.04%	4.37%	11.23%	16.42%
	(Updated Quarterly as of Jun. 30, 2000)				
	2.59%	(13.56%)	3.56%	10.90%	14.33%

Recent Pricing Data (as of Sep. 8, 2000)

52 Week NAV High & Date:	$26.61	9/08/99	**52 Week NAV Low & Date:**	$17.32	3/07/00
Last Distribution & Date:	$0.29	12/29/99	**Dividend Income(1):**	$0.29	
Estimated Ann. Dividend(2):	$0.28				
Offer Price:	$22.76		**Net Asset Value:**	$22.76	

Source: Tradeline.Com, a Platinum Equity Holdings Company

Top 10 Holdings	Key Statistics	
Waste Management	Sales Load (max)	0.00%
Marriott Intl. Cl A	Redemption Charge (max)	0.00%
FedEx	Expense Ratio	0.92%
General Motors	Management Fee	0.78%
Hilton Hotels	12b-1 Marketing Fees	0.00%
Canadian Pacific	PE Ratio	17.90
Trizec Hahn	Dividend Yield	1.12%
Knight-Ridder	Turnover Ratio	50.00%
Tricon Global Rest.	Beta Factor	0.78
Pioneer Natural Res. Canada	Total Assets	$3.29 bil.

VANGUARD GROWTH INDEX

Earl Osborn
Bingham, Osborn & Scarborough

Fund Profile

Looking ahead to 2001, I believe we'll have a much more volatile market than we've had in the past. If I'm going to own growth stocks, I want to branch out from a pure technology fund into a portfolio with much broader representation. In other words, I want to own growing companies regardless of what field they're in. Instead of just buying Lucent Technologies or Cisco Systems, I also want to own Wal-Mart and Procter & Gamble. Unfortunately, most growth funds are very heavy on tech. The advantage of Vanguard Growth Index is you get a very broad-based basket of stocks. In fact, technology comes in at around one-third of the portfolio—enough to give you solid exposure to this sector, but not too much that you put all of your eggs in one basket. Yes, you'll find Cisco, Lucent, Intel, and America Online in the portfolio. But Merck, Bristol-Myers, and Home Depot are in there, too. I really think you should look beyond the narrow technology class going in to 2001. This fund allows you to do that.

About the Manager

Vanguard Growth Index is managed by Vanguard's technology guru George Sauter, although it's really run by a computer. It is designed to track the S&P/Barra growth index, which contains the 250 stocks from the Standard & Poor's 500 index trading for the highest price-to-book multiple. Vanguard does a great job of indexing. It also has the lowest expenses, especially compared to the average large company growth fund. Plus, the fund's turnover is low.

Reason for Recommendation

I really like the broad diversification this fund provides. That's especially true because I don't think you're going to see stock market returns as concentrated in one sector or another as you have the past couple of years. I really think investors will be well-served by this fund.

Bottom Line

With Vanguard Growth Index, you get broad-based, steady participation in growth stocks, without overloading in technology, and all for a very low annual expense ratio.

Minimum Initial Investment: $3,000 ($1,000 for IRAs)

Contact Information: Vanguard Growth Index
Vanguard Financial Center, P.O. Box 2600
Valley Forge, PA 19482
800-662-7447
<www.vanguard.com>

BONUS PICK FOR 2001

FIDELITY VALUE

Symbol: FDVLX

My bonus pick is a very different fund. I'm guessing that there will be a rebound in value, or so-called old economy stocks, in 2001. These companies have real earnings, and should do better in a period of higher inflation and rising rates. That's because the assets of value stocks appreciate in a rising interest environment. Fidelity Value gives you exposure to these kinds of companies. It tends to focus on mid-cap value stocks, although manager Richard Fentin covers a pretty broad range. Plus, for an actively managed value fund, the expenses and turnover are quite low. The expense ratio runs around 0.61 percent, with turnover in the 36 percent range. (For more information on this fund, you can call 800-544-8888, or visit the fund's Web site at <www.fidelity.com>.)

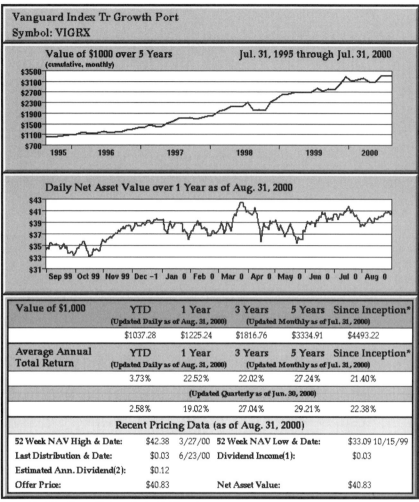

Vanguard Index Tr Growth Port
Symbol: VIGRX

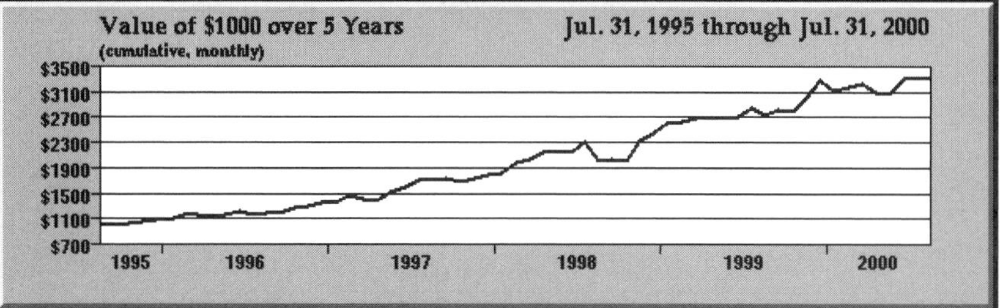

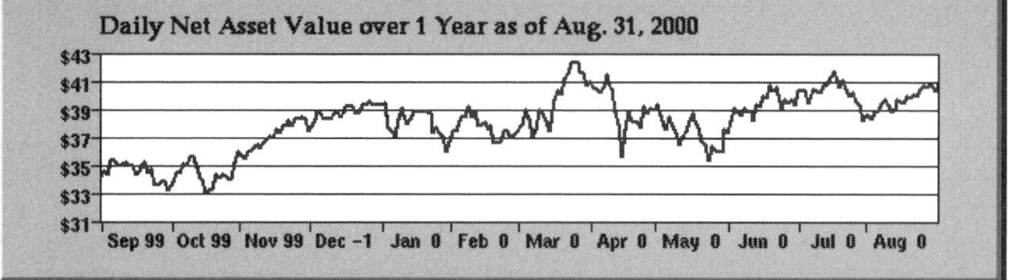

Value of $1,000	YTD	1 Year	3 Years	5 Years	Since Inception*
	(Updated Daily as of Aug. 31, 2000)		(Updated Monthly as of Jul. 31, 2000)		
	$1037.28	$1225.24	$1816.76	$3334.91	$4493.22
Average Annual Total Return	**YTD**	**1 Year**	**3 Years**	**5 Years**	**Since Inception***
	(Updated Daily as of Aug. 31, 2000)		(Updated Monthly as of Jul. 31, 2000)		
	3.73%	22.52%	22.02%	27.24%	21.40%
		(Updated Quarterly as of Jun. 30, 2000)			
	2.58%	19.02%	27.04%	29.21%	22.38%

Recent Pricing Data (as of Aug. 31, 2000)

52 Week NAV High & Date:	$42.38	3/27/00	**52 Week NAV Low & Date:**	$33.09 10/15/99
Last Distribution & Date:	$0.03	6/23/00	**Dividend Income(1):**	$0.03
Estimated Ann. Dividend(2):	$0.12			
Offer Price:	$40.83		**Net Asset Value:**	$40.83

Source: Tradeline.Com, a Platinum Equity Holdings Company

Top 10 Holdings	Key Statistics	
General Electric	Sales Load (max)	0.00%
Intel	Redemption Charge (max)	0.00%
Cisco Systems	Expense Ratio	0.22%
Microsoft	Management Fee	0.20%
Pfizer	12b-1 Marketing Fees	0.00%
Wal-Mart Stores	PE Ratio	46.60
Oracle	Dividend Yield	0.48%
Nortel Networks	Turnover Ratio	33.00%
IBM	Beta Factor	1.05
Lucent Technologies	Total Assets	$15.79 bil.

VANGUARD TOTAL STOCK MARKET

Sheldon Jacobs

The No-Load Fund Investor

Fund Profile

If you believe in indexing, as I do, for a portion of your portfolio, buying the Vanguard Total Stock Market is the ultimate no-brainer. This fund tracks the performance of the Wilshire 5000 index, which is basically a benchmark designed to replicate the performance of the entire U.S. stock market. When most people think of index funds, they think of the Standard & Poor's 500. That's an index composed primarily of large-company stocks. But, from time to time, small- and mid-cap stocks outperform large-caps. About one-fourth of the Wilshire 5000 is in small- and mid-cap stocks. So, regardless of whether large or small stocks are in favor, you'll benefit. If you're talking about investing for the long term, this is really the way to go.

About the Manager

One of the risks you face with any fund is that your manager will leave, to be replaced by someone less skillful. With an index fund, that's never a concern. But as index funds go, this one has a great manager in George Sauter of the Vanguard Group.

Reason for Recommendation

I really think it makes sense to keep up to half of your equity allocation in index funds. I personally wouldn't go above that. In fact, I was just at a meeting of financial planners. One of the speakers worked in Vanguard's index department. He was asked how much of your portfolio to index, and responded, "I don't know. Somewhere between 10 and 90 percent, but clearly not everything." That's really a nonanswer, but the point is even a guy who works as an indexer doesn't think you should index your whole portfolio. If you're a conservative investor, you don't want to index everything, because you shouldn't expose yourself to that much market risk. On the other hand, if you're an aggressive investor, you probably want to do better than average, and the only way to do that is through active management.

Bottom Line

According to statistics from Vanguard, between 1971 and 1999 there were only eight years when the Wilshire 5000 underperformed the average equity fund. I've been a proponent of indexing for many years and of all the index funds out there, this is my favorite.

Minimum Initial Investment: $3,000 ($1,000 for IRAs)

Contact Information: Vanguard Total Stock Market Index Fund
Vanguard Financial Center, P.O. Box 2600
Valley Forge, PA 19482
800-662-7447
<www.vanguard.com>

BONUS PICK FOR 2001

TIAA-CREF GROWTH & INCOME *Symbol:* TIGIX

TIAA-CREF is one of the oldest established money managers in America. The firm has run educational pensions for an eternity. The organization manages more than $225 billion in assets for 2 million participants in 8,000 educational institutions. About two years ago, the company began offering no-load funds to the general public. This is a fund with very low costs, a low minimum investment, and an interesting investment philosophy. Part of the portfolio is indexed to the S&P 500, and part is actively managed. If the index is beating the active managers, they'll overweight the index. If you get into a period where the reverse is true, the portfolio will become more actively managed. The managers can also invest up to 40 percent of assets overseas. It's a great concept. You couple that with about the second lowest expense ratio in the business and the lowest minimums available and you have one terrific investment. (For more information, call 800-223-1200, or visit their Web site at <www.tiaa-cref.org>.)

Vanguard Index Trust Total Stock Market Fund
Symbol: VTSMX

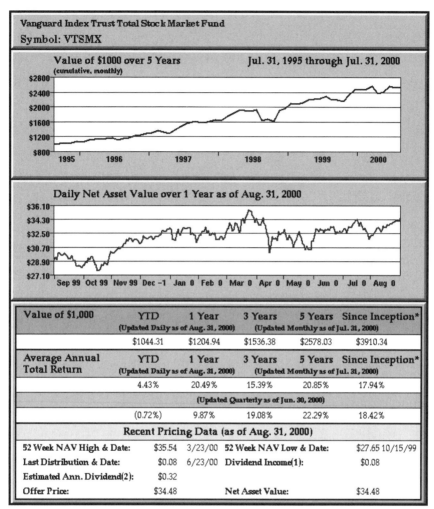

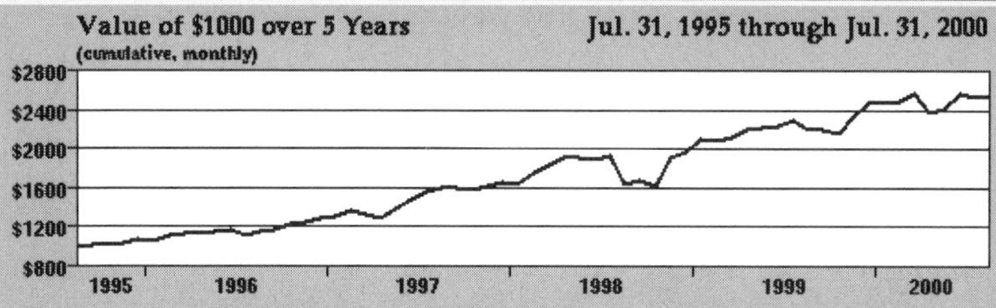

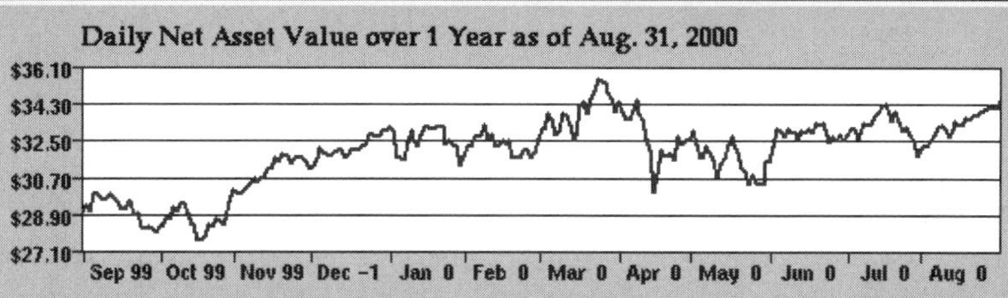

Value of $1,000	YTD	1 Year	3 Years	5 Years	Since Inception*
	(Updated Daily as of Aug. 31, 2000)		(Updated Monthly as of Jul. 31, 2000)		
	$1044.31	$1204.94	$1536.38	$2578.03	$3910.34
Average Annual Total Return	**YTD**	**1 Year**	**3 Years**	**5 Years**	**Since Inception***
	(Updated Daily as of Aug. 31, 2000)		(Updated Monthly as of Jul. 31, 2000)		
	4.43%	20.49%	15.39%	20.85%	17.94%
	(Updated Quarterly as of Jun. 30, 2000)				
	(0.72%)	9.87%	19.08%	22.29%	18.42%

Recent Pricing Data (as of Aug. 31, 2000)

52 Week NAV High & Date:	$35.54	3/23/00	52 Week NAV Low & Date:	$27.65 10/15/99
Last Distribution & Date:	$0.08	6/23/00	Dividend Income(1):	$0.08
Estimated Ann. Dividend(2):	$0.32			
Offer Price:	$34.48		Net Asset Value:	$34.48

Source: Tradeline.Com, a Platinum Equity Holdings Company

Top 10 Holdings	Key Statistics	
General Electric	Sales Load (max)	0.00%
Intel	Redemption Charge (max)	0.00%
Cisco Systems	Expense Ratio	0.20%
Microsoft	Management Fee	0.18%
Pfizer	12b-1 Marketing Fees	0.00%
Exxon Mobil	PE Ratio	35.50
Wal-Mart Stores	Dividend Yield	1.02%
Oracle	Turnover Ratio	3.00%
Citigroup	Beta Factor	0.98
IBM	Total Assets	$19.61 bil.

ARTISAN INTERNATIONAL

Walter Frank
Moneyletter

Fund Profile

Of all the international funds I follow, Artisan International has consistently been one of the better performers. This is a diversified international fund with a very broad and flexible mandate. A few years ago, the portfolio was heavily weighted in Europe. In fact, I remember seeing an interview with manager Mark Yockey where he said he wouldn't touch Japan. Today some of the fund's assets are in Japan, which has helped performance. The fund also has a substantial position in Canada, which is unusual. Artisan International is one-stop shopping for the entire world, excluding the U.S.

About the Manager

Yockey has done an excellent job running this fund since inception and was named Morningstar's manager of the year in 1998. He has an extremely good long-term record as well. He's an astute stock picker and has also proven himself to be adept at determining which countries to be in at any given time.

Reason for Recommendation

I recommend that investors maintain a substantial weighting to international stocks at this time because of the strong growth prospects abroad. Europe is essentially a year and a half behind us, in terms of the economic cycle. The Europeans aren't terribly interested in slowing the economy down, as the Federal Reserve is in the U.S. Growth is really picking up in Europe, especially in Germany and France. Interest rates are fairly low, and you're seeing a move from government pensions into privately financed defined contribution plans. As in the U.S., much of this money is going into equities. There are many reasons to believe that the European economy and overseas stock markets will grow at a fairly good rate in 2001.

Bottom Line

Artisan International has seen its portfolio grow dramatically recently, but I think Yockey still has a manageable asset base. So far, it certainly hasn't impacted his ability to stay at the head of the pack.

Minimum Initial Investment: $1,000

Contact Information: Artisan International
P.O. Box 8412
Boston, MA 02266-8412
800-344-1770
<www.artisanfunds.com>

BONUS PICK FOR 2001

MATTHEWS JAPAN

Symbol: MJFOX

Keeping with my international theme, I like what I see going on in Asia right now. That's why I've selected Matthews Japan as my bonus pick. This is a country-specific fund that is fairly new. It's run by the Matthews family of funds, which has a strong reputation for investing in the Pacific Rim. The firm is based in San Francisco, but managers Mark Headley and Jim Bogin travel to Asia frequently. They both have been analyzing Asian stocks for many years. Unlike most of the Japan-specific funds out there, Headley and Bogin are aware of valuations. In 1999, for example, many Japan-specific funds were up 200 percent-plus, but they were heavily invested in high-priced technology stocks. As a result, they got whacked as valuations came down and the market took a hit. On the other hand, Matthews Japan held up well in the downturn. I like Japan because I think the country has hit a bottom, as far as the economy is concerned. We're seeing many mergers and restructurings, and Japan has a zero interest rate policy. As a result, there is a huge flood of savings coming out of the postal savings system that will likely have nowhere to go but into equities. (For more information, call 800-789-2742, or visit their Web site at <www.matthewsfunds.com>.)

Artisan International Fd
Symbol: ARTIX

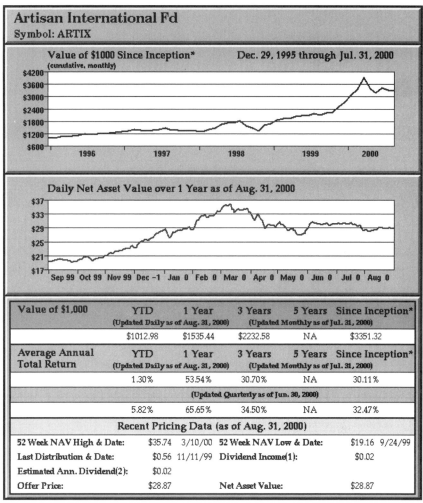

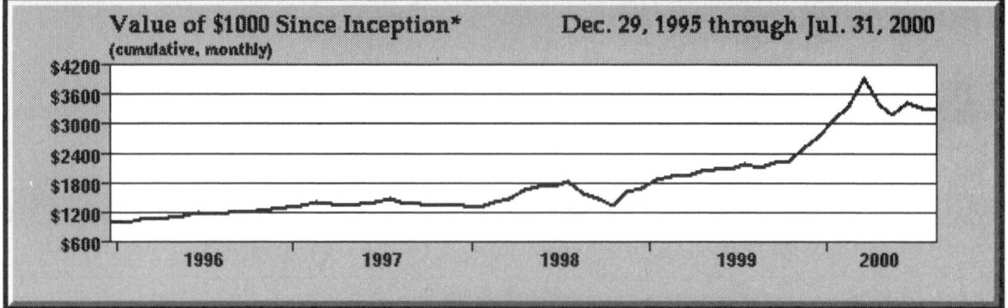

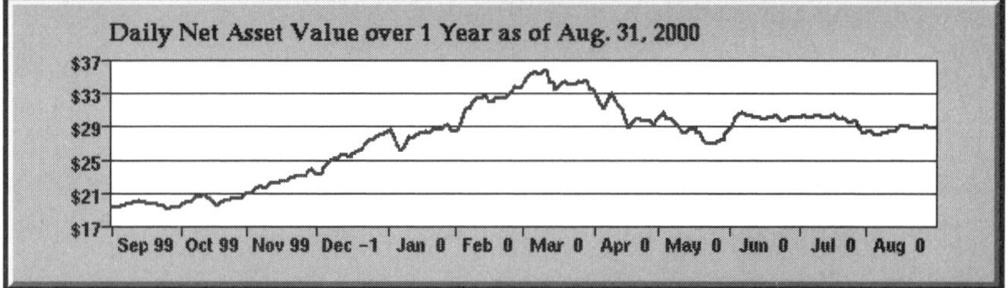

Value of $1,000	YTD	1 Year	3 Years	5 Years	Since Inception*
	(Updated Daily as of Aug. 31, 2000)		(Updated Monthly as of Jul. 31, 2000)		
	$1012.98	$1535.44	$2232.58	NA	$3351.32
Average Annual Total Return	**YTD**	**1 Year**	**3 Years**	**5 Years**	**Since Inception***
	(Updated Daily as of Aug. 31, 2000)		(Updated Monthly as of Jul. 31, 2000)		
	1.30%	53.54%	30.70%	NA	30.11%
	(Updated Quarterly as of Jun. 30, 2000)				
	5.82%	65.65%	34.50%	NA	32.47%

Recent Pricing Data (as of Aug. 31, 2000)					
52 Week NAV High & Date:	$35.74	3/10/00	52 Week NAV Low & Date:	$19.16	9/24/99
Last Distribution & Date:	$0.56	11/11/99	Dividend Income(1):	$0.02	
Estimated Ann. Dividend(2):	$0.02				
Offer Price:	$28.87		Net Asset Value:	$28.87	

Source: Tradeline.Com, a Platinum Equity Holdings Company

Top 10 Holdings	Key Statistics	
Granada Grp.	Sales Load (max)	0.00%
Lloyds TSB Grp.	Redemption Charge (max)	0.00%
AT&T Canada	Expense Ratio	1.38%
China Telecom	Management Fee	0.99%
Nippon Telegraph & Tele.	12b-1 Marketing Fees	0.00%
UnitedGlobalCom	PE Ratio	34.30
Prosiben Media	Dividend Yield	0.08%
Suez Lyon Eaux	Turnover Ratio	79.00%
UBS	Beta Factor	0.89
Nortel Networks	Total Assets	$3.63 bil.

CITIZENS GLOBAL EQUITY

Janet Brown
DAL Investment Company

Fund Profile

Citizens Global Equity is a fund that is heavily weighted in technology, media, and telecommunications—the fastest growing areas of our economy. Manager Sevgi Ipek is able to buy companies anywhere in the world. What's more, each company must pass through a series of social screens. While social screening is not my primary consideration when selecting funds, the result of the screening process is that Ipek is able to filter out many of the old industrial stocks. Companies that fail to pass the screens are often polluters or have manufacturing policies that aren't conducive to growth.

I like that a large percentage of the portfolio is invested outside the U.S. because I think that foreign markets in general are a better value right now. I expect growth outside of the U.S. to continue at a faster rate, simply because most foreign economies lag ours in terms of increasing productivity. We've seen tremendous gains in the U.S. going back to the 1980s. Most foreign economies lag us and should realize some of the gains we've seen from restructuring, cost-cutting, and technology. We're also seeing international cultures become more open to equity investing, which creates better demand for stocks. The most recent report shows that this fund has about 35 percent of its assets in the U.S., with 11 percent in Japan, 7 percent in the United Kingdom, and much of the rest in Western Europe.

About the Manager

Sevgi Ipek is a manager with a lot of experience. In addition to applying the required social screens, she looks for management policies that are in sync with what you would expect to find at a progressive company. The first social screen is that a company must not pollute and should increase the quality of life. As a result, tobacco and arms companies are automatically bumped out. The next screen looks at how workers are treated, how many women are on the board of directors, etc.

Reason for Recommendation

Again, I didn't choose this fund because of its social conscience. I chose it for its terrific performance. But it's a happy result that the screens lead to owning faster-growing companies with progressive management styles and policies. I also like the global nature of the fund. I prefer global funds to pure international funds, because I think you're better off letting the manager choose country allocations.

Bottom Line

This is a fairly low-risk way to add international exposure to your portfolio. It's a fund that takes advantage of growth in the new economy, without being very aggressive. I really think you're better off in a lower-risk fund going in to 2001. I would also recommend that you keep about 20 to 25 percent of your total portfolio in international funds.

Minimum Initial Investment: $2,500 ($1,000 for IRAs)

Contact Information: Citizens Global Equity
230 Commerce Way, Suite 300
Portsmouth, NH 03801
800-223-7010
<www.citizensfunds.com>

(Available without a transaction fee through Fidelity, Schwab, and TD Waterhouse.)

BONUS PICK FOR 2001

FIRSTHAND TECHNOLOGY LEADERS *Symbol:* TLFQX

I just love the Firsthand group. They're based in the Silicon Valley. I particularly favor the Firsthand Technology Leaders fund because we're seeing a flight to quality, and this fund favors the larger-cap technology stocks. I think we're going to have a lot of consolidation in this sector, and this fund is one of the safest ways to play this volatile area of the market. There's no doubt that technology is where the growth is at. Having said that, I probably wouldn't recommend that you keep more than 5 percent of your total portfolio in a fund like this. (For more information on this fund, you can call 800-662-7447, or visit the fund's Web site at <www.firsthandfunds.com>.)

Citizens Global Equity Fund
Symbol: WAGEX

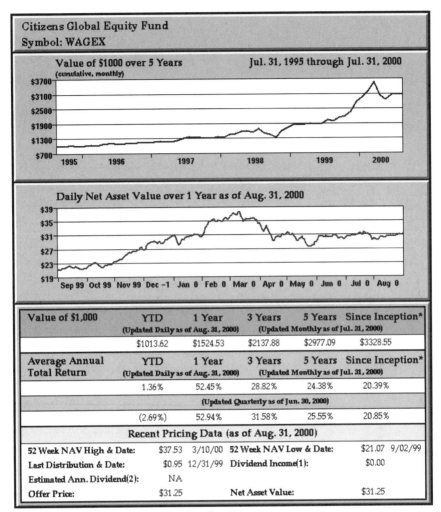

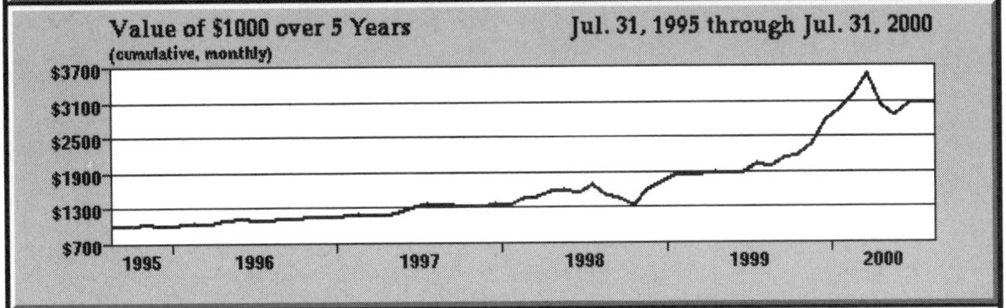

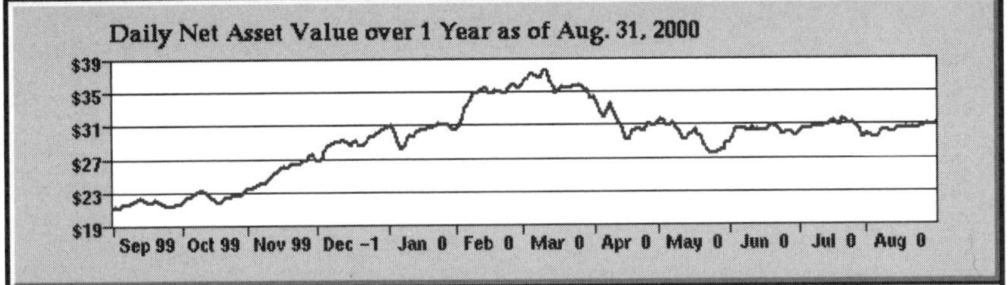

Value of $1,000	YTD (Updated Daily as of Aug. 31, 2000)	1 Year	3 Years (Updated Monthly as of Jul. 31, 2000)	5 Years	Since Inception*
	$1013.62	$1524.53	$2137.88	$2977.09	$3328.55
Average Annual Total Return	**YTD (Updated Daily as of Aug. 31, 2000)**	**1 Year**	**3 Years (Updated Monthly as of Jul. 31, 2000)**	**5 Years**	**Since Inception***
	1.36%	52.45%	28.82%	24.38%	20.39%
	(Updated Quarterly as of Jun. 30, 2000)				
	(2.69%)	52.94%	31.58%	25.55%	20.85%

Recent Pricing Data (as of Aug. 31, 2000)

52 Week NAV High & Date:	$37.53	3/10/00	**52 Week NAV Low & Date:**	$21.07	9/02/99
Last Distribution & Date:	$0.95	12/31/99	**Dividend Income(1):**	$0.00	
Estimated Ann. Dividend(2):	NA				
Offer Price:	$31.25		**Net Asset Value:**	$31.25	

Source: Tradeline.Com, a Platinum Equity Holdings Company

Top 10 Holdings	Key Statistics	
Tyco Intl.	Sales Load (max)	0.00%
AXA	Redemption Charge (max)	0.00%
Cisco Systems	Expense Ratio	1.96%
Glaxo Wellcome	Management Fee	1.00%
Nokia Cl A	12b-1 Marketing Fees	0.25%
Taiyo Yuden	PE Ratio	46.60
Vestas Wind Sys.	Dividend Yield	0.00%
Seven-Eleven Japan	Turnover Ratio	64.00%
Barclays	Beta Factor	0.80
Sun Microsystems	Total Assets	$353.00 mil.

MATTHEWS PACIFIC TIGER

Harold Evensky
Evensky, Brown & Katz

Fund Profile

Matthews Pacific Tiger is an emerging-markets fund that is solely focused on the Pacific Rim. It's predominately a small-company fund that invests in areas throughout the south Pacific, excluding Japan. Some of the biggest weightings are in Hong Kong, China, South Korea, Thailand, Malaysia, and Singapore. The portfolio contains an eclectic group of companies, including a number of financial, service, and technology stocks.

About the Managers

Although managers Paul Matthews and Mark Headley are based in San Francisco, they spend a lot of time out in the field traveling and visiting companies. Very simply, they look for good companies that are well managed with reasonable fundamentals. They really dig deep to understand and evaluate the accounting, raw data, and people running the operation. They look at every investment as buying interest in a company, not just as a stock. Matthews and Headley run a few other funds, but all are focused on this same general geographic area. Before starting the firm, Matthews was a manager with GT Management in Hong Kong, so he's definitely experienced in this part of the market.

Reason for Recommendation

I do feel it's appropriate for investors to have a small weighting in the emerging markets. By small I mean maybe 5 percent. I consider the area covered by Matthews Pacific Tiger to be different enough from the broad category that I overweight the Pacific Rim in my emerging markets allocation.

Bottom Line

This historically has been a very volatile fund. These markets are risky for a number of reasons, including politics. There is a domino factor in these smaller countries in that if one has a problem, it rapidly falls to another. Plus, people are very moody when it comes to the emerging markets. When these countries are hot, investors rush in; when they cool down, investors flee. Given this caveat, I am optimistic about the prospects for this fund in 2001. I might only keep 1 or 2 percent of the overall portfolio invested in a fund like this, but it will give you good diversification away from the U.S. market, which I think is important for every investor to have.

Minimum Initial Investment: $2,500 ($500 for IRAs)

Contact Information: Matthews Pacific Tiger I
456 Montgomery Street, Suite 1200
San Francisco, CA 94104
800-789-2742
<www.matthewsfunds.com>

(Available without a transaction fee through Fidelity, Schwab, and TD Waterhouse.)

BONUS PICK FOR 2001

OPPENHEIMER REAL ASSET

Symbol: QRAAX

Oppenheimer Real Asset gives you marketable exposure to the commodities market, which is rare in a mutual fund. I think commodities play a role in almost every portfolio for purposes of diversification. Oppenheimer created this fund a few years ago, but not without having to go through many regulatory hurdles. The fund is designed to closely mimic the Goldman Sachs Commodity Index, which is an index based on the actual world usage of commodities, as opposed to some sort of intellectually constructed benchmark. It is roughly two-thirds natural resources, oil, and gas, and about one-third agricultural. The portfolio is constructed based on making loans to high-quality, highly rated commodities firms. I typically keep about 5 percent of a portfolio in a fund like this, especially because commodities is the only general asset class that historically has been negatively correlated with both stocks and bonds. The biggest downside is that the A shares of this fund have a steep 5.75 percent sales load. But, given how unique it is, I think it's probably worth it. (For more information on the fund, call 800-525-7048, or visit the fund's Web site at <www.oppenheimerfunds.com>.)

Matthews Pacific Tiger Fd
Symbol: MAPTX

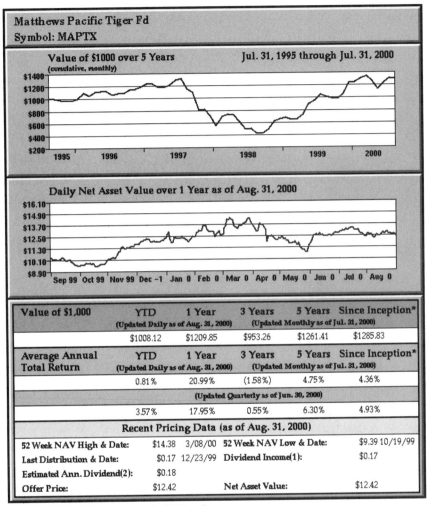

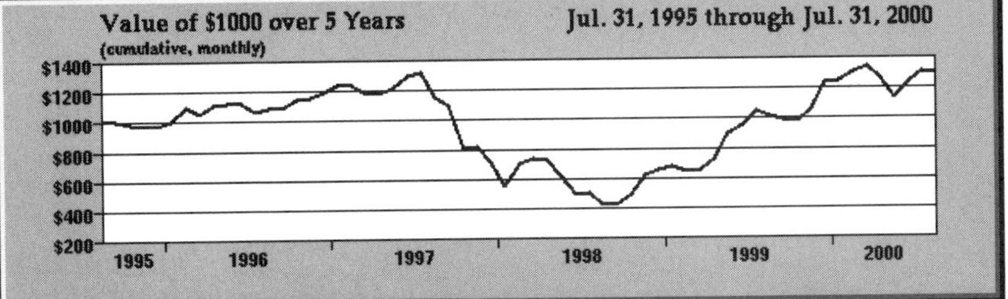

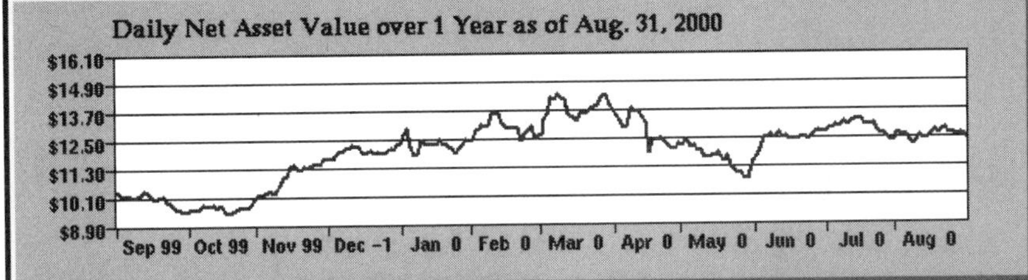

Value of $1,000	YTD	1 Year	3 Years	5 Years	Since Inception*
	(Updated Daily as of Aug. 31, 2000)		(Updated Monthly as of Jul. 31, 2000)		
	$1008.12	$1209.85	$953.26	$1261.41	$1285.83

Average Annual Total Return	YTD	1 Year	3 Years	5 Years	Since Inception*
	(Updated Daily as of Aug. 31, 2000)		(Updated Monthly as of Jul. 31, 2000)		
	0.81%	20.99%	(1.58%)	4.75%	4.36%
		(Updated Quarterly as of Jun. 30, 2000)			
	3.57%	17.95%	0.55%	6.30%	4.93%

Recent Pricing Data (as of Aug. 31, 2000)

52 Week NAV High & Date:	$14.38	3/08/00	52 Week NAV Low & Date:	$9.39 10/19/99
Last Distribution & Date:	$0.17	12/23/99	Dividend Income(1):	$0.17
Estimated Ann. Dividend(2):	$0.18			
Offer Price:	$12.42		Net Asset Value:	$12.42

Source: Tradeline.Com, a Platinum Equity Holdings Company

Top 10 Holdings	Key Statistics	
Li & Fung	Sales Load (max)	0.00%
Samsung Electronics	Redemption Charge (max)	2.00%
Legend Hldgs.	Expense Ratio	1.90%
Giordano Intl.	Management Fee	1.00%
Hutchison Whampoa	12b-1 Marketing Fees	0.00%
Hite Brewery	PE Ratio	25.10
Shangri-La Asia	Dividend Yield	1.35%
Via Tech	Turnover Ratio	99.00%
Asia Satellite Telecom	Beta Factor	1.56
Hana Bk.	Total Assets	$114.00 mil.

part 3

UP CLOSE WITH THE EXPERTS

GETTING TO KNOW WALL STREET'S FINEST

Now that you've read about the many stocks and mutual funds our distinguished panelists are buying in the year 2001, it's time to learn a little bit more about what makes them so great. What follows are biographies of each expert, presented in alphabetical order. You'll find a picture (so you can see they're not only savvy but also good-looking), followed by a brief overview of what they do and how they got where they are. Every profile ends with thoughts on the biggest mistakes investors make and strategies for success in the stock market. Also included are each panelist's occupation, birth date, educational background, market outlook, and the best and worst investments they've ever made.

Each luminary has a different way of choosing stocks and/or a unique field of expertise, so you will get a truly diversified list of disciplines and techniques to help you become a better buyer and seller of both stocks and mutual funds.

What characteristics do the world's greatest investors share? After doing some careful analysis of these profiles, I came up with five traits they all seem to have in common:

1. *They have adopted very specific strategies that they consistently follow regardless of what's happening with the overall market.* Clearly, there isn't just one technique that works all the time. Nevertheless, if you develop a system you understand and heed without fail, over time you will make a lot of money.
2. *The pros are highly suspicious of hot tips and anything recommended by a stockbroker.* Many go so far as to say people should avoid taking the advice of a broker altogether because most are mere salespeople who don't know much about the market to begin with.
3. *The masters don't pay attention to what they see and hear on the news.* Instead, they ignore the day-to-day direction of the Dow and focus on uncovering new ideas while closely following the holdings in their own portfolio.
4. *The wealthiest investors avoid market timing.* They are always fully invested, although the specific stocks and funds they hold might change depending on their outlook for such things as interest rates and the economy.
5. *The gurus all agree that diversification is the secret to achieving long-term investment success.*

It's interesting to note that only a handful of these experts actually majored in business or planned to invest other people's money for a living. That goes to show you don't need a Harvard MBA to become a first-class portfolio manager. It's also striking how open and easygoing most of these living investment legends are. Even though they work in a fast-paced, often frenetic industry, these folks have a great deal of confidence and faith in their decisions. They aren't constant traders yet are willing to accept both success and failure, and aren't afraid to move on when they're wrong. Without question, they understand the true essence of what makes the stock market work.

In addition to giving you a lot of insight into who these people are, the profiles will teach you how to pick stocks and mutual funds, when to sell, and what to expect from your investments in the future. You are sure to uncover valuable advice you can profit from for decades to come.

One last observation is that most of the panelists remain optimistic going into the new year, despite the increasing volatility in the market. Now let's hear more from them about how to properly pick your investments now and into the future.

SALLY ANDERSON

Kopp Investment Advisors

Sally Anderson always knew she'd leave Iowa someday and make it big in the business world. She just wasn't sure how until she got to college. "I went to the undergraduate business school at Northwestern when it still had one," she says. "After taking my first course in finance, I knew right away I had found what I wanted to do." After working for a year as a research assistant at a now-defunct Chicago brokerage firm, she moved on to Dain Bosworth Inc. in October 1965. She was an analyst in the research department for 26 years, eventually working her way up to the assistant director's position. When her former colleague Lee Kopp went off to start his own investment management firm in 1990, he asked her to join him as a senior portfolio manager and she accepted. The firm started out with $20 million in assets and now oversees some $7 billion, all of which is invested in emerging growth stocks.

It took Anderson a little time to get used to her new job. For one thing, though she was still using the same skills, she had to focus them differently. "I had worked primarily with the brokers at Dain Bosworth, trying to sell them on ideas that we thought were attractive," she recalls. "Now, suddenly I was out there looking for the ideas and then given the money in hand to immediately put to work." She was also used to following larger companies and had to adjust to navigating through the often treacherous small-cap waters that Kopp focuses its efforts on. "These smaller companies are more flexible and in earlier phases of their life cycles, which is why they grow faster," she observes. "That's why our firm has always been attracted to them."

In addition to managing private accounts for wealthy investors, Anderson helps to run the Kopp Emerging Growth Fund. She gets her investment ideas from all over the place, including trade shows, personal contacts, conferences, and Wall Street research. She looks for four main characteristics in every stock, the most important of which is a company's ability to grow by at least 20 percent a year. "We like to see 15 to 20 percent top-line growth and 20 percent or more bottom-line growth," she explains. Furthermore, she seeks out names that are relatively underfollowed by other firms. "Ideally, we like to find them when they're covered by three or fewer analysts, rather than 25," she says. "We feel those are typically less efficiently priced stocks. Therefore, if we can find them before the rest of the world does, we'll benefit not only from their earnings growth, but also when those earnings are reevaluated."

Anderson usually sticks with companies sporting a total market capitalization in the $300 million to $3 billion range. "We'll go lower or higher than that depending on the opportunities," she notes. "Our median market cap in the fund is $700 million." Lastly, she puts a heavy emphasis on visiting with company management. "This is a key factor in our investment decision," she insists. "We want to know what type of house they keep and the kind of interplay they have with their employees."

Unlike many small-cap managers, Anderson buys for the long term and doesn't like to trade frequently around her positions. "We're looking for stocks we can own for three plus years," she maintains. "If a company does extraordinarily well, we might be forced to trim back a position to make sure it's not overweighted, but we will stay with it for as long as things are continuing to play out. We let our winners run."

Even with the market's huge gains in recent years, she's still finding plenty of good ideas to choose from. The fund's current portfolio is currently weighted about 80 percent in technology stocks, with another 15 percent in health care. "We believe that tech was the growth engine in the 1990s and don't see that changing," she says. "It's an industry with the wind at its back." She notes that her technology holdings are quite diverse, with some of her biggest recent successes coming from companies with enabling technologies for communications.

Anderson's son and daughter are also in the investment field. She says she enjoys her job even more now than when she started more than 30 years ago. "To me, it is probably the single most exciting industry you could ever be in because every day is different," she observes. "The cast of characters changes, in terms of stocks, and you meet some very interesting and bright people."

Occupation: Senior Portfolio Manager, Kopp Investment Advisors
Edina, Minnesota

Birth Date: July 31, 1942

Education: BS, Northwestern University, 1964

Biggest Mistake Investors Make: "Being impatient and too quick to sell a good stock."

Best Investment: JDS Uniphase (Started buying in 1996 with a cost of under $1 and still owns it.)

Worst Investment: Western Digital (Began building position in 1995 for an average cost of $12.50; began trimming 20 percent of the position in the $40 range in the summer of 1997, and sold out the remainder in 1999 at $5 to $6 per share.)

Advice: "Find really good companies and stay with them."

Market Outlook: Cautiously optimistic

JOSEPH BATTIPAGLIA

Gruntal & Co.

Joe Battipaglia remains one of the most bullish investment strategists on Wall Street. He's been telling Gruntal & Co.'s aggressive clients to keep 100 percent of their assets in equities for some time now. But that's nothing new for Battipaglia. He's been positive on the market since getting into the investment business back in 1982. "There are really three reasons I feel so good about stocks," he explains. "In descending order, you have diminishing inflation, the fact that economic activity has been on an upswing, and a consumer confidence level that keeps improving. These conditions merit investors having a substantial exposure to equities."

He believes short-term rates will remain rather stable, with inflation running between 2 and 2.5 percent for the foreseeable future. That, in his mind, is a formula for continued gains in the market. "There are only two things, in my view, that will derail the bull market," he says. "The onset of a big recession in the United States or a new round of spiraling inflation. Without those, you have a continued strong market with a tendency for equity prices to go higher."

Battipaglia's father introduced him to the stock tables in *The Wall Street Journal* at a young age. But after earning an MBA from the Wharton School, he went into the corporate world as a financial analyst with Exxon. "My initial position was to work on five-year business plans," he says. "I learned what it meant to be in a pyramidal organization, where you were expected to advance only in your particular discipline." Battipaglia wanted to explore other opportunities. He was investing his own portfolio in stocks on the side and decided that might be fun to do full-time. "I liked the entrepreneurial and risk-taking aspects of the investment industry plus, structurally, investment firms are pretty much on a horizontal plane," he adds.

So Battipaglia got on the phone and started calling some of his classmates and contacts from Wharton. Within a few days, he had offers to become everything from an odd-lot bond trader to an institutional salesman. "In 1981, I took a position with a small broker-dealer out of Philadelphia called Elkins & Co.," he says. "I was a man of many hats. I did some analysis, helped out in the underwriting of investment banking, and worked on the rollout of an IRA product. As the bear market we were in at the time started to wither and die, Elkins decided to sell out to Bache, which viewed everyone at the firm as either a salesman or overhead. It was clear to me I had to tell them I was a salesman in order to keep my position. So I spent one year as a broker, thinking that would give me enough time to figure out what my other choices were."

In his search for new opportunities, he came across Gruntal & Co., which had just 300 brokers in the New York area and was looking to establish a presence in

Philadelphia. "The firm wanted to build up its research department, which consisted essentially of two people," Battipaglia notes. "I joined as the third person and started following anything that was interesting. My first recommendations included AT&T, Centocor, and Vanity Fair Corporation." In 1986, Gruntal asked him to come to New York, and four years later he was named director of research and given a larger staff of analysts. "I became head of our in-house money management business in 1993," he adds. "Then, in early 1997, I was named chief investment strategist and am now a partner as well."

There are two main focuses of Battipaglia's job. First, he gives an overall recommendation as to how much exposure clients should have to equities. As you know, for those willing to accept the volatility, he thinks that percentage should be quite high. And he doesn't expect this bullish environment to end anytime soon. What about the argument that stocks are overvalued, given the market's meteoric rise? Battipaglia doesn't buy it. "I think you've got to take a top-down approach to looking at markets and flip it over," he insists. "Whenever you come from a high inflationary period to a low inflationary period, assets can rise 15-fold to 20-fold during the next cycle. We still have a long way to go."

As part of his job, Battipaglia recommends specific companies that clients of the firm should consider investing in. His favorite themes currently include pharmaceuticals, technology, transportation, financial services, and telecommunications. "When evaluating individual stocks, I'm looking for what I would call an anomaly in the market," he shares. "That is, the market's valuation of the stock is not on point with the company's true fundamental condition. This could be caused by investors not realizing how strong the company's franchise is, an event that causes it to temporarily stumble, or a positive unexpected new product or development."

Occupation: Chairman of Investment Policy, Gruntal & Co. LLC
New York, New York

Birth Date: October 28, 1955

Education: BA, Boston College, 1976
MBA, Wharton School, University of Pennsylvania, 1978

Biggest Mistake Investors Make: "Not selling stocks based on a discipline. You need to know when you're going to sell before you go in."

Best Investment: Buying pharmaceutical stocks in the 1970s and holding on.

Worst Investment: Cambridge Biotech (Purchased in the late 1970s for around $6 and eventually went down to zero.)

Advice: "Have a clear sense of the broad fundamentals and stay focused on the creation of company value."

Market Outlook: Bullish

ART BONNEL

Bonnel Growth Fund

Art Bonnel is as bullish as ever about the prospects for the stock market, especially because the aging baby boomers seem to keep plowing money into equities at a frantic pace. In fact, Bonnel believes the Dow will hit 100,000 by 2025. "That reflects an average annual return of 9.25 percent, although historically it's been a bit higher," he says. "There will be corrections of 10 to 20 percent along the way, but there'll be buying opportunities."

Investing is literally a family affair for Bonnel. He runs the $400 million Bonnel Growth Fund out of his home in Reno, Nevada, with the help of wife Wanda. She uses her accounting background to scour through dozens of earnings reports and 10-Qs each day in search of companies growing fast enough to be considered by her picky husband. Art Bonnel then scrutinizes each candidate by subjecting it to a four-part test.

To begin with, earnings must be up from the previous year. "I don't care how much, I just want to see them up," he explains. If they're down, he passes or sells the issue if it's already in his portfolio. Next, the current ratio (current assets divided by current liabilities) should be 2 to 1. "If a company is having problems, for whatever reason, it shows up in the current ratio," he notes. Step three examines the amount of long-term debt on the balance sheet (he doesn't want to see it increasing), and the debt-to-equity ratio must be no more than 30 percent. Finally, Bonnel looks at insider holdings. He likes top management to own at least 5 to 15 percent of the company, reasoning, "I want them to be motivated to increase the value of their personal wealth."

If a company checks out in all four categories, Bonnel glances at a Standard & Poor's tear sheet for a brief description of the business and views a few charts. "I want to see a stock basing out or in a minor uptrend," he explains. "I don't want to catch a falling piano." A stock is unloaded if earnings go down or he sees meaningful selling by insiders.

Once Bonnel finds a promising idea, he likes to buy it at a reasonable price. "When I look at a company, I generally don't like to pay more than half the earnings growth rate," he insists. "In other words, if earnings are up 100 percent this year, I don't want a PE of more than 50. What I attempt to find are companies with PEs in the 20 range."

You'll notice he doesn't talk to company management or visit his potential investments. That's because, in his mind, the numbers don't lie, but people sometimes do. "Company officers can tell you anything they want and that things are great," he says. "I look at what the accountants tell us, not what company officers say they're doing. What's their debt level like? What are their current assets? You can tell me any story you want, but I want to see audited numbers."

In addition, he doesn't limit himself to any particular area of the market, meaning you'll find both large and small companies in his portfolio. "I'll buy anything that looks attractive," he says. "Sometimes I'll buy a company that hasn't been doing well for a couple of years but suddenly gets its act together, resulting in increased earnings."

While Bonnel claims his earnings-driven strategy works well in most markets, he warns it's not infallible, admitting he is wrong 35 to 40 percent of the time. Furthermore, when his companies report a disappointing quarter, they are often hammered by Wall Street. Still, he doesn't believe his discipline is unnecessarily risky. "In a bear market, good stocks go down, mediocre stocks go down, and poor stocks go down," he explains. "However, if you're in companies that are doing well, they will bounce back faster."

This strategy has helped Bonnel to produce an impressive record. Before being offered his own fund by United Services in 1994, he managed the MIM Stock Appreciation Fund for five years, generating an average annual gain of 18 percent. "I stick with this system through good times and bad," he insists. "There are slow periods when my style of investing goes out of favor, but then it tends to come back because I'm looking at companies that are growing."

Right now, he's especially interested in mid-cap stocks. "I'm finding some pretty good buys out there," he says. "The past few years have been difficult for this part of the market. Investors have been putting their money into companies with more predictable earnings."

Occupation: Portfolio Manager, Bonnel Growth Fund
Reno, Nevada

Birth Date: August 20, 1945

Education: BS, University of Nevada, 1968

Biggest Mistake Investors Make: "Watching stocks too closely and worrying about every tick."

Best Investment: QLogic (Bought for $5 in early 1999 and sold for $175 in early 2000.)

Worst Investment: Comtronix (Paid $20 a share and discovered the company was cooking the books; got out at about $4.)

Advice: "You can make more money with patience than brilliance. The true genius of investing is recognizing the direction of a trend, not attempting to pick market tops or bottoms. Also, if you find you have made a mistake, you should cut your losses."

Market Outlook: Bullish

ELIZABETH BRAMWELL

Bramwell Capital Management

Elizabeth Bramwell has been managing money for more than three decades. But growing up, she never had much of a financial vocabulary. Her father was a musician and never discussed the stock market. As a young girl, Bramwell dreamed of becoming a doctor and wound up majoring in chemistry at Bryn Mawr College. However, she found economics to be more exciting. So after graduation, she enrolled at the Columbia Business School, where she got an MBA in finance.

Among her Columbia classmates was famed money manager Mario Gabelli. Both began their professional careers as analysts at the same time at different firms, although they occasionally crossed paths. In 1985 Gabelli asked Bramwell to join his money management firm as director of research. Two years later, in April 1987, she was tapped to launch the Gabelli Growth Fund. Bramwell wrote the fund's investment philosophy and made all of the buy and sell decisions. From the start, Bramwell often posted better returns than her value-oriented boss, and the media took notice. Assets in Gabelli Growth quickly swelled to $700 million with some 60,000 shareholders. During her tenure, the fund posted an average annual return of 16.6 percent.

Following a highly publicized dispute, Bramwell parted ways with Gabelli in 1994 and started her own fund, Bramwell Growth, six months later. "I left [Gabelli] with the idea that if I were going to go out on my own, I too could start a business and succeed," she says.

Bramwell's investment discipline has evolved over the years. "When I started out, I worked on analyzing emerging public companies, so I like to own emerging, smaller names," she explains. "However, I also don't want to ignore some of the larger firms when they are big movers." In addition to running Bramwell Growth, which contains companies of all sizes, Bramwell Capital is subadvisor to the Selected Special Shares Fund, which concentrates on small-cap and mid-cap stocks. The firm also subadvises a fund sponsored by Sun America. In 1999, she started the Bramwell Focus Fund, a portfolio of 20 to 30 of her favorite stocks. "It's more aggressive than Bramwell Growth and reflects what's attractive to me today," she said. "It doesn't necessarily mimic the top holdings of my original fund."

Bramwell prides herself on being both a top-down and bottom-up analyst. "From a top-down standpoint, I think about things like inflation, interest rates, tax rates, currencies, and political events," she says. "I'm always thinking about the future, projecting earnings and the multiples on those earnings. I then relate those multiples to the underlying growth rates." Her ideal objective is to buy companies at a discount to their future growth rates.

From a bottom-up, more sector-specific perspective, she looks for industry-specific trends, such as accelerating use of technology. "Several things are happening that will be enormously positive for numerous technology companies," she maintains. "One is electronic commerce. Another is the explosion in new communications. I also think that the subsiding of the Y2K jitters will be positive for a lot of businesses in the technology sector." In addition, Bramwell is fond of companies that are big users and/or providers of outsourcing, which she sees as an expanding emerging trend.

Once Bramwell has determined which areas of the market she's most interested in, she begins looking closely at specific companies. "I'm trying to figure out how they're going to grow going forward with new products and markets," she explains. "Are the margins going to expand, and what's happening with tax rates? Do they need to raise more money, or will they buy back shares?" Attending conferences and company road shows that come through the Big Apple, where her office is located, provides useful insight. "Companies make 30-minute to 45-minute presentations in New York that are followed by a question-and-answer period," she notes. "Having other analysts and portfolio managers there [in the room] asking questions provides for a synergistic briefing."

Bramwell carefully monitors her holdings on a daily basis and looks for strong indications of change before deciding to move on. "I'll sell when I think the fundamentals are deteriorating or if the macroeconomic picture changes," she shares. "I'll also sell if I think I've found a better opportunity elsewhere. In that case, I'm willing to sell one stock to go into another."

Lately she's been finding a lot of attractive buys in smaller stocks, including some select IPOs. "There are some especially good opportunities in companies with market capitalizations under $5 billion, below which they start to lose a lot of institutional support," she adds.

Occupation: President and CIO, Bramwell Capital Management
New York, New York

Birth Date: December 1, 1940

Education: BA, Bryn Mawr College, 1962
MBA, Columbia University, 1967

Biggest Mistake Investors Make: "Being emotional."

Best Investment: Amazon.com (Bought in May 1997 for a split-adjusted $2.94 a share.)

Worst Investment: U.S. Satellite

Advice: "Understand what you're buying. Act with knowledge, not compulsively."

Market Outlook: Bullish

REUBEN GREGG BREWER

Value Line

Reuben Gregg Brewer admits he began college as a lost and searching soul. "I wasn't quite sure what I wanted to do," he says. "I found psychology to be really interesting, so I got a degree in that." After graduation, he took a year off, before his father offered to pay for him to get a master's degree. "A master's in psychology is pretty useless, so I decided to study social work," he recalls. "I was accepted to Columbia."

Earlier, Brewer's father had started an individual retirement account for him. When he went off college, his dad decided it was time for him to take charge of that as well. "I sort of dabbled in mutual funds and stocks," he says. "I also got into stupid things, such as penny stocks and frequent trading, figuring I could make a lot of money. I paid a price for those lessons, but I learned them well." Before long, he was hooked on investing.

Still, after college he planned on a career working with the elderly. "It was sort of a calculated decision," he admits. "I looked at the demographics of society and realized there were going to be a lot of older people. I figured if I got in early, I'd probably be in a management position by the time this trend peaked." But he was much more interested in investing. So, armed with his master's in social work, he began sending out résumés to brokers and other investment-related businesses.

"I quickly realized that since I hated sales I couldn't become a broker," he says. "I sent one of my résumés to Value Line, after seeing an ad in the paper. I got a call, came in, took a test, and the rest is history."

Brewer started out as a mutual fund analyst in 1997, and has quickly worked his way up to becoming manager of mutual fund research. "We put out a print publication, *The Value Line Mutual Fund Survey,* every two weeks," he notes. "We also have an online version and a monthly newsletter. My job is to give focus and be a driving force behind the department. I do a lot of editing and stay on top of what's going on in the industry." Brewer also writes the foreword for the annual *Mutual Fund Investor's Guide* by Kirk Kazanjian, which features Value Line data throughout.

Like its prime competitor, Morningstar, Value Line has a rating system for every fund it follows. Morningstar has stars, Value Line simply uses numbers. While the more stars the better under Morningstar's system, lower numbers rule under Value Line. For instance, a fund with a 1 rating is much better than one with a 5. "As you know, Value Line has a rich history in stock analysis," Brewer boasts. "We are now putting that knowledge base to work with mutual funds. We give people straightforward information that they need to make informed decisions. We also look at volatility differently, taking into consideration both upside and downside volatility. Morningstar only looks at volatility on the downside."

The rating system is purely a quantitative process, with no human judgment involved. However, Brewer's team of analysts do conduct regular interviews with portfolio managers and include that commentary in their research reports.

Brewer has fairly kind words to say about the fund industry in general, although he maintains there are really two sides to the business. "One is where the managers are making investment decisions for you," he observes. "While they aren't always correct, their ideas are generally well thought out. On the whole, mutual fund managers are very intelligent and do a good job. But the flip side is that the companies that sell the funds are all about gathering assets under management. They're always trying to create new products, which may not be in the best interest of investors. In other words, they'll create a biotech fund, just because biotech happens to be hot. But it may not be a good idea for investors to concentrate money in this area. As they say, it's a case of caveat emptor."

Away from the office, Brewer spends his time playing trumpet and reading. "I'm a pretty sedate guy who is happy just going home and opening a book or making music with my trumpet," he says.

Occupation: Manager of Mutual Fund Research, Value Line
New York, New York

Birth Date: November 20, 1972

Education: BA, Purchase College, 1994
MSSW, Columbia University, 1997

Biggest Mistake Investors Make: "Following the crowd."

Best Investment: Westinghouse (Bought several years ago before its merger with CBS. It gave him an entry into the Internet space, without buying a volatile IPO.)

Worst Investment: American Heritage Fund (Purchased in 1994 just because it had a low share price. In the months that followed, the price got even lower. The lesson: Don't judge a fund by its net asset value.)

Advice: "Always do your own research before making an investment."

Market Outlook: Cautious

JANET BROWN

DAL Investment Company

Janet Brown's approach to investing is the exact opposite of traditional asset allocation. "We believe a sure way to underperform is by allocating a percentage of your portfolio to an underperforming sector and stick with it through thick and thin," she says. "I think many of the asset allocators out there are coming around to our way of thinking." In other words, instead of owning a little bit of everything, including large, small, and international stocks at all times, she believes in going only with the winners in the current market cycle. As this book went to press, that was predominately aggressive growth stocks, although value was starting to make a comeback. "I believe your best chance for beating the market is by following the leaders."

Brown and her former boss, Burton Berry, devised a unique strategy for selecting funds in the late 1970s. They call it "upgrading." The results of their research are printed each month in *NoLoad Fund*X,* a newsletter published by Brown's firm. "The first thing we do is classify the funds in our database by risk," she explains. "We then look at current performance over the past 12-, 6-, 3-, and 1-month periods. Next, we take a simple performance average during those four periods, give funds in the top 15 some bonus points, and rank each one by its performance-based score." It's a purely quantitative process, which calls for purchasing funds based on returns alone. The background of a manager isn't really a consideration. The best five funds in each risk category are recommended for purchase. When a fund's performance drops, thus booting it out of the top five, Brown recommends switching into another winner. There are some exceptions, however. She tells investors not to put more than 25 percent in international or small-cap funds, even when they are the best performers, because they are too risky.

The logic behind this system is pretty straightforward. Every fund manager has a certain investing style that works well in some environments and poorly in others. "For instance, aggressive growth stock pickers have been doing well until recently because that's where the market leadership has been," Brown says. "But there will be periods when value managers do better. There are also certain sectors that come and go out of vogue. Investing is quite cyclical because of changing economic fundamentals. It's easy to identify areas of outperformance after the fact, but they're impossible to forecast."

Brown's discipline calls for staying fully invested at all times. If it works as designed, you'll always be in the right place at the right time. "The system should continually keep you in those funds that have gotten it right because they're in the best stocks or sectors. They might even be in cash if the market's going down," she adds. A high-performing fund usually maintains its momentum for an average of six months, though Brown says some have stayed in the spotlight for as long as two and one-half years.

Following the leaders means paying capital gains taxes each time you make a trade. In retirement accounts, that's not a concern. But in taxable portfolios, Brown admits it doesn't always make sense to switch around so much. "You really have to look at whether upgrading will result in enough increased performance to make the trade pay off," she admits. "To be truthful, in the last few years it often hasn't because you've been able to get good results in almost all domestic market environments."

Brown entered the fund business through a rather unconventional channel. After graduating from college with a degree in architecture and art, she went off to Brussels with a friend. She needed a job and wound up working for a large insurance brokerage firm as a fund administrator. "The company sold mutual funds, mostly to U.S. servicemen," she recalls. "In order to do my job, I had to get licensed. I began to study investments, and particularly funds. I quickly concluded that no-loads were the way to go." Unfortunately, her European employer only peddled load funds, which carried steep 8.5 percent sales charges. Brown moved back to San Francisco three years later and thought about becoming a stockbroker. "I knew I wanted to be in the investment business but found brokers did more sales work than investment management," she says. "I also felt there was a conflict of interest between the broker and the client as it was a commission-based relationship. Then a friend of mine introduced me to Burt Berry, who had started an investment firm using only no-load funds. He hired me as his assistant in 1978 when we had less than $10 million under management. The two of us developed this upgrading strategy." In 1997 Berry sold most of the firm to Brown and her partners.

Brown's upgrading system seems to be effective and has consistently been given high marks by *The Hulbert Financial Digest.* "It's not complicated, but it really does work," she says.

Occupation: President, DAL Investment Company
San Francisco, California

Birth Date: November 10, 1950

Biggest Mistake Investors Make: "Having a short-term outlook and not riding through corrections."

Best Investment: Firsthand Technology Value (Bought it in 1999 and it has more than doubled.)

Worst Investment: Continuing to own value funds through the late 1990s, even though they performed poorly relative to growth.

Advice: "Take a long-term view and only stick with funds that are doing well in the current environment."

Market Outlook: Bullish

JAMES COLLINS

Insight Capital Research & Management

"In all the years I've been in this business, I've never seen as much day-to-day volatility as we're having now," says Jim Collins of Insight Capital Research & Management. "To tell you the truth, I don't think this volatility is going to end anytime soon. We better learn to live with it."

Collins began following the stock market in high school for an unorthodox reason. He wanted to own a manufacturing plant some day and knew he would have to come up with capital to do it. He figured learning about stocks would give him the knowledge he needed to raise cash. But things didn't turn out as he planned. "After graduating from college with an engineering degree, I went into the Navy," he reflects. "For about ten years, I tried everything conceivable out there to get an edge on the marketplace."

After his tour of duty was over, he joined General Electric as an engineer and spent his off-hours trading stocks. He managed to turn $1,500 into $487,000 in just four years. "I hadn't been at GE very long before I was making more money trading stocks than I was as an engineer," he confesses. "I was pretty much a speculator and trader in those days. I ran a concentrated portfolio of over-the-counter stocks. I typically held no more than six to eight names at a time, with most of the money invested in three issues." His portfolio eventually zoomed to $1.5 million before plummeting back down to $30,000 after a series of bad gambles. "I took that money, married a lovely girl from Asheville, North Carolina, and as soon as I graduated from the Harvard Business School, we took off for Europe and spent the whole $30,000 traveling for three months," he says. "I never looked at it as money. I just looked at it as a score. My thinking is still pretty much the same. I want to rack up as big a score as I can."

So far, that's exactly what he's done. His firm is ranked in the top tier of all money managers in the nation. His *OTC Insight* newsletter has been the number-one investment newsletter over the past five, eight, and ten years, according to *The Hulbert Financial Digest,* producing an annualized return of 69.6 percent during the past five years, and 46.2 percent over the last decade.

Collins's first professional job in the industry was working as a stock picker for a mutual fund company in 1967. He later became a stockbroker before starting his own firm in 1983. "I'm primarily a fundamentalist in what I do," he explains. "I have a three-step buying process: running quantitative screens, doing fundamental analysis, and then what I call performance analysis. Performance analysis for me is really taking a look at the relative strength of a stock."

He maintains a database of around 8,000 stocks, which he screens every morning. "First and foremost I like to find stocks with a track record of beating the market over a long period of time," he reveals. "The primary purpose of the screening is to see if a company has a track record of beating the market. Then I move on to fundamental analysis to verify that the industry looks good and that the company is a notch ahead of the rest of the players in its business. I then like to dig deeper to see that earnings are indeed growing rapidly, preferably by 20 percent a year or better, and that there is a solid cash flow."

Because he demands such strong growth, he most often gravitates toward smaller stocks that trade over the counter. The average company in his portfolio should grow its earnings by 33 percent in 2000. "The number-one reason I'll sell a stock is because it's not beating its benchmark index," he adds. In his non-tax-efficient accounts, this can lead to extremely high turnover.

Even though Collins specializes in small-cap stocks, his firm, Insight Capital, invests money across the board. He even runs a value portfolio, although he's known for being a heavy momentum player. But his definition of value is a little different from most. "We're really looking for growth companies that are out of favor for whatever reason," he says. "Sometimes a company will miss a quarter or get downgraded. We'll watch to see where it bottoms, but we don't try to go bottom fishing. We try to pick it up after it turns back up. So we're following the trends with some of the fallen angels."

When Collins wants to escape the hustle and bustle of the investment world, he and his wife travel. They recently took a trip to South America and occasionally go hiking in England. As for the future, Collins thinks interest rates could come down in 2001, which would lead to a continued strong market. "The longer term economic picture for this country is about as attractive as it has ever been," he says. "I especially like mid-cap stocks and think they will do very well going forward."

Occupation: President, Insight Capital Research & Management
Walnut Creek, California

Birth Date: August 26, 1934

Education: BEE, Georgia Tech, 1956
MBA, Harvard Business School, 1963

Biggest Mistake Investors Make: "Panicking and hitting the sell button at the wrong time; being greedy and thinking there's easy money to be made."

Best Investment: Cisco Systems (First bought it in 1991 and still owns it.)

Worst Investment: Gantos (Purchased shares of this clothing company in the 1980s for between $9 and $12 per share; got out around $5.)

Advice: "Focus on the fundamentals of a company and keep your money in stocks on an up-trend."

Market Outlook: Bullish

ELIZABETH DATER

Warburg Pincus Asset Management

Elizabeth Dater is convinced small-cap stocks will continue to do well in the coming year, although she hopes the winning names will broaden out a bit more. "Most of the action we're seeing is in companies with market capitalizations above $1.5 billion," she notes. "This shows investors still favor the liquidity provided by the bigger names. But the value is clearly there. Companies in the Russell 2000 are growing by 33 percent a year, yet the index is trading at 20 times earnings. That's a huge relative discount to the S&P 500."

Dater is a growth investor who looks for tiny, well-managed companies with the potential to become the large blue chips of tomorrow. "If I'm successful, the businesses I follow will have very little recognition when I start investing in them but a lot by the time I'm ready to sell," she says. "I look for companies with proprietary products and services along with access to the capital they need to fund their growth. I like companies with low debt to equity and a high return on equity because these tend to be the most profitable businesses." Most important, Dater takes a close look at management, which she believes is essential for determining whether an upstart will succeed or fail. "Management must be able to articulate a clear vision and business plan that I can benchmark them to and watch as the plan progresses," she explains. "I also like management to have an incentive to hold an equity ownership position to make sure its interests are aligned with the shareholders."

Because many small-cap companies don't make much money, especially in the early stages, it isn't always easy to determine how much they are worth. Dater's rule is to buy companies trading at a PE ratio below their growth rate. She also diversifies among 75 to 85 names to spread out her risk. "I rate each company in my portfolio as either a core holding or changing dynamic," she adds. "At least 75 percent are core holdings. These are companies with the strongest earnings momentum, unique business models, and best management. The other 25 percent, the changing dynamics, are put on close watch to make sure they grow as I expect. This would include the Internet stocks. If they don't work out, they get replaced."

It seems only fitting that Dater wound up as a panelist on the PBS program *Wall $treet Week with Louis Rukeyser* shortly after launching her career in the investment business. She's been a great communicator interested in the performing arts all of her life. As a young girl, she was a dancer and planned to teach drama. But after graduating from Boston University in 1966, she instead decided to tour the world as a flight attendant for Pan American World Airways.

Two years into this vocation, she got married, which in those days essentially meant forced retirement from the airline. Dater hopped on over to a temporary employment agency that specialized in helping former stewardesses find new careers. "They sent me to Wall Street working for Lehman Brothers," she recalls. "The first year on the job I sat in Bobby Lehman's office answering phones. He was ill at this point, and I talked to his estate lawyer every day. His lawyer told me I should consider a career in this business. I spent a few days on the trading desk with a couple of high-pressure institutional salespeople and really got into it." Before long, she was working for the department full-time, picking up some accounting and economics courses at night.

As luck had it, Dater began her adventure in investing right at the peak of a roaring bull market. "I then had the unique opportunity of spending the next 11 or 12 years waiting for the next one to come around," she quips. "It got pretty rough in the mid-1970s." Dater left Lehman Brothers in 1971 to become an assistant portfolio manger at Fiduciary Trust Company. "I worked my way up to the research department, where I became an analyst," she says. "I developed a fair amount of expertise in the area of media communications, which was a very underfollowed industry at that point. There was this funny little business called cable just starting up to help improve the reception of TV signals. I was one of the first people to cover that industry."

By the time she left Fiduciary Trust to join Warburg Pincus in 1978, a year after becoming a panelist on *Wall $treet Week,* she was a vice president. "When I joined Warburg Pincus as a securities analyst, it was very small with only $300 million under management. As there were only a few of us here, I viewed it as a real entrepreneurial opportunity, which is why I made the switch." Warburg Pincus's roots are in venture capital, a market Dater was no stranger to. Many of the media companies she followed were little more than tiny upstarts when she began covering them. Today she heads up Warburg's small-cap and postventure capital effort and also runs a few mutual funds.

Occupation: Managing Director, Warburg Pincus Asset Management
New York, New York

Birth Date: May 13, 1945

Education: BFA, Boston University, 1966

Biggest Mistake Investors Make: "Not sticking to their own investment beliefs."

Best Investment: Affiliated Publications (First bought as an IPO in the early 1970s and ultimately made 30 to 40 times her original investment.)

Worst Investment: WPP Group (Purchased in 1988 for $12 and wound up selling out for around $3 a few months later.)

Advice: "Stick to your investment philosophy and don't sell good companies too early."

Market Outlook: Bullish

MICHAEL DiCARLO

DFS Advisors

Mike DiCarlo believes small-cap stocks have begun a run that should last for some time to come. "We're already seeing signs of this in earnings," he says. "Bigger companies are faltering, while smaller companies are doing great. Small-caps are still much cheaper relative to the larger stocks." The tinier names were out of favor through much of the mid-1990s. DiCarlo attributes that largely to the growth of indexing. "The S&P 500 funds, which have received huge inflows, rank the companies in their portfolios by market capitalization, just like the index," he explains. "Of course, the biggest companies get the most money, and the smallest companies get the least." DiCarlo thinks, in addition to attractive valuations, small-caps should be standout performers going forward because investors are starting to index their money to broader benchmarks, like the S&P 600.

DiCarlo has always had a knack for making money. Even as a teen, he had his own business managing a number of local bands. It was a profitable venture, and DiCarlo found himself with an abundance of cash. He reasoned the best place to put it was in the stock market. "Having run my own company, I was familiar with the kinds of things companies faced every day and that helped me to make investment decisions," he says. In college, he prepared for a career in politics. But, as graduation day grew closer, he had a change of heart. "The more I saw my politician friends having to go through lots of scrutiny, the more I said that's not for me," he recalls. So he took a job as a bill processor with John Hancock. He worked his way up over the years, eventually taking over management of its small-cap Special Equities Fund in 1988. He later became the company's chief equity officer.

Because he's always been an entrepreneur at heart, it came as no surprise when he left John Hancock in July 1996 to form his own investment firm with two other partners. "It was something I always wanted to do and the timing just felt right," he says. "I had been at John Hancock for 18 years and was looking for a new challenge." DiCarlo continued to manage Special Equities through mid-1998, and also runs a hedge fund. His hedge fund concentrates exclusively on small-cap stocks, and occasionally takes on more risk by shoring and buying exotic securities. "I think small-cap companies are interesting because they attack a niche in the market, which is easily definable," he shares. "It's clearly one of the riskiest areas, but if you have a disciplined approach to doing things, you can take out and mitigate some of that risk."

DiCarlo uses four yardsticks to measure his stocks, all of which can be applied consistently in any kind of market or economic environment. "First, I try to find companies that are growing by 25 percent or better before the momentum investors get a hold of them. Ideally I want to sell to the momentum players," he says. "Next, I look for companies that are self-financing and in a leadership position in their particular market. Finally, and most importantly, I look for management that's focused on generating shareholder gains. You've got to sit down with the managers and grill them about their business, what their margins and new products look like, how their competition is doing, and what their exit strategy is. Then you go talk to vendors, distributors, customers, competitors, anyone you can to make sure what you're being told by the top of the house is actually being executed throughout the entire company. You also want to see management have a lot of their net worth tied up in the company."

Most of DiCarlo's companies have market capitalizations between $100 million and $1 billion when he makes his initial purchase, although he'll hold his winners even if they grow beyond that range. "If a company continues to give me the kind of growth I bought it for in the first place, I'll stay with it even if it exceeds those parameters," he says. "I'll get rid of a stock when it goes down 12 percent from what I paid for it. Also, because I'm always fully invested, if I find a new candidate for purchase, I'll sell one holding to buy another."

DiCarlo maintains there are four things you need to be successful in the investment business, and an MBA isn't one of them. "It takes hard work, skill, luck, and, most importantly, common sense," he says. "We all try to make this job, for whatever reason, sound more complicated than it really is."

Occupation: Founding Partner, DFS Advisors
Boston, Massachusetts

Birth Date: March 6, 1952

Education: BA, University of Massachusetts at Boston, 1980

Biggest Mistake Investors Make: "Not getting rid of their losers."

Best Investment: Infinity Broadcasting (Started buying as an IPO, and it was eventually taken over by Westinghouse.)

Worst Investment: Hunter Environmental (Paid up to $5 a share for the stock several years ago, and it dropped down to $1 in one day.)

Advice: "When it comes to investing, always reassess what you've done, but only after you've given it time to play out as you expected."

Market Outlook: Bullish, especially on small-cap stocks

HAROLD EVENSKY

Evensky, Brown & Katz

Many consider Harold Evensky to be the father of financial planning in the United States. Now he's busy taking his crusade for the profession to other parts of the world. "There are 13 countries offering the Certified Financial Planner (CFP) mark," Evensky observes. "I'm on my way to South Africa to speak to a financial planning conference there, and my book was just translated into Japanese. The industry is actually growing faster outside of the U.S. right now." That's just more proof the financial services industry is truly global in nature.

After a short stint running his own construction company, Evensky became a stockbroker more than 20 years ago. But he quickly found he wasn't very good at cold calling to round up clients. "I read about financial planning, which was something brand-new back then," he recalls. "I enrolled in a program to learn about it and started giving seminars on financial planning to develop my business." He soon decided to target more sophisticated and wealthy clients, though his employers weren't comfortable with how he did business. So in 1985 he rejoined his old partner from the construction business and went out on his own.

"Our firm was opened as a financial-planning practice," Evensky explains. "We set up our own broker-dealer in order to maintain total control and flexibility. We did big, multi-hundred-page comprehensive plans for a very substantial fee and then implemented them on a commission basis." When discount broker Charles Schwab introduced a program allowing independent planners to trade no-load mutual funds with minimal transaction costs, Evensky switched over and became a totally fee-based advisor, charging his clients a percentage of their assets under management instead of a load or commission. "We are not money managers," he says. "We hire money managers [usually through mutual funds]. Our focus is on the asset allocation, not the selection process."

Once Evensky and his staff prepare a plan, they begin the process of finding the right funds by looking for managers who invest in specific asset classes. He uses both index and managed funds, although he now weights index funds more heavily than before. "We use active managers in areas where we believe there's a possibility they'll outperform net of costs and fees, namely in small-cap growth and international," he says.

When it comes to active funds, Evensky doesn't like eclectic managers who are willing to buy anything. "We also don't look at specialty funds," he confides. "The managers at specialty funds tend to be the newest ones. It's where they're put to try their teeth. We generally don't want managers with huge concentrations in any one area, and we stay away from domestic managers with excessive foreign positions."

Next, he eliminates all candidates with high fees and consistently poor performance. "We avoid those in the bottom half of their asset class for the last five years or the bottom third for the last three years," he notes. "Our experience says if they've been that consistently close to the bottom, they'll probably stay there." He then checks to see if the fund has grown too large, if it's run by a manager with a trackable record, and whether it has a high degree of turnover (which he doesn't like). "In addition, we absolutely, irrevocably avoid what I call the *Money* magazine fund of the last ten minutes," he emphasizes. "We think that is a guaranteed solution for buying high and selling low. When it comes to the individual manager, we're looking for commitment, brains, and passion. We reject what we consider to be pomposity, simplicity, and marketing hype."

As a final step, Evensky will often consult with his fellow members of the Alpha Group, a consortium of financial advisors from around the country that uses its muscle to encourage positive changes in the fund industry. In recent times, the Alpha Group has put pressure on fund companies to cut costs. "We'll reject managers solely on the basis of high fees," Evensky boasts. "The reason it hasn't been more of an issue [for everyone else] until now is because returns have been so high that no one has noticed how much they were paying."

The financial-planning profession has come a long way since Evensky joined it, especially over the last few years. "We've seen amazing growth," he observes. "The industry has gone through a huge amount of turbulence. But the end result is that the people who have stayed in it and those who are entering it today tend to have a very serious commitment to the concept and philosophy of planning as a process."

Occupation: Partner, Evensky, Brown & Katz
Coral Gables, Florida

Birth Date: September 9, 1942

Education: BA, Cornell University, 1965
MA, Cornell University, 1967

Biggest Mistake Investors Make: "Not knowing what they want to accomplish and not having an investment plan."

Best Investment: Starting his financial planning practice.

Worst Investment: Managers Intermediate Mortgage Fund (Bought it four years ago, and when interest rates spiked up, he lost 15 percent of his money.)

Advice: "Make a plan before you invest."

Market Outlook: Cautious

AL FRANK

Al Frank Asset Management

Al Frank isn't afraid to admit he's a naturally cheap guy. "I'll still go to a discount gas station a mile away to save three or four cents a gallon," he concedes. "I like to get things on sale, and when I travel, I always look for the lowest fare." Frank traces his frugality back to his childhood. Both of his parents were uneducated tailors who never had a lot of cash.

As a youngster, Frank was bored with homework and wanted to do nothing more with his life than work at a print shop. "I had no intention of going to college," he admits. "I was a mediocre student. I graduated in the lowest quartile of my high school class." But because many of his classmates enrolled at Los Angeles City College, Frank decided to join them. "It was the best educational institution I ever attended," he contends. "I was still planning to be a printer and thought I'd take a business major for two years to learn how to run my print shop. But after one semester, I decided I didn't want to be a business major after all." Frank transferred to UCLA with dreams of becoming a cinematographer. He practically flunked out and enlisted in the Army instead. After his discharge, he hitchhiked to New York, working briefly for the *New York Times.* He then married his first wife and came back to California to earn a bachelor's degree at UC Berkeley. Next, he moved to Las Vegas, then back to New York, and over to Europe before returning to California to get two master's degrees at California State University, Los Angeles. At the same time, he worked on a Ph.D. at UCLA.

Frank is unquestionably a man who loves adventure. But his search for what to do with his life ended one day after his mentor at UCLA introduced him to the stock market. He quickly developed a passion for it. "I was studying the stock market while working as an assistant professor," he recalls. "In 1977 one of my friends suggested that I write an investment newsletter, and another wanted me to manage money. I decided to register with the SEC and started *The Pinchpenny Speculator,* which is the original name of my monthly investment newsletter *The Prudent Speculator.*" It was just a hobby at first. Frank mailed out around 100 letters and managed some $65,000. That all changed in 1983, when *The Hulbert Financial Digest* crowned his publication the year's number-one performer. "All of a sudden I had 1,000 subscribers and then 6,000," he exclaims. "Before long, I was grossing $2 million a year." Everything was going great until the crash of 1987. Frank was fully margined, and his model portfolio lost more than 55 percent of its value that year. "I personally had a $2 million portfolio," he recalls with dread. "After the crash, it was worth $400,000. I made the money back in two years, but most of the subscribers I lost never returned."

Frank merged his asset management company with another firm in Minneapolis at the end of 1999 and now works out of his home in Santa Fe, New

Mexico. John Buckingham, who joined Frank in 1987 during his senior year at the University of Southern California, is now the firm's director of research, and does most of the actual stock research. He is also chief portfolio manager of the Al Frank Fund. Buckingham works out of the company's Laguna Beach headquarters. Frank and Buckingham follow about 850 companies at any given time and pay close attention to such fundamental factors as price-to-book value, price-to-cash flow, price-to-sales, and PE ratios along with debt and return on equity. "In the beginning, when I was doing this myself, I just used Barron's. Twenty years ago you could find stocks selling for six times earnings, 60 percent of book value, and yielding 6 percent," Frank remembers. "They were called 'The Triple Sixes.'"

His computerized database is much more sophisticated now but stocks that cheap are hard to find in today's market. Nevertheless, Frank's overriding goal remains the same: to uncover stocks that he expects to double within three to five years. "Once I spot a company that looks promising, I send for 10-Ks and 10-Qs," he adds. "I then estimate a value for each stock, and if the current selling price is below 50 percent of my target, it's a buy." Frank rarely visits a company or talks with management. "I've never found a chief executive who didn't see the problems at his corporation as anything but opportunity," he notes. Frank is a big believer in diversification and has learned a lot from studying the work of his mentor, Benjamin Graham. "His was one of the first books I ever read," Frank reveals. "Graham's idea that you should buy undervalued stocks because they provide a cushion of safety was very impressive to me."

Occupation: Chief Investment Strategist, Al Frank Asset Management
Laguna Beach, California

Birth Date: April 19, 1930

Education: BA, UC Berkeley, 1956
MA, California State University, Los Angeles, 1962–1965

Biggest Mistake Investors Make: "Being impatient, panicking out before the market realizes the value of a corporation, and not doing your homework."

Best Investment: SunAmerica (Bought for a split-adjusted 38¢ a share in 1980 and sold for $50 in 1997.)

Worst Investment: A couple of savings and loans that were forced out of business and went down to zero in the 1980s

Advice: "Realize that if you have a good system, you'll be right about your investment decisions around 75 percent of the time. But if you're right just two out of four times, you'll make a great return."

Market Outlook: Bullish

WALTER FRANK

Moneyletter

Economics has been a lifelong passion for Walter Frank. After serving in the Armored Division for three years during World War II, Frank earned an undergraduate degree in history and literature at Harvard University. Then, after spending a year in Paris working for Radio Free Europe, he returned to study economics.

"Economics was incredibly important when I was growing up during the 1930s," he says. "I further realized while working as a correspondent for Radio Free Europe that economics was at the basis of everything, and I wanted to know more about it."

Frank also had a strong interest in stocks. "As soon as I got back to Harvard, some friends of mine inherited a fair amount of money and wanted to know if I would be interested in managing their portfolio," he recalls. "I said, 'yes.'"

That sparked a career that has lasted close to 50 years. Frank's first job after college was writing a monthly newsletter for a New England bank. "After a while, the bank asked me to consult on the general economic outlook for their trust department," he says. "Meanwhile, I picked up a couple of more portfolios on my own and started to build up a reasonably sized advisory business."

In the mid-1960s, he and a partner on Wall Street formed a hedge fund, which they ran through the beginning of the bear market in 1973. "We went long stocks, like the aggressive growth funds of today, and that was a good period for it," he recalls. "We bought IPOs and played all of the games, but we didn't short stocks."

In a bull market, that's wonderful. But when the great bear emerged, it was a disaster. "The hedge fund didn't survive," he laments. "I wandered in the wilderness for a while. I continued to consult, write the newsletter, and do articles for *The Economist.* I even consulted for Congress at one point."

He ultimately left the stock market altogether and began playing around in real estate when it was hot during the early 1980s. "Then, in 1985, an opportunity came for me to work on *Moneyletter,* and at the time I needed to accept the offer," he says. The newsletter has gone through numerous owners since Frank came on board, and was most recently purchased by PRI Publishing in Massachusetts.

Frank not only writes *Moneyletter,* but also does market forecasting and selects the recommended funds. He considers overall asset allocation to be the most important part of his job. "The first thing I do is look at the economic outlook, mainly in terms of my view on interest rates, because this determines the justifiable price-earnings ratio for stocks," he explains. "Then I examine the various asset classes, both in the United States and overseas."

Next, he decides whether it makes more sense to be in equities, bonds, or cash, and to what degree. "I spend no time on whether I want aggressive growth, value, or high or low beta," Frank admits. "That's because I developed a computerized fund selection system to go along with the asset allocation strategy that chooses the funds automatically for me."

You might think of it as a momentum strategy, because it only takes into account performance of periods of about one year, without regard for who is actually managing the fund. "One of the things you'll find if you use a momentum strategy like this is there is the danger of having five funds in your portfolio that all turn out to be, for all intents and purposes, exactly the same," Frank warns. "So I do some fundamental work to make sure this doesn't happen."

Frank is convinced that funds are the best way for most people to invest. "Despite what Peter Lynch says, I don't think individuals should be investing in individual securities, unless they make it a full-time job," he argues. "The ordinary Joe is in no position to compete with the institutional world in terms of knowledge, and knowledge is what makes this whole thing go."

While Frank has watched the mutual fund industry grow exponentially over the past few decades, he thinks it has much more steam left. "If we have some bad markets, some funds aren't going to make a lot of sense and you'll see them disappear and be bought out," he predicts. "However, I don't see that the fund industry has anywhere to go but up. The assets may go down in bad years, but they'll be back."

Occupation: Editor and Chief Investment Officer, *Moneyletter*
Baltimore, Maryland

Birth Date: March 31, 1924

Education: BA, Harvard University, 1949
MA, Oxford College, 1952

Biggest Mistake Investors Make: "Having a lack of patience, plus the inability to hold on and look ahead."

Best Investment: Loew's (Bought in the late 1960s, and the stock multiplied several times.)

Worst Investment: Several high-tech IPOs he purchased in the early 1970s, one of which went completely broke

Advice: "Know your limitations, and don't be too greedy."

Market Outlook: Cautious on the U.S., bullish on international

SETH GLICKENHAUS

Glickenhaus & Co.

Seth Glickenhaus expects the Dow Jones Industrial Average to trade between 7,500 and 12,000 through August 25, 2014. That's a good reason to be invested in cash, right? "To the contrary," Glickenhaus insists. "From 1966–82, the Dow went from 1,000 to 1,000, yet we made a ton of money. I think the same thing will happen during the next number of years. Some stocks in the average will triple, some will lose a lot, and others will do very little. It's a matter of owning the right stocks." As a result, he advises investors to avoid index funds, which he feels have become too popularized to be effective anymore.

Glickenhaus is one of the most established and respected value investors on Wall Street. At 86, an age when most people do very little, Glickenhaus still works full-time at his New York investment firm. This colorful manager once had dreams of becoming a medical doctor. But, after graduating from Harvard some 67 years ago, he was convinced by Herbert Salomon of Salomon Brothers to give up a chance to go to law school (his second choice) in favor of working as a broker. "I agreed to take a job with him for three months on the condition that if it didn't work out, I'd go back to school," Glickenhaus recalls. "It worked out, but I left in 1938 because I was generating about $25,000 a week in profits for the firm, and they were paying me just $48."

He managed to earn his law degree by going to night school and went on to work for a little brokerage shop that folded a few months after he joined it. "The owner was a dipsomaniac," Glickenhaus contends. He first thought it served him right for leaving what could have been a cushy future at Salomon. But then Glickenhaus and one of his colleagues had an idea. They convinced the defunct brokerage shop's principals to let them take over, after promising to return the $25,000 the principals had invested in the company. "They agreed, and in a few months we had paid them back and turned it into our own firm," he recalls. "We ran it through 1946, although I went off to war for a while, and my partner took over until I came back." That was when Glickenhaus started what, in effect, was the first hedge fund. "If someone had invested $10,000 with us, by the time we wound the fund up 13 years later, that person would have walked away with something on the order of $300,000."

Glickenhaus made out much better, because he and his partner were entitled to 50 percent of the fund's profits. At that point, Glickenhaus was a multimillionaire and figured his performance so far would be a tough act to follow. Glickenhaus next decided to finally pursue his dream of becoming a medical doctor at the age of 46. "I did my premed work at Columbia and was admitted to the Einstein Medical School," he says. "But the lure of Wall Street got to me again. I quit school and started my own firm, Glickenhaus & Co. All I did at first was trade for my own account. This went on for about ten years."

Then some rich friends asked him to manage their retirement accounts, and he agreed. Since that time in 1972, he's developed an impressive record that, until value grew out of favor in the late 1990s, placed him among the top 1 percent of all investment managers in the nation.

Glickenhaus calls himself a cautious investor who is more concerned about downside risk than the quality of earnings. "When I look for a stock, I want to find outstanding management," he reveals. "I'm also very price conscious. I love overlooked companies that have come down in value for one reason or another that I feel is invalid. I also like companies with a lot of cash flow that will be used to buy back the stock." Furthermore, he seeks out names that are either industry leaders or low-cost producers, and he wants to buy them for less than their intrinsic value (or what a reasonable person would pay for the entire business). "I look for stocks selling for very low price-earnings multiples," he adds. "I also examine a company's dividend policy and profit margins."

Glickenhaus deals almost exclusively with large-cap stocks. He has several strict sales rules. "Let's assume I buy a stock and I think its price is going to go up 80 percent in two years," he offers. "If its price does go up that much and it's not a bargain any more, I'll sell it. Another reason for selling is if a stock goes up too much too fast. I'll get rid of it to avoid losing my gain."

Don't look for Glickenhaus to slow down any time soon. "I've decided I'm going to retire when I'm 125," he says, "That means I have a good 39 years left."

Occupation: Senior Partner, Glickenhaus & Co.
New York, New York

Birth Date: March 12, 1914

Education: BA, Harvard College, 1934
LLB, New York University Law School, 1938

Biggest Mistake Investors Make: "Managing their own funds without professional guidance."

Best Investment: Chrysler (Bought when Lee Iacocca first came on board.)

Worst Investment: An environmental company (he forgets the name) that went from $23 to zero in 1994

Advice: "Carefully research your investments and pay attention to downside risk. Also, beware of current trends."

Market Outlook: Bullish on select stocks; bearish on others

SHELDON JACOBS

The No-Load Fund Investor

Sheldon Jacobs has made a career of forecasting. In an earlier life, he spent 25 years predicting which shows people would watch on television for both ABC and NBC. Now he predicts which mutual funds will perform best in the future. He also has a forecast for how long the seemingly nonstop growth of the mutual fund industry will continue. "Until the next bear market comes along," he says. "Then we'll probably get a fairly sizable amount of consolidation."

One reason Americans are in love with funds, Jacobs surmises, is because there's really no better financial alternative available right now. "Real estate returns were great through the 1970s and part of the 1980s, but that's not true anymore [in many parts of the country]," he explains. "In a real sense, the stock market's the only game in town."

Jacobs first discovered no-load funds in the early 1970s, while working in television. He was instantly hooked. He went on to write his first book, *Put Your Money in Your Pocket,* in 1974 and began publishing a quarterly no-load fund newsletter from his kitchen table five years later as a sort of hobby. When the bull market took off in 1982, Jacobs walked into his boss's office at NBC, just four years shy of his scheduled retirement, and quit his job. His new mission in life was to teach others how to successfully invest in funds. His *No-Load Fund Investor* newsletter now has around 18,000 subscribers. He also publishes two annual mutual fund guides and manages some $400 million in discretionary accounts along with partner Bob Brinker, host of the popular ABC radio weekend program *Moneytalk.*

Jacobs is clearly a big believer in funds. "I own only one individual stock, and I'm a professional in this field," he maintains. He notes that funds have two distinct advantages: diversification and professional management. There is, however, one exception to his all-fund rule. "You should buy equities through a mutual fund unless you know more about a stock than Wall Street does," he offers. That doesn't mean getting a hot tip from a broker or the Internet. Instead, he's referring to the inside information one gains through working for a particular company or industry. As he puts it, "Everybody owns IBM, so there's no edge for the individual investor. There's only one negative to buying mutual funds instead of individual stocks. You can't control the tax situation. You're at the mercy of when the portfolio manager decides to take his capital gains. Other than that, I don't think there's any reason to buy individual stocks." He also argues that almost everyone should have a significant equity component in his or her portfolio. "If you're wealthy and don't need the money, you should keep a minimum of 60 to 70 percent in stocks, no matter what your age," he insists.

Jacobs admits that funds are less advantageous as a vehicle for purchasing Treasuries, although he believes junk bonds should always be bought through funds because of the diversification they provide.

What's the best way for investors to select individual funds? "You start with past performance, then you adjust it for other factors, such as where you think the market's going, which stock groups will be hot, the size of the fund, things like that," he says. "You've got to get beyond the numbers." But Jacobs admits it was a lot easier for him to pinpoint which television shows would be popular in his former career than picking which funds will act best in the future. "If I just had to do a guesstimate, I could have probably made a run-of-the-mill prediction on television audiences with an error rate of maybe 2 or 3 percent," he says. "On mutual funds, if I get within 25 percent, I'm doing great."

Jacobs concedes he failed to predict how enormously popular funds would become when he entered the business full-time in 1979. "I bought an existing newsletter when I started *The No-Load Fund Investor,*" he recalls. "The man who sold it to me said that the mutual fund newsletter would never be as big as his other publication, which focused on stocks, because more people buy stocks than funds. He was wrong. I think funds are the only sane way to go. If you do it on your own now, you're competing against all of these professionals. It makes more sense just to hire them. Plus, they'll do a better job. Over and above their picking prowess, they'll diversify properly, and they'll be there every day."

Jacobs predicts the market's future direction from here will remain up, although he's somewhat cautious right now and has 50 percent of his growth portfolio sitting in cash. As for his own career, Jacobs still keeps a busy schedule, even though he often thinks of slowing down. "I've been telling everybody that I'll consider retirement in the year 2001," he says. "But I honestly don't have any firm plans either way right now."

Occupation: Publisher and Editor, *The No-Load Fund Investor*
Irvington-on-Hudson, New York

Birth Date: January 29, 1931

Education: BA, University of Nebraska, 1952
MBA, New York University, 1955

Biggest Mistake Investors Make: "Not taking enough risk."

Best Investment: Mutual Shares (Recommended in the first issue of his newsletter in 1979 and held on until manager Michael Price left in 1998.)

Worst Investment: "I can't remember any major disasters."

Advice: "Diversify."

Market Outlook: Cautious

VIVIAN LEWIS

Global Investing

Vivian Lewis once lived a life most journalists dream about. She was a foreign correspondent who covered stories throughout Western Europe during the 1960s and 1970s. During that time, she lived in London, Brussels, and France. Like most who wind up in glamorous jobs like this, she got into the business by accident. After graduating with a history degree from Radcliffe in 1962 at the age of 20, she planned on a career in academia. "I got married to a foreign correspondent while I was working on my PhD thesis, and we ran out of money," she explains. "I didn't think a married woman should ask for tuition assistance from her dad, so I took a job with *Business Week* as an office assistant. A year and a half later, I was bureau chief in Brussels."

When Lewis got pregnant with her first child, the magazine immediately fired her. "When I say this today, people ask why I didn't sue them," she says. "They told me if I sued them I would never get another job in journalism, and I believed them. I was scared to make waves about being treated badly." Fortunately, she managed to land on her feet and went to work for such publications as *The Economist* and *Institutional Investor,* writing about foreign companies and the financial markets. The magazines were thrilled to have her on retainer because she was stationed overseas, which saved them from paying her travel expenses.

"When my husband was posted back in the United States by his employer, the *New York Times,* 11 years ago, I went sashaying into the *Institutional Investor* offices and said, 'Hi, I'm here.' Their faces dropped. I told them this was their opportunity to make use of my brilliant European connections in the United States. They replied, 'We're not going to send you to Europe and let you run up expense accounts. It was great having you write for us while you were over there and we could get you cheap, but now it's a different story.'" Lewis looked in the mirror and realized she was in her 40s and not immediately employable. "The reason I started *Global Investing* is because I decided there was a niche in the market and I needed a job," she admits. "I was covering this stuff for the institutional market but wanted to cover it for U.S. retail investors who were not, and still are not, being given any information about internationalizing their portfolios."

Global Investing is a monthly newsletter that highlights select foreign stocks that trade as ADRs in the United States. "ADR stands for American depositary receipt," Lewis points out. "These investment vehicles were invented in the period right after the first World War for a specific purpose—for foreign-based companies to raise money on U.S. capital markets. Shares of securities from these overseas companies are deposited in a foreign bank, and a U.S. bank creates a certificate to prove they are there. You then trade the receipts, which settle in the United States under the same system as U.S. stocks." Lewis still takes about ten trips a year to uncover new ideas. She spends most of her time in Europe, which she knows well. She also has a team of freelance stringers from around the world who contribute stories and ideas to her publication.

Although Lewis is a big advocate of foreign investing, she cautions against buying shares directly through overseas markets instead of using ADRs. "Most people do not have custodial accounts on foreign exchanges," she reasons. "If you want to buy foreign stocks rather than ADRs, there are all kinds of obstacles for retail investors. The minimum trades are much higher in foreign markets, and they don't like limit orders. Plus, you don't get 1099s or the same kind of information regarding quarterly and annual results as you do with the ADRs. You're also not treated as well when it comes to rights offerings and stock splits."

Admittedly, it's not easy getting good information about a company in another country when you live thousands of miles away. That's why Lewis, who speaks several foreign languages, calls evaluating ADRs more of an art than a science. "For one thing, you should know more about the country and other stocks in the industry when considering a foreign stock," she advises. But why take such risks? Isn't it a hassle to research and find foreign companies? Wouldn't it be better to just keep your portfolio invested in U.S. stocks that you could keep a close eye on? "No," Lewis insists. "You shouldn't put all of your eggs in one basket. Two-thirds of the stocks in the world are outside the United States. It's idiotic to ignore them. I think people should have one-quarter to one-third of their portfolio invested overseas."

Occupation: Publisher, *Global Investing*
New York, New York

Birth Date: June 19, 1951

Education: BA, Radcliffe College, 1962
MA, University of California at Berkeley, 1963

Biggest Mistake Investors Make: "Being too short term–oriented."

Best Investment: The Japan Fund (Bought it while living in Europe throughout the 1980s. Her earliest investments had returns of some 5,000 percent.)

Worst Investment: Bitech (This is a Canadian company that drills for oil in northern Russia. She bought the stock for $4 in 1997, and at last check it was trading for around 50¢.)

Advice: "Take a long-term view, especially when it comes to foreign investing."

Market Outlook: Bullish on the United States and Japan, but cautious on Europe

BOB MARKMAN

Markman Capital Management

Bob Markman has had a change of heart. Although he once bought the academic argument that to make the best returns over time you need a diversified portfolio, including exposure to both small and large stocks in the United States and overseas, he no longer believes that. "I think people overdiversify," he says. "The whole financial services industry has blown it by recommending so many asset classes. When you own this much stuff, you have no chance of doing well in a bull market and aren't going to be protected in a bear market."

So this Minnesota investment advisor, who specializes in mutual funds, says he's decided to put the vast majority of his clients' money in just one part of the market—large-company U.S. growth stocks. "A lot of the advice on asset allocation is based on old data and is flawed," Markman insists. "The world this is based on no longer exists. Things have changed. The market is telegraphing this message to us. That's why large companies have done so well in recent years." Markman doesn't like small-cap funds either, because the premise behind them doesn't make sense to him. "They are, by definition, always selling their most promising companies as they grow larger just because they fall out of a certain range in terms of market capitalization," he says. Markman also thinks investors should avoid international and value-oriented funds. "Value stocks are doomed to underperform," he predicts. "The real action in this economy is in the tech end. Almost by definition, a tech stock is never going to be a value stock. The typical growth portfolio has no technology in it."

Lest you think Markman is hitching a ride on the current hot sector of the moment, he insists he plans to keep all of his money in large U.S. multinational growth stocks for "as far as the eye can see, certainly for the rest of my lifetime." He's also bullish on the market for about that same time span. "This is the world we were too embarrassed to even hope for," he exclaims. "Our planet is going through a productivity and technological explosion with hardly any inflation on a global basis. What's more, we have a regulatory environment that's more benign than ever. And even though Washington is using phony numbers, we've got a budget that's basically in balance and likely to go into surplus. Any one of these things could have been the catalyst for a bull market. But we've got them all together at the same time. I don't think anyone can possibly predict how high this market will go."

If all that weren't enough, Markman also notes that the country's demographic makeup favors a continued rise in equity prices for some time to come. "We have this huge bulge of baby boomers moving through their 50s," he observes.

"As everybody knows, that's when most people start saving for retirement more aggressively. This is only adding fuel to an already hot fire."

If things had been different, Markman might be managing the futures of some big Hollywood stars instead of investment portfolios. After graduating from Northwestern University, he worked at the William Morris Agency before leaving to pursue a career in advertising. In 1980 he became fascinated with the financial planning field, which was still in its infancy. He took a job selling load funds with Private Ledger. But the idea of charging his customers a commission each time they purchased a fund never made sense to him, especially after the crash of 1987. "It occurred to me that even if someone had shown me *The Wall Street Journal* two weeks in advance, and I could have known there was a crash coming, I couldn't have done anything about it," he reflects. "I had all my clients' money in load funds and didn't have the discretion." That prompted him to go out on his own, managing money through no-load funds on a fee-only basis.

Today, Markman manages around $700 million in both private accounts and three "fund-of-funds" (mutual funds that invest in other funds). The idea behind these investments is that instead of choosing ten different stock funds on your own, for example, you can simply put your money into a fund-of-funds and let the manager research and select the underlying funds for you.

Markman prefers concentrated funds, which generally own less than 30 stocks. Unlike some of his colleagues, Markman spends little time interviewing individual fund managers, although he concedes the person pulling the trigger is important. "It's rare to find a manager who is a real jerk," he reveals. "The benefits of interviewing managers might be outweighed by the risk of falling for a relationship with them."

Occupation: President, Markman Capital Management
Edina, Minnesota

Birth Date: August 30, 1951

Education: BA, Northwestern University, 1973

Biggest Mistake Investors Make: "Confusing volatility with risk."

Best Investment: Rydex OTC (It has more than doubled since he purchased it in 1997.)

Worst Investment: Rydex Ursa (A fund that shorts the market. He bought it in July 1996 at a market bottom.)

Advice: "Simplify, cancel your subscription to *The Wall Street Journal,* and spend more time with your kids."

Market Outlook: Bullish

CAPPY McGARR

McGarr Capital Management

In addition to having a winning hand at investing, Cappy McGarr is also getting his feet wet in politics. He was appointed by President Clinton to the Kennedy Center Board of Trustees and is chairman of Democratic Senator Tom Daschle's leadership political action committee. But he admits he could never run for an elected office himself. "I like making money too much," he says. McGarr makes plenty for the partners of his Dallas-based hedge fund. Since the $220 million fund's founding some 15 years ago, he has showered investors with an annualized return of 26.68 percent compared with 18.93 percent for the S&P 500. And he's done it without employing some of the exotic strategies used by some of his colleagues. Not bad for a guy from San Angelo, Texas, who had no career goals growing up, let alone a desire to invest.

McGarr wound up on Wall Street almost by accident. He majored in both journalism and government in college but found the jobs he was qualified for didn't pay much. So he went back to school for an MBA and landed a job with Goldman Sachs after graduation. After spending a year in New York, the firm transferred him to Dallas. Four years later, he decided to go into business for himself. Today, it takes at least $1 million to get into his hedge fund.

When he originally went out on his own, McGarr raised money for various private business deals. He launched his fund in 1984. Despite having the freedom to do whatever he wants, McGarr avoids speculating in currencies, commodities, futures, or derivatives. Instead, he invests his concentrated portfolio of 10 to 15 names primarily in large-cap, household-name stocks, which have an average market capitalization of $11 billion. He likes these big companies because of the liquidity they provide.

The most adventurous thing McGarr does is short anywhere from 5 to 40 percent of the portfolio, although he maintains it always makes sense to have a bias toward the long side. "Over time, managements get up every day to make money for their shareholders," he says. "They may execute a wrong strategy, be in a bad business, or be unintelligent. But if they have integrity and are trying to do what's right, the only goal management should have is to increase shareholder value."

McGarr admits hedge funds have been given a bad rap over the past couple of years, especially after the fiasco with Long-Term Capital Management in 1998. But he claims it hasn't impacted his business one bit. "Whenever you pay someone an incentive fee to manage money, as you do in a hedge fund, there is inherent risk associated with that because the manager is always trying to make more money for himself," McGarr explains. "Another problem with some funds is disclosure. I think it's very important for managers to disclose what positions they hold."

McGarr believes earnings are what ultimately drive stock prices, although the people in charge are also important. That's why he checks to make sure the executives of any potential investment have their own personal wealth on the line. "I spend a lot of time looking at management and what they own of their own company," he says. "I want to see what options they have and how much stock they are mandated to own. That's very important because if management owns stock, they're obviously going to have the same interests as the shareholders because they are shareholders." McGarr adds that he invests all of his own liquid money in his fund.

In addition, a strong financial standing and reasonable share price are essential. "A solid cash flow and earnings growth rate is very important to me," McGarr explains. "If you can find a company selling below its growth rate, by definition you're buying a stock that's cheap. So I obviously try to purchase stocks that are selling below their growth rate. In other words, their PE sells at a discount to their growth rate."

A final requirement for every stock McGarr owns is that it must be a proven leader. "I like companies that have a dominant market share and are number one or two in the areas they deal in," he says. "I find all of this out by constantly pouring over research, reading periodicals, and running computer screens." On the short side, McGarr does intense research looking for companies that are doing something wrong. "I will only short a company outright if its balance sheet doesn't make sense or management is doing something that I don't consider to be forthright," he shares. "I don't do many outright shorts. When I do, I make sure I've done my homework."

Occupation: President, McGarr Capital Management
Dallas, Texas

Birth Date: August 1, 1951

Education: BA, University of Texas at Austin, 1973/1975
MBA, University of Texas at Austin, 1977

Biggest Mistake Investors Make: "Having a lack of patience and investing for the short term."

Best Investment: Dell Computer (Originally bought in 1990 for a split-adjusted price under $10 and still owns it.)

Worst Investment: PageNet (Purchased in 1996 for $19 and finally sold out several months later for half that amount.)

Advice: "Invest in good companies with outstanding fundamentals for the long term."

Market Outlook: Bullish

RONALD MUHLENKAMP

Muhlenkamp & Company

If Ron Muhlenkamp is right, momentum investing will continue to be popular in the year ahead, but for all the wrong reasons. "I think the momentum stocks will be moving on the downside," he says. "I'd much rather own financials, consumer cyclicals, and other economically sensitive stocks at this stage of the game. The market is acting as if we have gone through a recession, even though we haven't, and these stocks are cheap."

As an engineering student at MIT, Muhlenkamp took a few business courses to broaden his education. By the time he graduated, he was married with two kids. He went on to get an MBA at Harvard, intending to gain a better understanding of the production process for the time when he became an engineer. "My goal was to eventually make enough money so I could retire and farm and live the way I wanted to," he says. "I wound up studying marketing and corporate finance at Harvard." When he graduated in 1968, he decided the job offers that came his way weren't very interesting. He discovered a few of his classmates planned to start an investment firm in New York and decided to join them. "I had never owned a stock or bond, nor had I taken any investment courses," he says. "That turned out to be quite an advantage." By the end of their second year in business, Muhlenkamp and his partners had a modest $3 million in assets. He felt his future potential at the firm was limited, so he left to join the research arm of an insurance company.

In the early 1970s, stocks went down more frequently than they went up. Muhlenkamp made it his job to find out why. "All of the studies up to this point proved that 4.5 percent was a normal interest rate for bonds and 17 was the normal PE for stocks," he remembers. "As PEs went from 17 to 15 to 7, Wall Street analysts kept telling me about stocks they thought were cheap. I'd ask them what the company was worth, and they couldn't tell me. So I did some basic work to arrive at values for companies. I really wrote another chapter from Ben Graham's book, only my chapter showed how evaluation criteria change with inflation. I've used the same stuff ever since, and it's worked beautifully."

Muhlenkamp concluded that as inflation changes, there is a lag time before the public realizes it. "When we had high inflation and low interest rates in the 1970s, it was a great time to borrow money," he points out. "That trend reversed in roughly 1981, but all through the 1980s people still believed you could make a lot of money buying a big house with a mortgage. They didn't change their mind until 1990. Public fears, if you will, set the attitude of the marketplace. Where a guy like me makes money is by exploiting the difference between these fears and reality." With stable inflation and interest rates, he is convinced stock prices in coming years will move solely in line with earnings.

Muhlenkamp began his own investment firm in 1978, running private accounts for individuals. He launched a mutual fund in 1988 and now oversees some $300 million. His goal is to provide clients with the best overall total return, regardless of whether that means investing money in stocks or bonds. "To me, inflation is the rate at which your money is shrinking," he says. "What I'm trying to do is make money after taxes and inflation. I have found over the years that if inflation is 3 percent, I'm not interested in owning bonds unless I can get 3 percent over that, or 6 percent. Similarly, I'm not interested in owning stocks unless it looks like I can get a return of 5 or 6 percent over inflation."

Most of the time, Muhlenkamp's money is in equities. One reason is that management works for the shareholder and against the creditor. "You don't know of any company executive who owns bond options," he observes. "Can you name a company you'd rather lend money to than own a piece of?" He won't buy a stock unless it will give him a return on equity (ROE) greater than 15 percent. And he wants to purchase it for a PE ratio below the ROE. "I say I like to buy Pontiacs and Buicks when they go on sale. I don't want to buy Renaults at any price," he says. "The other thing I'll sometimes do is look for clumps of value. In 1990 all of the banks looked cheap; I concluded any bank that didn't go bankrupt was a buy."

While he's primarily interested in the fundamentals, Muhlenkamp, an avid motorcycle enthusiast, often decides to sell based on technical indicators. "I learned a long time ago that you can't find out the bad news in time for it to do you any good," he says. "So I always set price targets. If one of my stocks gets fully priced or stops performing and I can't figure out why, it's usually best to start selling some."

Occupation: President and Portfolio Manager, Muhlenkamp & Company
Wexford, Pennsylvania

Birth Date: February 9, 1944

Education: BS, Massachusetts Institute of Technology, 1966
MBA, Harvard Business School, 1968

Biggest Mistake Investors Make: "Running with the crowd. In other words, buying based on impulse or the fad of the moment instead of on research."

Best Investment: Green Tree Financial (Bought in 1990 for $1.50 per share. It was acquired in 1998 for more than $40.)

Worst Investment: In high school, he put two summers' worth of work money (about $1,100) in an Ohio savings and loan that went bankrupt.

Advice: "Buy stocks the way you would buy a used car. Do your homework, and get something you plan to own for a while. If you wind up with a lemon, sell out and move on."

Market Outlook: Bullish

MICHAEL MURPHY

California Technology Stock Letter

How much technology should you own in your investment portfolio? "Take 100 and subtract your age," says tech guru Michael Murphy. "The result is the percentage you should keep in technology stocks. I think most people will find they are severely underinvested in this area of the market." And despite the huge gains in these stocks seen during the 1990s, Murphy thinks there's plenty more to come. "The underlying growth in computing and communications is still very strong," he insists. "The visibility for the semiconductor business in particular is better than I've ever seen it, and many new drugs are getting approved, which will be good for biotech companies."

Murphy began his career in technology stocks as a computer programmer with American Express in 1968. He was asked to analyze the company's investment operations and spent 18 months researching the stock market to better understand his assignment. A short time later, he was tapped to become a computer analyst, and ultimately wound up on the investment committee managing money.

He launched the *California Technology Stock Letter* in 1981 after spotting an unfulfilled need in the area of technology stock research. "There was really nothing for individuals that provided fundamental analysis of these companies," he recalls. He also writes *Technology Investing,* a publication for more novice investors, and the *Overpriced Stock Service,* which offers advice for shorting stocks. In addition, he manages some technology-related mutual funds.

Murphy covers both computer-electronics and what he calls "medtech-biotech" companies, noting there's a big difference between the two. "On the medtech-biotech side, you are dealing with development-stage firms," he explains. "In the electronics and computer area, you don't mess around with development-stage companies."

That's because there's a real model and path set up for getting legitimate electronics companies funded and profitable before they go public, most commonly with the help of venture capitalists. But such support isn't normally available to biotechnology companies, and they often have no choice but to offer stock. "It costs so much money to develop a drug and there is no way for venture capitalists to keep these things private through to profitability," Murphy contends. "They take them public early, but keep a close eye on them to make sure they stay on track."

On the computer-electronics side, Murphy wants to buy companies that show at least 15 percent annual growth in both profitability and return on equity. However, he's somewhat of a bargain hunter and only willing to pay a fair price. To determine what that is, he begins by calculating a potential candidate's "growth flow" rate, which represents earnings plus research and development per share.

He then calculates the share price-to-growth flow rate, and if the result is ten or less, the stock is usually a buy. Ironically, the more a company spends on R&D, the less Wall Street usually likes it because it depresses current earnings. Murphy has a different opinion. "R&D is where new products come from," he insists. "New products are what create all this sales growth, regardless of what the economy's doing, and usually new products carry higher profit margins."

Murphy has another approach for evaluating medtech-biotech companies, which he points out carry more risk. "The capital markets pay people to assume risk, and these are clearly risky development-stage companies," he says. "But when they ultimately succeed, you can make 30 to 40 percent per year compound rates of return." Unfortunately, you can't use the growth-flow exercise to evaluate attractiveness, because most of these companies don't have any earnings. "So we have a measure that we can call the 'M-score,'" he offers. "We look at how much money they've spent on research and development in the last five years and add that up." He then examines the stock's total market capitalization. The ratio between the market capitalization to R&D gives him the stock's M-score. "In normal times, this ratio will be eight to ten, which is fair," he says. "On the other hand, in tough times, it will fall to three or five. The lower the M-score, the better."

Other things to look for when evaluating technology companies, according to Murphy, are the quality of each company's scientific advisory board (it should be composed of prominent, well-published names) and whether they have any blue chip marketing partners. But the bottom line, as is often the case when it comes to investing, is to use common sense. "If a company makes something that you think is goofy, whatever it is, don't mess with it," Murphy cautions.

Occupation: Editor, *California Technology Stock Letter*
Half Moon Bay, California

Birth Date: December 29, 1941

Education: BA, Harvard College, 1963

Biggest Mistake Investors Make: "Acting without information. Buying on tips and not even getting an annual report."

Best Investment: Chiron (Bought it for $1 nine years ago.)

Worst Investment: Telios Pharmaceuticals (Purchased for $8 and it ultimately went bankrupt.)

Advice: "Buy stocks in a growth universe but use value criteria. Don't try to make money in things that aren't growing, but don't get sucked into the momentum investment theory."

Market Outlook: Bullish

WILLIAM NASGOVITZ

Heartland Advisors

Small company value stocks are selling at record low valuations, according to a man who spends his life following such investments. Bill Nasgovitz is the president and chairman of Heartland Advisors, a Wisconsin investment management firm. The Heartland Value Fund, which Nasgovitz comanages, is one of the oldest micro-cap value funds in the business. "Valuations today look like where they were in 1974, when I rediscovered the teachings of Benjamin Graham," Nasgovitz says. "I think we're past the inflection point of this 'Nifty Fifty-like' craze, and small-cap value stocks are poised to outperform for years."

Nasgovitz began investing as a teenager, using paper route money to buy shares in companies based in his hometown of Milwaukee. He's always been a fan of undiscovered opportunities, which is what originally led him to mine for stocks in waters few others dare to wade. He's an expert at investing in those tiny companies with market capitalizations of less than $100 million. While it may seem there aren't a lot of choices in this area, especially given how far the stock market has risen in recent years, the opposite is true. Nasgovitz estimates that of the 14,000 or so publicly traded companies out there, around 90 percent meet his criterion, in terms of market value.

After spending time after college as a broker at Dean Witter, he started his own advisory group in 1982. His company suffered greatly during the crash of 1987. However, he quickly recovered and the firm now manages some $2.5 billion in both private accounts and several mutual funds. Although Nasgovitz himself continues to focus on micro-caps, he has expanded his firm's list of offerings to include large- and mid-cap stocks as well. "I like micro-caps because they represent the fastest growing part of the U.S. economy," he says. "These stocks perform best over the long term, and it's a job finding something that nobody else knows about." Indeed, although Wall Street is starting to give these tiny gems more attention, they remain in relative oblivion compared to their larger brethren.

Nasgovitz traces his entrenched value investment philosophy back to the bear market of 1973-74, when the Dow crumbled and the average stock plummeted by 70 percent. He reread Benjamin Graham's work and vowed to only buy stocks based on a list of specific value parameters. "Low PE, low price-to-cash flow, low price-to-book value, financial soundness, things like that," he explains. "What we're trying to do is capitalize on the upside potential of small stocks, but limit the downside risk."

He locates candidates through all sorts of channels. He and his analysts look for such characteristics as financial soundness, positive earnings dynamics, high insider ownership, capable management, and some kind of catalyst in each company they consider. "The catalyst has become increasingly important in recent years," he adds. Nasgovitz has built up a library of micro-cap ideas over the years that he revisits from time to time to see if their value parameters have been met. He also gets hundreds of external research reports each year.

"We're looking for companies that not only have a value safety net, but also have upside potential," Nasgovitz says. He notes that stocks in this area generally have a small number of outstanding shares, so prices can gyrate tremendously from day-to-day, making them much more volatile than larger companies. That's why he admits individual investors need to own at least two dozen different micro-cap stocks to have a properly diversified portfolio. His value fund has close to 270 names.

"This is a very inefficient market and prices rarely equate the true worth of a company," he adds. "We like to discover companies selling for a ridiculous price." Although he's a fundamental analyst, Nasgovitz always views stock charts to see where a company has been, and therefore, its potential once the price recovers. He likes to buy at bases and sell into uptrends. Nasgovitz rarely touches initial public offerings, although he files them away for future consideration after the early excitement has subsided.

Nasgovitz admits his discipline requires patience, because the market often takes time to recognize value. But he's willing to wait up to two years to see a story unfold as expected. If nothing happens by then, chances are he'll take his money off the table and move on. He'll also sell once a stock's value is realized and it moves from being undervalued to overpriced.

To thaw out from the cold Milwaukee winters, Nasgovitz bought a home in Santa Barbara, California, where he has set up a branch office of sorts. "I love the weather, and you can actually grow a garden there," he exclaims.

Occupation: President and Chairman, Heartland Advisors
Milwaukee, Wisconsin

Birth Date: October 8, 1944

Education: BA, University of Wisconsin, Madison, 1966

Biggest Mistake Investors Make: "Not paying attention to what's going on in the bond market."

Best Investment: Interdigital (First bought in 1996 at an average cost of $6. It got all the way up to $80 in just a few years.)

Worst Investment: Maxicare (Purchased for $10 a few years back. At last check, it was trading for around $1.)

Advice: "Pay attention to competitive returns in the bond market, and equate those returns to earnings yields from stocks."

Market Outlook: Bullish on small-caps; cautious on the broad market

LOUIS NAVELLIER

Navellier & Associates

Louis Navellier admits his reputation is changing. He was once known as a premier small-cap specialist. Now he writes a newsletter called *Louis Navellier's Blue Chip Growth Letter,* which is devoted to large company stocks. And while he used to just manage a handful of small-cap aggressive growth mutual funds, he now oversees value, large-cap, and international portfolios as well. Why the sudden expansion? "We're a big firm now and have specialists in all of these areas," he insists. "There are 55 of us and over time we've added all of these new areas."

Navellier likes to compare his investment strategy to flying a plane. "I'm on autopilot," he says. "I run my computer-based models every weekend and follow them religiously. The best way to think of it is if I were flying an airplane, I wouldn't look out the window. I would just read my instruments."

It's no secret that professional managers have had a difficult time keeping up with the S&P 500 in recent years. Navellier maintains that's because all but 28 of the stocks in the S&P are efficiently priced, making it tough for any one person to gain a competitive edge. "Stocks usually get inefficiently priced because of the flow of funds," he says. "Any time a stock's being discovered or institutionalized for the first time, or when Wall Street hasn't properly discounted the fundamentals, it is inefficiently priced."

The only way you can beat the market, according to Navellier, is by finding and buying those inefficiently priced stocks. That's why he focuses on finding stocks in all capitalization ranges that are most neglected by the major institutions. He determines whether a stock is inefficiently priced by looking at its so-called alpha factor. "A stock's return correlated to the market from week to week over the past year is the beta, and the return uncorrelated to the market is this mysterious alpha factor," he explains. "There are a lot of stocks out there that are totally correlated to the market, and 85 percent of big-cap stocks have alphas at or near zero."

Navellier first began honing his investment skills as a finance student in the late 1970s. He didn't buy the conventional wisdom that the stock market was always efficient. "I knew back then there were money managers beating the market," he recalls. So with the help of two professors, he developed several computer models to prove he was right. It's a system he has refined over the years and still uses today. "I'm continuously testing and monitoring what works on Wall Street and rebuilding my models," he says. "I'm really more of a modeler than anything else."

In other words, Navellier uses his computer to find out which stocks and characteristics the majority of investors are in love with at the present time. His theory is that if you want to beat the market, you must buy stocks that aren't simply moving in tandem with it. He puts his database of 9,000 stocks through several bottom-up screens each week. Predictably, he starts off by calculating each company's alpha factor. "I then take the alpha, divide it by a stock's volatility, and get a reward-risk ratio," he says. "The quantitative screens are designed to stack the odds in my favor, and that's what I try to do. The whole process is automated. There's no subjective judgment to it at all."

The computer puts his entire list of stocks through 36 back-testing models, which check various ratios such as price-to-book, dividend discount, cash flow, and PE, along with earnings momentum. "I'm trying to find what Wall Street likes fundamentally [at any given time], because what it likes does change," Navellier reasons. "I'm overlaying fundamental anomalies on my high alpha stocks to tilt the odds in my favor." Based on the results of this and the risk-reward ratio, the computer sorts each stock in terms of relative attractiveness, and the top 10 percent form Navellier's buy list. Right now, Navellier says, Wall Street likes growth at a reasonable price. He also says the market has matured and is now demanding fundamentals, including strong earnings growth.

As a final step, he uses an optimization model to determine how to mix and match the final list of stocks to get the highest returns with the least amount of risk. "The model will often say put 5 percent in this stock, 2 percent in this stock, 3 percent in this stock, and so forth," Navellier reveals. "What it's trying to do is find stocks that complement each other and represent different industry groups while attempting to lower the overall volatility."

Navellier is highly diversified and has a strong sell discipline. He keeps his average holding 9 to 11 months. "As a stock moves up in price, it tends to become risky," he says. "My allocation model will tell me to cut back, not because it's a bad stock, but because it's getting increasingly less predictable."

Occupation: President and CEO, Navellier & Associates
Reno, Nevada

Birth Date: November 22, 1957

Education: BA, California State University, Hayward, 1978
MBA, California State University, Hayward, 1979

Biggest Mistake Investors Make: "Putting all of their eggs in one basket."

Best Investment: CMGI (Bought in April 1998 and it jumped almost 1,700 percent in less than one year.)

Worst Investment: Digitran Systems (It suspended trading and ultimately went down to zero.)

Advice: "Sell good stocks to buy better stocks."

Market Outlook: Bullish

VITA NELSON

The Moneypaper

Even though some Internet brokers now execute trades for as little as $5, Vita Nelson pays a better price to buy most of her stocks—nothing. How does she do it? By going directly to the company and investing through what are known as dividend reinvestment plans, or DRIPs. Many of the largest companies offer such programs. To get in, you normally have to buy your first share through a broker. But once you're a shareholder and have signed up for the DRIP, you can both reinvest your dividends and buy additional shares of stock at little or no charge. Granted, some companies are more generous than others. Nelson prefers those that give the most benefits free to DRIP participants. She claims they often turn into the best investments too.

Nelson's rise to becoming queen of the DRIPs was an unconventional one, to say the least. In fact, she owes much of her success to the word *divine.* "When I first graduated from college, I went to work at *Mademoiselle* magazine, which seems as far away from the financial markets as you can get," she concedes. "After being there for about a year, I found myself using the word *divine,* and it was associated with a blouse. I figured that was enough, and it was time to get out of there." In other words, she felt she wanted to do something more substantial with her life. So she began looking through the help-wanted section of the newspaper and was attracted to, of all things, an opening as an apprentice in the municipal bond department at Granger & Company. "I was home sick and kept interviewing over the phone," she remembers. "It was in 1960, and even though the company wasn't expecting to have a woman, I got the job."

She learned the bond business from the ground up at Granger. "My boss had to teach me what an eighth of a point translated to," she admits. "I started out bidding on short-term bonds, and after a while, I was on my own and had millions of dollars that I had to keep busy in the market." Several years later, when Nelson and her family moved to Westchester County, she decided it wasn't practical to keep her job at Granger, even though the company offered to make her manager of municipals. She instead took some time off to raise her three children and decided to reenter the publishing business in 1969, this time founding *Westchester Magazine.* She sold it in 1980 and began what is now known as *The Moneypaper.*

"It was originally called *A Financial Publication for Women,*" she recalls. "I looked for strategies to reduce risk because I knew women were risk averse. But it was very hard to market to women using traditional direct mail. I didn't change the focus, but after realizing everything was equally appropriate for men, I changed the title after four years."

What made her especially popular with subscribers was her reporting on DRIPs. "I'm always looking for ways to diversify and minimize risk," she says.

"I first found out about dividend reinvestment plans in 1984 in an article in *The Wall Street Journal.* There was a list of companies you could invest in without going to a broker. I started writing about them immediately. In the next issue, I published a portfolio of companies that had these programs and told people what they had to do to enroll in them. It just kept growing from there." Today she also publishes the biweekly *Direct Investing* newsletter and the regularly updated *Guide to Dividend Reinvestment Plans.*

About 1,100 companies offer DRIP programs today, a number that is quickly growing. Again, the catch is that most plans require you to purchase at least one share of stock through a broker before you can enroll. That's become less of a problem now that you can trade stock for just pennies a share. Nelson also has a service that will get you your first share of stock and register you for the DRIP for around $15. She has even started her own mutual fund of DRIPs for those who don't want to do the direct investing on their own. It is designed to track an index of DRIP stocks she created. The index has bested the performance of the S&P 500 most years going back to 1994. The downside to all this, Nelson says, is that some companies now charge fees for their DRIPs, including McDonald's and Walt Disney. She hastens to add that most DRIPs remain attractive and there is almost always a no-fee alternative in every industry.

"For people with limited resources, in terms of research and finances, DRIPs give you a way to diversify without having to go into a mutual fund," Nelson notes. "Small investors with just $500 can spread their risk among 10 or 20 different companies for only $25 a shot. If you had to pay a commission each time, this would be impossible. DRIPs also encourage people who would not otherwise get into the market to get in, and that's the most wonderful part of it."

Occupation: Publisher and Editor, *The Moneypaper*
Mamaroneck, New York

Birth Date: December 9, 1939

Education: BA, Boston University, 1959

Biggest Mistake Investors Make: "Having a lack of patience and reacting with emotion. Also, not having a strategy."

Best Investment: Phelps Dodge (It's the only stock she has traded frequently.)

Worst Investment: Unocal (Bought on a hot tip in the early 1980s.)

Advice: "Start investing early. Never do anything unless you're following a rational plan."

Market Outlook: Bullish

EARL OSBORN

Bingham, Osborn & Scarborough

Earl Osborn loves market volatility. "Diversified portfolios, like the ones we construct for our clients, shine in that kind of environment," he says. Before getting into the investment business, Osborn was an attorney. "I'd always thought about going to law school," he recalls. "I enjoyed the precision of the law and was intrigued by the intricacies of the legal system." While working in private practice, he found himself handling a lot of cases in the areas of business, valuation litigation, and securities law. He was also good at working with computers. So when his former Amherst College buddy Bob Bingham suggested the two form their own investment management firm, Osborn jumped at the opportunity.

"I came into this business, not because I was unhappy with law, but because I enjoyed investing more," he says. "When we originally established our company, we used loaded funds (funds sold with an up-front sales charge). It was the only system set up where you could manage complete portfolios, because you had the brokerage servicing arms of the mutual fund companies." In 1990, when Charles Schwab created a system allowing financial planners to electronically trade no-loads and keep everything on one statement, Osborn's firm switched over and began charging clients on a fee basis. "Schwab allowed people like us, who before had to work on a combination of fees and commissions, to work solely on a pure fee basis," he adds.

Today the firm manages $500 million through both open-end mutual funds and exchange traded index tracking shares, such as QQQ, which represents the Nasdaq 100. "Our primary belief is that it is the market which determines returns more than the individual fund," he explains. "In other words, let's say you're in a technology fund. Over the past year or so, you're going to have the highest returns of any mutual fund. It may appear that is due to the manager, but it is really due to the fact that your fund invests in technology companies, which have been the market's best performers."

Therefore, when putting portfolios together, the first question Osborn asks is, "Where's the best place to be in the market right now?" The answer is often determined by a proprietary computer model he developed. "We'll go back historically and look for those particular forms of diversification or combinations of markets that give us the most efficient portfolios," he says. "We want to put together a portfolio offering the maximum return for the particular level of risk we're willing to accept." Typically, he keeps at least 30 percent of his clients' money in stocks at all times, both domestic and foreign, but won't go above 80 percent unless a client demands it. "That's because once you get a mix of 70 to 80 percent stocks, the last 20 or 30 percent you add historically has not increased returns at all, though it has increased risk," he observes. In terms of global diversification, his current equity model calls for a split of 80 percent in the U.S. and 20 percent overseas, with the majority of his domestic allocation devoted to value stocks.

Once Osborn determines where he wants to be, the next step is finding the right vehicles to get him there. Much of the mix involves index funds. "We probably use 40 or 50 different indexes," he says. "All of our fixed-income portion is indexed. That's because expenses have a much greater impact on the fixed income side, and index funds are the most cost-efficient. We also index a majority of our equity money, especially for the large-cap portion of the portfolio. When you move into small company U.S. stocks, we start to incorporate more managed funds, based in part on our belief that managers have a better chance of beating the averages in these less-efficient markets. It's also hard to find good indexes in this area."

When he does use active management, Osborn looks for four primary characteristics: consistency of performance, cost structure, low turnover, and depth of management. "We're not necessarily looking for the best-performing fund over recent time periods," he explains. "We're looking for funds which have shown an ability to consistently give above-market returns over a number of market cycles. We want below-average expense ratios. Turnover is also important, because the trading spread among stocks, especially for smaller companies, can run as high as 6 percent. And we look for organizations with a consistent philosophy and the ability to manage a wide range of funds effectively through different managers. That way we're not reliant on any one star manager."

Looking ahead, Osborn says stocks are still the place to be, although he expects returns in the new millennium will be lower than they were in the 1990s."

Occupation: Partner, Bingham, Osborn & Scarborough
San Francisco, California

Birth Date: April 5, 1948

Education: BA, Amherst College, 1970
JD, Hastings College of Law, 1975

Biggest Mistake Investors Make: "Going after the hot deal and being overwhelmed by performance numbers, both for stocks and mutual funds; they buy what's up without understanding why."

Best Investment: Buying S&P 500 index funds in 1995 and holding on.

Worst Investment: Several real estate limited partnerships he purchased in the 1980s, in which he lost 80 percent of his money

Advice: "Look for consistency. Worry about the fund that's gone up much more than the market, as well as the one that's gone down much more."

Market Outlook: Bullish

L. ROY PAPP

L. Roy Papp & Associates

Call Roy Papp old fashioned, but he isn't interested in buying any Internet or biotech stocks, even though he now runs his own small-cap fund. "It's hard for me to accept the concept of buying stocks that are going to lose money every year for the foreseeable future," he says. "My guess is at least a quarter of the Internet stocks out there will be gone in the next year or so."

Papp's preference is for solid, proven companies with global domination. Papp has lived and traveled all around the world during his long and colorful life. After serving in the military, Papp studied economics at Brown University. He went on to get an MBA at the Wharton School before being recruited by the Chicago investment firm Stein, Roe & Farnham. "I started out as an accounting man in training working specifically for Wells Farnham," Papp says. "I was really a glorified clerk, but I worked my way up to becoming a senior partner in the firm."

Along the way, Papp was also involved in politics, which led to an appointment on the Fannie Mae board in 1969. A few years later, he got a personal invitation from President Ford asking him to become the U.S. ambassador to the Asian Development Bank in Manila. "My wife and I decided to accept, and I resigned from both Fannie Mae and Stein Roe."

As a bank director, Papp helped to decide which countries got loans. Although he didn't do any investing as part of this role, he still played the market with his own personal money. "Because I was in Manila, I was never awake when the New York Stock Exchange was open, and I got the *New York Times* about two weeks late," he says. "It was clear to me I could not buy stocks that required quick judgments. So I focused on companies that I felt comfortable owning for three or four years. This was in 1975. Stocks were so cheap at that point, it wasn't hard to find things that were attractive. I learned to just sit with my investments and hold on. As it turned out, I made more money being on the other side of the world using that philosophy than I did actively managing accounts at Stein Roe."

After his term on the Bank ended, Papp and his wife headed for Phoenix, where he started his own investment shop. At first he managed money for friends out of his home. Once his business grew, he recruited his son Harry and Harry's wife, Rose, to join him in the firm. Today, L. Roy Papp & Associates manages some $1.3 billion in both private accounts and four mutual funds.

Papp's a big believer in the amazing economic growth that continues to take place around the globe, so much so that he started a fund in 1991 called America-Abroad. But he exploits this potential through buying U.S. multinationals instead of foreign stocks. "I think you're a lot safer that way," he maintains. "You don't expose yourself to currency risk, you avoid having to deal with varying accounting standards, you save on operating expenses, and you don't have to worry about the political instability inherent in some countries. Most important, you have SEC protection. You don't get this when you buy foreign stocks. We've had very few financial scandals in the United States over the last 50 years. That's an enormous plus."

Sticking with American companies, according to Papp, also lets you invest in the future instead of the past. "The big businesses in smaller countries are involved in steel, cement, and infrastructure," he observes. "You can't export this stuff. They're behind the rest of the world, not in front of it like we are in the United States. Our economy is based on technology, which is the future. That's worth a much higher premium."

As for the argument that owning foreign stocks helps to increase the diversification of your portfolio, Papp considers that to be nonsense. "World markets tend to move in the same direction," he insists. "There is one major difference. If we catch cold, everyone else gets pneumonia. Conversely, if others catch cold, we usually aren't affected. For example, everyone said that when Japan got into trouble in the 1980s we would too. But we didn't."

When Papp searches for investment ideas, in addition to a global business plan, he looks for companies growing at a good rate. "I don't want them doubling every year because that can't be maintained," he notes. "The ideal rate for me is 20 or 25 percent a year, but a good rate is 12 percent. And I want to buy stocks at a multiple at or near that of the overall market." He also prefers monopolies but will settle on leaders in their industry. He'll let go of a holding once it trades for a 50 percent premium over its intrinsic value. "Because that number changes every day, I don't think you're wise setting a specific price," he says. "There are really three good reasons to sell a stock: you screw up, the industry changes, or the company is so successful that it becomes overpriced."

Occupation: Managing Partner, L. Roy Papp & Associates
Phoenix, Arizona

Birth Date: March 18, 1927

Education: AB, Brown University, 1951
MBA, Wharton School, University of Pennsylvania, 1955

Biggest Mistake Investors Make: "Trying to get a high yield or return; you always wind up buying poor quality because high return equals high risk."

Best Investment: Richard Irwin (Bought in 1975 for $10.50 a share; Dow Jones acquired the company a month later for $26.)

Worst Investment: A North Sea oil stock he purchased in the 1960s, on which he lost most of his money

Advice: "Stick with quality companies, even when it comes to investing in the Internet."

Market Outlook: Bullish

MARGARITA PEREZ

Fortaleza Asset Management

Being female and Puerto Rican is an unusual combination in the world of finance. However, Margarita Perez maintains it hasn't been much of a factor in her successful career. "It's investment returns that really drive this business," she insists. "If you are doing a good job, I don't think anyone is going to worry about your gender or race." Perez makes money for her mostly institutional clients by investing in the securities of small-cap growth companies. "I find that they are growing very fast and are a lot of fun to follow," she says. "I also have access to top management. I can talk to them, look them in the eye, and really get a sense of the direction they're taking."

Perez moved from her native Puerto Rico to Chicago at the age of 14. She was always good with numbers and figured she'd become a math teacher. "At DePaul University, I was introduced to accounting and finance for the first time and thought it was great," she recalls. "I realized I could do something other than just teach math to someone. So I decided to pursue accounting for a while and eventually became a CPA." She took a job with Borg-Warner's treasury department, while going to school at night to get an MBA in international business. "At Borg-Warner, I was given a chance to join the in-house pension investment group," she says. "Once I tasted that side of finance, I was hooked." When the corporation became privately held in 1989, her department was downsized, and she decide to start her own investment management firm. As it turned out, Borg-Warner was one of her first clients.

Perez gets her investment ideas from many channels, including regional brokers, screening through computer databases, attending investment conferences, and her own in-house research. "I'm not a quant [someone who only looks at the numbers]," she maintains. "I really practice fundamental, bottom-up stock picking." She has learned over the years that there are several key factors usually found in successful small-cap stocks. To begin with, even if a company doesn't have a long history of being publicly traded, it must have been around for some time for her to get interested. She further searches for companies with conservative accounting policies. "Currently, one of the things we're focusing on is how revenues are recorded," she explains. "We like companies that take a conservative stand and defer revenues on the more complicated projects." Perhaps most of all, she wants her companies to have experienced management. "In real estate, location is everything," she rations. "In small-cap stock investing, I think management is everything. They must have the ability to execute the business plan. Fortunately, most of the time top executives in smaller firms are very accessible. It's easy to get to the CEO."

Perez shuns stocks with a lot of leverage on the balance sheet. "Most of my companies have no debt," she insists. To make the final cut, they must register top-line growth of at least 20 percent. "I often say you've got to have the revenues driving the earnings," she points out. "It can't just be a restructuring story. If the revenues are not rising, eventually the growth won't be there." She prefers to buy these stocks at a reasonable price, but is willing to pay up for strong growth. "Generally, I like to stay at one times the company's growth rate," she says. "If I can get it lower than that, that's ideal. It is essential that you do a real peer comparison. If a company has a big lead over the competition, I'm willing to pay a premium for that."

Before making a purchase, Perez always sets a sell target going in. "It's very easy to fall in love with a fast-growing company," she admits. "If you don't have a sell discipline in place, you can get in trouble." Perez will unload a stock if it meets her target, if the fundamentals change, or she uncovers a more attractive opportunity. Her portfolios are highly diversified, holding an average of 65 different names. Turnover can be as high as 150 percent a year. She claims it's simply not possible to be a buy and hold investor when you're dealing with small-caps. "This is an evolving market," she explains. "There are always new entrants. I'm a firm believer that you should take your profits."

Perez still travels back to Puerto Rico, especially now that she has two clients there—a bank and a university. She even had the commonwealth in mind when naming her firm, Fortaleza Asset Management. "It means fortress and fortitude in Spanish," she points out. "I found that name to be particularly meaningful, because those of us dealing with the small-cap growth area need all the fortitude we can get."

Occupation: President, Fortaleza Asset Management
Chicago, Illinois

Birth Date: May 14, 1954

Education: BS, DePaul University, 1978
MBA, DePaul University, 1981

Biggest Mistake Investors Make: "Not having a long enough time horizon and being too anxious; people buy stocks expecting to make a million dollars tomorrow. You have to give your investments time to work out."

Best Investment: Powerwave Technologies (Bought for around $6 in 1998 and still owns it.)

Worst Investment: Comptronix (She purchased for $7 in 1994 and it went down to $2.)

Advice: "Develop a plan, know your tolerance for risk and time horizon, and invest accordingly."

Market Outlook: Bullish

MARCUS ROBINS

RedChip.com

Like many of the companies he follows, Marcus Robins has reaped dot-com riches for himself. In late 1999, investment banking firm Roth Capital Partners bought a majority interest in his firm, and helped to spin-off RedChip.com, an online source for investment research on small-cap companies. Robins's Portland-based company also publishes the biweekly *Red Chip Review* newsletter, a publication that specializes in analyzing small-caps.

Robins has lived in Oregon all of his life. Early on, he felt destined to get into medicine. He worked in one hospital or another from the time he was a freshman in high school to the day he graduated from college. But after getting his bachelor's degree, Robins had a change of heart. He decided instead to enroll in graduate school, not to become a doctor, but to get into money management. It was quite a change, though not that far-fetched, as he had been fiddling with the stock market since he was in the fifth grade.

Armed with a master's in administration, in 1979 Robins went to work as a broker at a small investment boutique in Portland. "It turned out I wasn't very good at sales, but I was good at analyzing companies," he recalls. "So I was the foundation of what became our research department. Five years later, I helped found another local boutique before moving to the institutional side." In 1988 he got his first shot at money management when he joined Capital Consultants and became primary manager of the WestCap Small-Cap Growth Portfolio. "It was a $100 million western state–based small-cap fund that consisted solely of individually managed accounts," Robins explains. "I wanted to start a public mutual fund, but my boss didn't, so I decided it was time to do something else."

Then two monumental things happened in his life. First, he was about to turn 40 and began rethinking the direction of his career. Then he made a remarkable killing in a small-cap stock called American Pacific. "It's a specialty chemical company, which drew on my background in medicine and chemistry," he says. "In May 1988, the company's only facility blew up, and the stock went down to $2. But American Pacific was an expert at producing ammonium perchlorate, used in solid rocket motors to supply oxygen. The U.S. government essentially put the company back in business within 18 months. At the end of 1991, the stock was discovered by two major brokerage companies. It had gone from $2 to $40 when I sold out on February 29, 1992." Although Robins won't say how much he made from his investment, he claims to have owned "a ton" of the stock.

He cashed out, quit his job, and made plans to start his own publication geared toward small-cap company research. He taught a finance course at Portland State University at the time and recruited several of his best students to help analyze companies in the basement of his home. The first edition of *The Red Chip Review* was published on August 2, 1993. "The philosophy behind my business was quite straightforward," Robins confides. "At that time, the institutional research and brokerage arena was concentrating more and more on the biggest 500 or 1,000 companies. But the best performance historically has come from small-cap stocks. I wanted to start the Morningstar of small-cap and micro-cap stocks. It would be a source of unbiased and independent research on these companies, which is something no one else offered."

There are around 11,000 tiny companies trading on the over-the-counter market, although Robins only considers about 4,500 of them to be legitimate. Of those, he's winnowed down the list of the most promising candidates to just 300. Those are the ones he covers and assesses for his readers during the course of the year. For Robins, 20 is a magic number. "My ideal company is one growing earnings by at least 20 percent annually, with a return-on-equity prospect of 20 percent, insider ownership of at least 20 percent, and institutional ownership of less than 20 percent. If I can find that kind of stock and then buy it for a multiple of less than 20, it's probably a pretty good bet." Of course, he believes good management is of utmost importance and avoids what he calls "Slick Willie" executives who own little or none of their company's stock. "I like down-to-earth managers with a lot of their wealth tied up in the business," he discloses.

Robins always sets a price target when he buys a stock, which is constantly being reevaluated as the stock moves up (or down) in price. After years of doing research on small-caps, Robins maintains he's learned that when it comes to evaluating top management, five warning signs indicate trouble ahead: black shirts, great tans, double-breasted suits, hair pieces, and tons of jewelry. "These almost always let you know you're dealing with problem people that you should probably stay away from," he adds.

Occupation: CEO and Editor-in-Chief, RedChip.com
Portland, Oregon

Birth Date: December 8, 1953

Education: BS, Willamette University, 1976
MAd, Willamette University, 1979

Biggest Mistake Investors Make: "Selling quality companies too soon."

Best Investment: Calgene (Bought for $8 in late 1998 and it jumped to $187 within four months.)

Worst Investment: Boyd's Wheels (Bought in 1997 for $12, got out at $4, and it ultimately went to zero.)

Advice: "Avoid stocks or sectors where there is euphoria or a consensus of opinion."

Market Outlook: Bullish

JOHN ROGERS

Ariel Capital Management

The prospects for value stocks have never been better, according to John Rogers. "I think value is going to have a long-lasting and meaningful run here," he says. "I've never seen such a discrepancy between growth and value in my entire career. I think value can go up while growth is destroyed. And I especially like small-cap value stocks." That's not surprising to hear, since Rogers specializes in small- and mid-cap companies.

As a kid growing up in Chicago's Hyde Park area, Rogers's dad used to give him stock as a present for Christmas and birthdays. The elder Rogers was worried that his peers in the African-American community didn't know enough about the stock market. "It was important to him that his son didn't grow up with that hole in his learning," Rogers says. He took the lesson to heart.

At the age of 18, his dad gave him total control over the portfolio he had been building over the years. That's when he began to think about investing as a possible career. He majored in economics at Princeton and started off in the business as a stockbroker with William Blair & Company. Unfortunately, he never liked that job very much. "I was already developing my own investment strategy based on a long-term, patient, value-oriented discipline," he says. "Being in the brokerage industry didn't really make sense. You had to make transactions happen in order to get paid, which forced you to think only about the short term."

Two years later, Rogers and a friend joined forces and started their own investment management firm. "We opened an office on Michigan Avenue in Chicago with dreams of starting a money management and mutual fund company," he remembers. "The thing we had going for us is we were both lifelong Chicagoans, so we knew a lot of people and could get in some doors." The two went to parents, family, friends, and their brokerage clients to raise seed capital before launching the Ariel Fund, which at the time was legally run as a partnership. "It was a way of building a track record," Rogers concedes. "Starting in the summer of 1983, I had about $500,000 under management. Every quarter after that I would go to prospective clients and say, "I'm 24 years old, but here's how I've done, and this is what you will get if you hire me.'" Today he oversees more than $2.5 billion in private accounts and mutual funds.

"I call myself a contrarian value investor," Rogers says. "There are three things I focus on. First, I want stocks that are cheap and out of favor. I look at the PE and price-to-cash ratios first. Then I try to figure out what a reasonable person would pay for the business if it were to be sold. I like companies selling for no more than 13 times next year's true cash earnings and a 40 percent discount to private market value." His firm concentrates solely on companies with market capitalizations below $5 billion. Rogers claims to find most of his investment ideas through reading. "I read all of the business publications that are out there as well as mutual fund newsletters and books," he reveals. "I am constantly searching for companies and industries that are doing well." However, some of his best buys come from reading stories about companies that are having trouble. If an article is negative on a stock, Rogers often gets an itch to check it out further. "I spend a lot of time trying to truly understand the management team of every company I consider," he adds. "I want to know all I can about the team's background. My experience has been that when you encounter any type of disaster down the line, it's usually because of a problem with management."

In addition, Rogers puts each company through a series of social screens. "I stay away from industries I do not think are right for me long term," he reasons. "I avoid tobacco stocks and those that aren't environmentally friendly. I am convinced companies that aren't concerned about the environment will have a hard time being successful. I also try to be sure that there's a culture in the companies I invest in that appreciates diversity. I believe these social screens lead me to making better investment decisions."

Even though small-cap stocks have been out of favor the past few years, Rogers has remained faithful to his discipline. In fact, he's been selling some of his larger stocks to buy smaller ones, because he thinks the values among tinier names are more compelling.

Ariel's motto, "Slow and steady wins the race," alludes to Rogers's aversion to pulling the trigger. "The major reason I'll sell a stock is if I lose confidence in the quality of the product being produced or management's ability to grow the business at above-average rates over the next three to five years," he adds.

Occupation: President, Ariel Capital Management
Chicago, Illinois

Birth Date: March 31, 1958

Education: BA, Princeton University, 1980

Biggest Mistake Investors Make: "Buying stocks that are popular; they wind up jumping on the bandwagon after it's too late."

Best Investment: T. Rowe Price (Started buying after the crash of 1987 for $5 a share. He still owns it.)

Worst Investment: Golden Books Family Entertainment (Purchased the stock in April 1987 for $8. Sold out for 12¢ in September 1998.)

Advice: "Work at investing in industries in which you truly understand why a company is going to do well."

Market Outlook: Bearish on growth, but bullish on value

STEPHEN SAVAGE

The No-Load Fund Analyst

In the unpredictable world of mutual funds, one thing appears to be certain: "You should keep away from those funds that are ranked poorly," insists Steve Savage, editor and publisher of *The No-Load Fund Analyst.* "It's tough to tell whether a highly rated fund will stay that way. But the bad ones almost always remain dogs." That information is useful because if you eliminate all the stinkers from the list of the 12,000 potential funds competing for your money, you presumably have several thousand fewer names to choose from.

Savage knows a lot about fund ratings. He's devoted most of his career to compiling them. He initially got into the investment area through journalism. In college, Savage was hired by a Canadian newsletter publisher to write for one of its New York–based investment publications. "I got a chance to interview some pretty well-known fund managers," he says. He joined the publisher full-time after graduation and convinced his bosses to let him start a mutual fund research publication, called the *Blue Book of Mutual Fund Reports.* It featured single-page research write-ups on each fund, similar to what Morningstar and Value Line do today. "I went out and bought a computer and learned how to set up my own database and generate my own full-page reports," he says. "I put the whole thing together myself."

The service was marginally successful. However, the publisher faced hard times after a postal strike in Canada and decided to shut the publication down after one year. That was in 1986, right about the time when a then unknown firm called Morningstar launched its first fund research publication. Savage left the company to start his own fund newsletter but had a difficult time building a subscription base. He decided to sell out after just seven months to work as an editor with Wiesenberger, a company known for its meticulous fund research and performance-tracking service. "That job schooled me in the real fine points of mutual fund data and statistics," Savage says.

After being named director of his division, he was charged with modernizing and computerizing Wiesenberger's massive database. "We still had stuff that was being tracked on index cards and hand calculators," Savage notes. "I brought in the resources to build a computerized database and put up a PC network. What used to take 20 hours to calculate now could be done in 30 minutes."

In the winter of 1993, Savage learned that the CEO of Value Line wanted to talk with him about a job. "I called to politely turn her down and we wound up talking for six hours," he remembers. "They wanted to build a mutual fund information division from the ground up, applying the Value Line formula to mutual funds, competing head-on with Morningstar." Savage was intrigued by the challenge and accepted the offer.

"The day I started, there was nothing more than a drawing on a page of what Value Line wanted to do," he says. "There were no computers or research analysts, and I was supposed to get the product together in six months." By working late nights and weekends, Savage's team almost met the deadline, and the *Value Line Mutual Fund Survey* was born in 1993. He helped the company to develop both print and online versions of the product.

In May 1999 he became editor and publisher of *The No-Load Fund Analyst,* an Orinda, California–based monthly publication featuring in-depth research on actively managed funds. "We focus on doing a high level of research to find those managers who are likely to succeed in the future," he says. "We're not just looking for what's hot or chasing trends." Savage is also helping to increase the publication's Web presence and working to develop a product for financial advisors.

While Savage personally has a bias toward active management, he concedes indexing makes a good core holding for many portfolios. *The No-Load Fund Analyst* even calls them acceptable alternatives for active funds in its model portfolios. Savage also has no problem with investors owning some individual stocks as well. "My ideal fund is run by a manager with an established track record, a philosophy and discipline that make sense, and a support team of researchers and analysts that will help the manager sustain his or her record," Savage adds. "I honestly don't think there are a lot of managers out there who are able to outperform their benchmarks. But there are some. And if you do the work, you can find them."

Occupation: Editor and Publisher, *The No-Load Fund Analyst*
Orinda, California

Birth Date: June 23, 1961

Education: Attended Hunter College

Biggest Mistake Investors Make: "Chasing fads."

Best Investment: Invesco Technology Fund (Bought in December 1995 and sold in January 2000. The fund more than tripled.)

Worst Investment: Budget Group (Purchased for $29.50 in 1998 and sold for $10.50 a few months later.)

Advice: "Discipline is the single most rewarded trait in investing."

Market Outlook: Bullish

THURMAN SMITH

Equity Fund Research

If you're looking for great ideas in mutual funds, keep your eye out for brand-new portfolios run by experienced managers. That's the advice of Thurman Smith, who takes pride in uncovering these small gems. Smith publishes the *Equity Fund Outlook* newsletter, which has a small but loyal subscriber base made up largely of professional financial advisors. He's known for his ability to spot promising new funds before the rest of the crowd, which he especially likes because of their flexibility. "Everything else being equal, a new fund can be much better than an old one, mainly because of the smaller asset base," he says. "The managers are able to be more flexible and move more quickly. Most people tell you only buy funds with a five-year track record. I think that's bad advice."

Smith views mutual fund research as a bilateral process. "It requires using both sides of the brain," he surmises. "You begin by screening funds using the performance numbers and then you look at the fundamentals." Smith uses various computer programs he developed over the years to examine these statistics. He actually got started in the business as a computer applications programmer for several different investment companies, including State Street Bank and Fidelity Investments. After doing this for awhile, he decided he'd rather be the actual investment manager instead of just creating programs that allowed other people to do it. Because he already had an MBA in finance and investing, he decided to start his own investment firm and immediately began putting money to work for clients using no-load mutual funds.

"I like funds because your universe is under control and you solve the problem of diversification for clients who don't have large accounts," he explains. "An account under $1 million would probably be better off in funds rather than in individually managed stocks in terms of efficiency, reward-risk, diversification, and expenses."

Smith spends much of his day in front of his computer running screens to uncover tomorrow's top performers. "I realized it was possible to evaluate managers by using some computer tools to generate reward-risk ratios for individual funds. This type of analysis is more useful for evaluating funds and predicting their performance than simply using calendar period figures," he reasons. "I had developed enough software and data to generate a newsletter prototype, and I launched *Equity Fund Outlook* in 1988, figuring if I had all this information, I might as well get something out of it and some national exposure as well."

Smith's custom-built system may sound complicated, but the rationale behind it isn't. "I compare up and down market performance over the past three years," he explains. "During that time, we've had 12 up periods and 6 down ones. That's more useful than looking at beta or standard deviation or anything else I can find. I examine the actual behavior of the funds relative to the Wilshire 5000 index in those up and down periods, which have nothing to do with calendar periods." Smith's database contains 300 funds, which he selects using other computerized products, including Morningstar, and by reading various financial publications.

Once he's run his screens, he gives each fund a grade, which determines whether it winds up on his buy or sell list. To get an "A," a fund must do well in good markets and not fall as much as its peers in bad ones. "Given the same risk level, it would have to have the highest growth potential or reward factors, as measured by its up-market performance," he points out. However, even if a fund is explosive during bull markets, he won't even consider it if it goes into a free fall when the market turns south.

Once Smith finds a fund with good numbers, he moves on to evaluate it more closely, including analyzing the person running the show. "The data are just the initial ABC screening," he admits. "I want to know who's behind the wheel." Smith will sell and replace a fund once its growth and risk numbers start to deteriorate. He's certainly not afraid to pull the trigger. Turnover in his momentum-based tax-deferred portfolios can be as high as 100 percent a year, although he admits he's trying to keep that number down.

Smith notes that one style seems to consistently land on top. "Growth at a reasonable price is a discipline that tends to continually do the best," he reveals. "This technique captures both the growth potential of a stock while paying attention to the price you pay for it."

Smith follows equity funds only. He contends that even the most conservative investor should stay away from bonds. "Bonds just don't return enough, and they don't necessarily offset movements in stocks," he maintains. "If you're nervous, you could use an equity-income or value fund instead."

Occupation: President, Equity Fund Research
Boston, Massachusetts

Birth Date: May 9, 1942

Education: BA, University of North Carolina, 1965
MBA, Babson College, 1976

Biggest Mistake Investors Make: "Not having a properly diversified portfolio."

Best Investment: Vanguard Capital Opportunities (Purchased in 1998 and still owns it.)

Worst Investment: Oakmark Small Cap (Bought this fund in 1995, right before it fell out of bed.)

Advice: "Hunt for newer, smaller funds run by managers with good records."

Market Outlook: Bullish

LOUIS STANASOLOVICH

Legend Financial Advisors

Louis Stanasolovich really believes in diversification, even when it comes to mutual funds. "On a $500,000 portfolio, I might use 13 to 15 funds, depending on the circumstances," he says. Stanasolovich's first rule of mutual fund investing is to buy the manager, not just the fund. "I won't invest in a fund without getting to know the person who is running it," he claims. "I also ask for biographies of all the key analysts and traders, because a lot of turnover among your underlying staff will create chaos in the organization."

Stanasolovich notes that his main reason for getting to know the manager is to make sure the investment approach parlayed on paper and in marketing brochures is accurate. "I send out a questionnaire to each manager I'm considering with about 120 questions on it," he shares. "It covers everything from what they manage privately to how much is in their funds. It also asks about all the members of the management team, how long those people have been around, and how they are compensated [he likes those that get an incentive for good performance]." His favorite funds are run by smaller, boutique investment firms where the manager is also an owner. He also prefers fund companies that don't know how to market as that allows their asset base to remain relatively small. As a result, he tends to avoid families like Fidelity and Putnam.

Stanasolovich has an accounting background and started out as a cost analyst for U.S. Steel Corporation after college. "I was trying to find somewhere to put the extra money I was making, and all I knew about were credit unions, savings bonds, and things like that," he reflects. "A buddy of mine was taking an investment course, and I joined him." Soon after completing the class, he read about the International Association for Financial Planning (IAFP), an industry trade association, and decided to get into the business. He joined a financial planning and asset management firm after receiving his securities license and started his own company, Legend Financial Advisors, seven years ago.

"Most of my clients come in with money they've either invested on their own or through a broker who was selling a product," Stanasolovich says. "It's hard to tell whether someone earning a commission is working in your best interest. I would say 97 times out of 100 they aren't. I work strictly on a fee-only basis and believe that's the future of the brokerage industry. It's what the investing public wants. It used to be that half of my clients would start off by asking how I'm compensated. Now I'd say the number is closer to 95 percent."

Stanasolovich builds each portfolio by first figuring out which investment styles and markets he wants to target. Then he puts money to work by buying funds that represent each of those asset classes. "I do it on a valuation basis," he says. "Right now, in an all-equity portfolio, I'd have about 30 percent in U.S. securities, divided roughly equally among small and large stocks, with 20 percent international, 5 to 7 percent in real estate funds, and the rest in what I call "uncorrelated" assets, such as commodities, arbitrage funds, and the like."

He generally prefers using funds because they give him more options and have documented performance records. "I believe when you buy a private manager, you're buying sex appeal," he insists. "You can get a huge amount of diversification by using several funds rather than just placing your money with one manager. I believe you need to have all of the major styles covered and it's not practical to do that using individual managers. You have to use funds." However, because of client pressure, Stanasolovich has also started to use private managers, and even picks individual stocks himself for some portfolios.

Although Stanasolovich may occasionally use a Standard & Poor's 500 index fund for the large-cap U.S. growth portion of a client's portfolio, he generally prefers to go with active managers. "When you're buying big stocks, your universe is maybe 200 securities," he rationalizes. "Therefore, if an active fund is buying 50 or 60 stocks, those stocks aren't going to perform much differently than the S&P 500. So in that case it makes sense. But I don't think it makes sense for small-caps at all. There are about 8,000 small stocks to choose from, so a manager can definitely add value."

Even though Stanasolovich likes to personally get to know each fund manager, he admits that's not easy for the average investor to do. Therefore, he recommends reading the various financial publications and only looking at funds with excellent performance when running your initial screens. "I watch all of my funds very closely to make sure they're keeping up with the indexes for their investment style," he says. "I don't have a lot of turnover, maybe two or three funds a year."

Occupation: Founder and President, Legend Financial Advisors, Inc.
Pittsburgh, Pennsylvania

Birth Date: February 5, 1957

Education: BS, Pennsylvania State University, 1979

Biggest Mistake Investors Make: "Reading the news, taking for granted it's correct, and then projecting it into the future."

Best Investment: Caldwell and Orkin Market Opportunity Fund (Bought it in 1997, and it went up about 40 percent in 18 months.)

Worst Investment: An oil and gas penny stock he purchased in the 1980s that went belly-up.

Advice: "Hire a good advisor and/or seek out good sources of information."

Market Outlook: Cautious

MICHAEL STOLPER

Stolper & Company

If you own more than four mutual funds, you've got too many in the eyes of Michael Stolper. Stolper is a man with feet on both sides of the mutual fund fence. As an investment advisor and president of a firm that matches wealthy individuals with money managers, he often recommends funds to his clients. But as a director and shareholder of three fund companies, he empathizes with the business concerns these companies face, including the need to pay an enormous amount of overhead. Therefore, he's not as concerned about fund expenses as some other advisors are. "My attitude on fees is that if you don't like it, don't buy it," Stolper says. "If you think you're buying a Camry and it's priced like a Lexus, go down the street. There are thousands of products to choose from. You're buying intellectual skills. I want the best skill I can get, and I'm perfectly willing to pay up for it."

This Oklahoma native has had a lifelong interest in the stock market, although he's not exactly sure why. "I just sort of got the bug," he says. "I thought it was a fascinating business. It looked like easy money without a lot of work. That's probably what appealed to me." After earning a master's degree in finance, Stolper originally planned to get into investment banking, which he viewed as the most glamorous job on Wall Street. Unfortunately, the big firms weren't impressed with his degree from the University of Oklahoma. "I ended up in the retail brokerage business," he shares. "I was 22 and not well-credentialed, so that was the only avenue available to me." He took a job with Bateman, Eichler in 1968 and began using investment advisors to manage money for his clients in the early 1970s. "It became clear to me that it was easier to make judgments about people managing money than about individual securities," he maintains. "I was choosing stocks on my own and also had some clients who were being advised. The advisors were doing better than I. So I had to reluctantly acknowledge that these people were more clever and capable of investing the money." A short time later, Stolper founded a firm specializing in matching the rich with the right people to oversee their portfolios.

While Stolper uses both funds and individual managers, he insists that when clients leave the decision up to him, funds are always his preference. "The main advantage to funds is simplification," he says. "The main disadvantage is their tendency to overdiversify." When it comes to choosing funds, however, the manager in charge remains his most important consideration. "That's the only thing that matters," Stolper contends. "If you don't believe that, you should just find an index and put your money there."

Judging managers isn't easy though. "What you're looking for is a pattern of success," Stolper explains. "I not only want statistical data, but also to talk with these folks. I want to believe there's something intellectually compelling about them. Typically, my worst mistake has been hiring bright guys who weren't moneymakers. Some people will dazzle you with their intellect, but they can't put the numbers up."

Stolper reveals that the best managers he's come across tend to be socially underdeveloped. "We interview about 150 to 200 firms a year in their offices," he says. "One thing you'll always find in great managers is that all they can talk about is stocks. There's a clear change in the conversational pattern and body language when that subject comes up."

A more difficult decision for him is deciding when to sell a fund. "The reality is you sell when you run out of patience," he admits. "We're real slow to add names. If you run a screen, you'll find 88 percent of underperformance is style driven. In other words, the market doesn't like what the manager is buying, yet they own the same stocks that attracted you to the fund in the first place. If I can't find anything else wrong, I'll stick with the manager and go back to sleep."

In fact, Stolper says his goal is to find a manager he can invest with, go into a coma for five to ten years, and wake up feeling good about his decision. That's not always easy in this day of fund manager musical chairs, but if you can latch on to a manager like that, you should sit back and enjoy the ride. And, as previously mentioned, Stolper believes you can achieve all the diversification you need with just four funds. "I'd probably divide my assets equally among the four funds," he says. "I'm less concerned about asset classes and more interested in having a team of great managers running the portfolios."

Occupation: President, Stolper & Company, Inc.
San Diego, California

Birth Date: August 15, 1945

Education: BA, University of Oklahoma, 1967
MBA, University of Oklahoma, 1968

Biggest Mistake Investors Make: "Thinking and overmanaging their investments."

Best Investment: Investing in three privately held mutual fund companies (Janus, Meridian, and the Pasadena Group)

Worst Investment: An oil limited partnership he bought in the 1980s that became worthless

Advice: "Never forget that in this business you make most of your money by just showing up. The influence of participation and compound interest is substantially greater than cleverness or asset allocation."

Market Outlook: Bullish

ROBERT STOVALL

Prudential Securities

Bob Stovall grew up on Wall Street. His first job at age 14 was as a messenger for the brokerage firm Reynolds & Company, where his father also worked. After graduating from the Seton Hall Prep high school in the middle of World War II, he was accepted at Harvard, Yale, Georgetown, and the University of Pennsylvania. His dad told him to skip college and just learn bookkeeping. But his mom pressed on and recommended Pennsylvania's Wharton School, primarily because it was cheaper to take the train there than to Boston or Washington. And, except for a brief tour of duty with the U.S. Army in Italy, he's been on Wall Street ever since graduation.

"I got my start as a junior analyst answering wires at E.F. Hutton way back in the 1950s," he recalls. "I was then a partner or voting stockholder of several different major firms, including John Nuveen and Dean Witter Reynolds, from 1960 through 1985." He is now a senior market strategist with Prudential Securities in New York and says he enjoys the business now as much as when he started. "It's a chance to make a good living and help people," he maintains. "It's exciting."

When it comes to choosing stocks, Stovall has a unique strategy. "I look for groups that have underperformed their norm," he explains. "I believe that the market itself is the main determinant of price action, whether you're talking about stocks, paintings, precious metals, or any category of investment. The market is the tide. That's as much as 50 percent of the price action. The tide was in our favor in stocks throughout much of the 1990s. The second most important factor is the sector or industry. That's the wave. The third is the stock itself."

To assess the various sectors, he looks at a wide array of research, including data put out by his son Sam, an editor and investment strategist for Standard & Poor's and a major proponent of rotational sector market movements. Once Stovall identifies attractive and undervalued sectors, he looks for the very best companies in those groups and remains invested in them until the rest of the world catches on and drives their share prices higher. "When the thrill goes away, I move on to another sector," he says. He oftentimes applies this same discipline to closed-end mutual funds, buying those that are selling below their net asset values and hanging on until that gap is closed. "For example, when the emerging markets are on everybody's tongue, you sell it and when they become submerging markets you mark them for purchase at some later date," he adds. He's not one to time the market and is generally always invested, though he gets more conservative when he feels the tide has turned.

While he's a big believer in the importance of international diversification, Stovall believes you can achieve that by sticking with companies on the New York

Stock Exchange. "Specifically in the Dow 30, you've got companies like Procter & Gamble, Philip Morris, Minnesota Mining & Manufacturing, and Merck," he observes. "They all get 40 to 60 percent of their sales from overseas."

Stovall divides his time between Florida, Pennsylvania, and New York. (He lives in the first two and works in the third.) He's a recognizable figure on radio and TV, including a long-standing stint as a regular panelist and "Hall of Fame" member on the PBS series *Wall $treet Week with Louis Rukeyser*. He was featured in the book *Growing Rich with Growth Stocks* and is a professor of finance at New York University, where he teaches a new generation how to succeed in the stock market. "I give them a historical bent and throw in a lot of humor," he says. "I think the students find my classes to be interesting and entertaining." Does he worry that too many people who have never experienced a long bear market are managing money these days? "Not really," he admits. "I suppose it could accentuate the drop, but I'm not convinced that is going to happen."

Occupation: Senior Market Strategist, Prudential Securities
New York, New York

Birth Date: February 16, 1926

Education: BS, University of Pennsylvania, Wharton School, 1957
MBA, New York University, 1957

Biggest Mistake Investors Make: "Selling their winners too soon, and holding their losers too long."

Best Investment: E.F. Hutton and Dean Witter Reynolds (These are two firms he used to work for. He says his return on both stocks has been enormous, especially when you factor in that the companies have split and spun-off many times.)

Worst Investment: International Art Schools Convertible Bonds (He bought them for their high yield about 20 years ago. Unfortunately, the company turned out to be a fraud, and the bonds went down to zero.)

Advice: "Be patient. Take a little longer than you think is necessary to buy something and be very patient before you give up on it."

Market Outlook: Cautious

ED WALCZAK

Vontobel USA

The past few years have been quite frustrating for Ed Walczak. "I've been a money manager since 1984 and this has been my most trying time ever," he says. "I've never seen a discrepancy like this between growth and value stocks. Some value managers tell me it's been worse than the 1973–74 bear market. I hope this is just a once every 25 years event." In addition to struggling with poor relative performance, value managers like Walczak have also seen their portfolios shrink, as impatient investors seek higher returns elsewhere. But he says the bargains available to him have never been better, and for the first time in many years, his fund now holds less than 10 percent cash.

As a kid growing up in Norwich, Connecticut, Walczak dreamed of one day becoming a garbage man. "It was neat to see those guys get out there and toss cans into the air," he says. "I thought it was a cool profession as a boy and still do." The only son of a professional baseball player, Walczak decided to study government in college and thought about going to law school. "Instead, I got a graduate degree in international economics before going on for my MBA," he recalls.

His first job was working in the finance department at Ford Motor Company in Ann Arbor, Michigan. "I did that for a little over a year, but it just wasn't as interesting as I thought it would be," he shares. A headhunter then offered him a job in the General Motors Treasury Department in New York. "The most intriguing thing I did was conduct research on why the Japanese could build cars cheaper than us in the late 1970s," he notes. After less than three years at GM, another headhunter offered to bring him to Wall Street.

He landed a job working in institutional sales for Sanford C. Bernstein & Co. in 1982. "I liked the culture there, however I got tired of making the same sales calls over and over again," he admits. "I then decided to switch from sales to being a junior portfolio manager at Lazard Freres in late 1984." After a few years there, yet another headhunter came with an offer he couldn't refuse—the chance to manage money on his own at Vontobel. "I had never heard of Vontobel," Walczak concedes. "I did some research and found out that it seemed to be a reputable Swiss bank. That was 12 years ago."

Walczak now runs $138 million in various portfolios, including the Vontobel US Value fund. His investment style has evolved over time. At first, he combined both the quantitative and qualitative traits he learned from his first two jobs on Wall Street. "It was more of a Graham and Dodd approach, emphasizing low PE and low price-to-book stocks," he says. "Then I kind of hit the books, and the more I read about Warren Buffett's work, the more I realized how much I agreed with his style." Walczak proceeded to dig up Buffett's old annual reports and became a self-described "Buffett Moonie."

"Just like Buffett, the quality of a company is the most important thing I look for in a potential investment," he says. "I keep my eye on such things as high returns on capital, shareholder-oriented management, elements of a franchise, predictable earnings, and free cash flow. The company should also be involved in an unregulated industry."

After that, he examines whether the company sells for a cheap price. "This involves figuring out its intrinsic value, or what it's really worth," he explains. "I try to go out a number of years in the future and make a reasonable guesstimate about whether the current returns can be sustained for several years into the future. If so, I'll come up with some earnings and free cash flow estimates going forward and discount those numbers back to the present using today's level of interest rates. I usually use the ten-year bond. I look for value in stocks the same way I do for bonds. I am really looking at a company's prospective future returns compared with what I could get in a risk-free 10-year or 30-year government bond. For me to be seduced out of a risk-free investment, a stock has to offer sufficient increments of return."

Walczak holds a pretty concentrated portfolio, like Buffett, although he's found so many good values lately, his fund now owns around 25 different companies. He says he only owns around eight stocks in his own personal portfolio, because he doesn't believe in overdiversification. His sell discipline is equally straightforward. "I'll get rid of a stock for one of two reasons," he notes. "If my thesis for buying has deteriorated, which is a nice way of saying I'm wrong, or if the stock becomes fully valued."

Occupation: Chief Investment Officer, Vontobel USA
New York, New York

Birth Date: September 17, 1953

Education: BA, Colby College, 1975
MA, Columbia University, 1976
MBA, Columbia University, 1978

Biggest Mistake Investors Make: "Chasing historical performance; being too short term–oriented."

Best Investment: Buying regional bank stocks at distressed prices in 1990; many more than doubled in subsequent years

Worst Investment: Not owning many technology stocks (They don't fit his valuation criteria but have done well in the market.)

Advice: "Be disciplined and, like Warren Buffett says, wait for the pitch. Don't buy unless there's something that's really attractive and undervalued."

Market Outlook: Bullish on value; cautious on growth

JOHN WALLACE

RS Investment Management

When a friend of John Wallace's first suggested that he get into the securities business, Wallace figured it must have something to do with "locks." Why should he think otherwise? After all, he had been living as far away from Wall Street as you can imagine: Ecuador. Wallace fell in love with the South American country after spending a year there studying college Spanish. "I liked it so much, I went back in 1979 and started an import/export clothing manufacturing business with a partner from Denmark," he says. "We were selling hand-knit sweaters, hats, and some cotton skirts and tops."

While the company was successful, Wallace quickly grew tired of it and ultimately turned the reins over to his girlfriend, before the two returned to her hometown of New York. "We got married and she said somebody's got to work for a living," he recalls. "So I went back to get my MBA at night. At the same time, I had a friend in the money management business, and he set up some interviews for me."

As it turned out, Wallace was in the right place at the right time. About three months after having lunch with Diane Jarmusz, then a portfolio manager at Oppenheimer & Co., he was offered a job as her assistant. "That was in 1986, which means I started in this business when I was 32," he says. "This is really a second career for me." Jarmusz ran the Oppenheimer Equity Income and Total Return funds, and Wallace helped her out. A short time later, the firm launched what it called the Main Street Fund and told Wallace he could manage it. "Oppenheimer was very entrepreneurial back then," he says. "It was known as a shop that would give its people a chance to run money sooner compared to other fund companies."

His big break came in 1990, when Jarmusz decided to do something else and gave Wallace control of the Total Return fund. His performance was so good, both Main Street and Total Return quickly ballooned in size. "When I left, Total Return had about $1.8 billion and Main Street around $2.5 billion," he says. At one point, Main Street was the number-one fund in the country over a five-year period under Wallace's leadership. This strong performance captured the attention of San Francisco–based Robertson Stephens Investment Management, which offered Wallace a chance to run its new Growth and Income Fund in 1995. Since then, two big things have happened. First, the name of the fund has been changed to RS Mid-Cap Opportunities. Perhaps more importantly, Wallace now is a part-owner of the company. He and several colleagues bought the firm from Bank of America in 1999, and renamed it RS Investment Management.

Wallace defines investment management as an art, not a science, and he continues to refine his stock-picking skills as the years go by. "I come to work every day literally trying to find stocks that I think have the potential to double within two to three years," he shares. "If I'm able to do that, I'm compounding money for shareholders at 25 to 30 percent annually." Of course, that's easier said than done. So how does he find such stocks? He begins by looking for a catalyst that can drive earnings and therefore the stock price higher. "It could be a new management team, a new product launch, new markets they are expanding into, a restructuring, or a realization of an undervalued asset," Wallace explains. "Finding this catalyst is all based on information flow. I'm in constant communication with the sell-side research firms, meeting with managements and suppliers, and talking with other traders and brokers."

Although he has a growth bias, and tends to concentrate on small- and mid-cap issues, valuations do matter. "I like stocks trading at two-thirds to 80 percent of their growth rates," he maintains. "I do occasionally invest in IPOs and some of the faster-growing high PE names."

Wallace sets a price target for each holding in the portfolio using a simple formula of A times B times C. "'A' is the forward earnings estimates of the company," he points out. "'B' is the market multiple of the S&P 500. 'C' is whether or not the company deserves a premium or discount to that multiple." As a stock approaches 90 percent of that target, and assuming there's been no fundamental change, he'll get rid of it. He also sells part of his position in any stock that goes down 15 percent or more from his entry point (although he's had to become more flexible in today's wildly volatile market), or if he finds a better place to put the money.

Occupation: Portfolio Manager, RS Investment Management
San Francisco, California

Birth Date: April 8, 1954

Education: BA, University of Idaho, 1978
MBA, Pace University, 1987

Biggest Mistake Investors Make: "Not understanding how their money is being managed. A lot of mutual fund shareholders are betting on five-year track records where the guy who produced this performance isn't even there anymore."

Best Investment: InfoNow Corp. (Bought for under $1 in 1997 and started selling it for around $15 in late 1999.)

Worst Investment: Iwerks (Purchased as an IPO for $18 in 1993. It immediately doubled before crashing down to $3 in about one year. Wallace got out around $6.)

Advice: "Do your homework. Understand your money manager's process. Look at the stocks in your portfolio and see if they are the types of names you can sleep with at night."

Market Outlook: Agnostic. "We keep getting later and later in the bull market," he says.

MARTIN WHITMAN

Third Avenue Funds

Ask Martin Whitman what direction the market is headed in and he's apt to give you an honest answer. "How do I know?" he replied when that question was posed to him for this book. "This is one strange market. I've never seen a time when we've had so many speculative excesses and cheap stocks all at the same time." The past few years have been pretty tough for investors like Whitman, who prefer cheap stocks to the more expensive, fast-growing issues that seem to grab the financial headlines these days.

As a so-called vulture investor, Whitman loves to read the new low list in *The Wall Street Journal.* "I want to buy what's safe and cheap," he says. Whitman earned his vulture reputation by building a career out of investing in distressed companies that others expected to go out of business. "There's almost nothing I go into where the near-term outlook isn't terrible," he points out. It's a field of expertise he got into almost by accident. "After serving in the Navy, I originally planned to teach economics," he remembers. "But after finishing graduate school, I saw there wasn't much of a future for me as an academic, so I went to work on Wall Street."

He started in research before moving into investment banking, managing private money, and ultimately doing control investing. Whitman first began specializing in distressed companies in the early 1970s, when he decided to start his own firm. "I wanted to do corporate finance, but didn't have a lot of money," he says. "There were two fields that were wide open, where I didn't have to compete with big firms like Morgan Stanley and Goldman Sachs. They were bankruptcy and shareholder litigation. I built quite a reputation in both areas." Originally, Whitman just gave advice to troubled companies. But he soon realized he could make more money by investing in them instead as a portfolio manager. Today, in addition to managing private accounts and two mutual funds, he teaches a course on control investing at Yale.

Whitman invests in both the stocks and bonds of distressed companies. The instrument he uses depends on where he sees the most opportunity. "In all cases, the companies I'm buying have cash well in excess of total book liabilities," he points out. "I also won't pay more than a 60 percent premium over book value and rarely pay more than 12 times what the company's historic net income has been. This is designed to simulate the pricing a first-stage venture capitalist would pay if he were financing a private company."

When it comes to investing in severely troubled companies, Whitman almost always prefers secured debt over common stock because he wants to own the most senior issue available in case of any potential reorganization. "For credit securities, I always assume there will be a credit default," he notes. "Then I figure out how I will come out in the event that happens."

Although Whitman describes what he does as a form of value investing, he pays little attention to traditional indicators of value, like dividend yields and PE ratios. "Graham and Dodd (the two noted authorities on value investing) are all screwed up," he maintains. "I analyze companies just like Warren Buffett does. I examine the values in the business and stop. The basic analysis of all the amateurs, including Graham and Dodd, is to try and determine at which price a stock will sell. You carry an awful lot of excess baggage with that kind of methodology." He also couldn't care less about the overall market. "That's only important to incompetents who want to make a lot of money by charging fees for stuff like asset allocation," he maintains. "For people who know about the companies they invest in, the market is immaterial. There are always bull and bear markets."

Whitman's portfolio turnover averages less than 15 percent a year. "Most of my companies get taken out through mergers and acquisitions," he says. "If I'm doing everything right, there ought to be a lot of takeovers in any six-month or one-year period. I will sell a stock on my own if I conclude I've made a mistake or find out the guy in charge is a crook." Two warning signs are when management starts to "burn" cash or the company has a successive string of bad operating results. Whitman admits that some 20 to 30 percent of his stocks turn out to be total clunkers. However, the gains from his winners more than make up the difference.

As for his own future, Whitman insists he has no immediate plans to retire. "I'd become a tennis pro if I could, but I don't think that's likely to happen," he says.

Occupation: CEO and Chief Investment Officer, Third Avenue Funds
New York, New York

Birth Date: September 30, 1924

Education: BS, Syracuse University, 1949
MA, New School of Social Research, 1956

Biggest Mistake Investors Make: "Not paying attention to fundamentals and not being price conscious."

Best Investment: Nabors Industries (Paid 40¢ a share for the stock in 1987, and it's now worth around $20. He's also a director of the company.)

Worst Investment: Union Federal (Bought for $2 a share in 1993, and it ultimately went to zero.)

Advice: "Buy extremely well-capitalized companies and don't pay more than 50¢ for every dollar you think it might be worth presently as a private company."

Market Outlook: Cautious

DAVID WILLIAMS

U.S. Trust

While many value investors simply go after down and out companies that aren't very good businesses, Dave Williams looks for good companies that have simply stumbled along the way. "I'm looking for attractively priced stocks, but not necessarily those that are being given away," he insists. It's a formula that has made his Excelsior Value and Restructuring Fund one of the top-performing value funds in the country.

Williams majored in art history at Yale in the 1960s and was a Navy pilot for five years. "After that, I went to Harvard Business School and decided I would like to manage money," he recalls. "My first job was working at T. Rowe Price [in 1974] managing private and pension accounts. For the six months I was there, the market went down like clockwork every day. It was an unbelievable period to be exposed to investing." It got so bad that the firm brought in a psychologist to help managers deal with belligerent clients who were furious about getting negative returns. "They kept saying, 'Why should we give money to you when we can get 4 or 5 percent from the bank without taking any risk?' And they were serious," Williams notes. "Now, of course, no one would think of putting their money in a savings account while the market is doing so well."

Nevertheless, Williams isn't apathetic. He has no doubt we'll go through another period like 1974 again. It's just a matter of when. "It all has to do with inflation," he insists. "For the time being, I think inflation's under good control and won't be a problem for the foreseeable future. However, there will come a time when we have higher inflation and the market will take a beating because of it."

Williams spent five years at T. Rowe Price before starting his own investment firm with a partner in New York. They weren't making much money, so Williams took a job with Horizon Trust as chief investment officer in 1981. Six years later, he joined U.S. Trust. "For the first couple of months, I was in charge of a new product that was marketed to smaller accounts of between $250,000 and $2 million," he says. "Most of the proceeds were invested in our mutual funds. Then they asked me to manage larger accounts. My fund was launched in 1993. Today I run about $2 billion altogether."

Like the quirky name of his fund suggests, Williams looks for companies selling at value prices that often are going through some type of restructuring. "I try to find companies that are under a cloud," he explains. "They've disappointed Wall Street for one reason or another. I really like companies that are in difficulty but have done something to indicate they recognize the problem and are addressing it. Often the companies I invest in sell for relatively cheap prices. By that I mean they have low PE or price-to-cash flow ratios. They also often have new CEOs who are changing what the old management botched up."

Finding companies under a cloud and on the bargain table isn't hard. The challenge is separating those that belong there from those that are unduly being punished yet have a lot of promise. Williams concedes you can never be sure about this, although he feels like he improves his chances by scheduling an in-person meeting with management. "It may be psychological, but it does give me more confidence when I hear the story from the horse's mouth rather than secondhand from a Wall Street analyst," he says. "You get a sense of how good members of management are by how they talk. You also learn whether their plan for their company makes sense. If I get a good feeling from management, more often than not it turns out to be a successful investment."

In today's market, Williams prefers to buy companies trading for a below-market multiple. "By mere chance, the stocks in my portfolio have consistently sold at about a 33 percent discount to the S&P 500 since day one," he offers. One way he reduces risk is by maintaining a well-diversified portfolio of some 85 names. "I always have something that's working," he adds. "I have both big and small companies and keep roughly 10 percent overseas."

In the current market, many of the restructuring plays Williams is finding fall more into the category of spin-offs and consolidations. "Companies are trying to refocus their businesses, instead of having to lay people off," he says. "As a result, the kinds of companies I'm buying are changing somewhat. I used to own a lot of industrial and cyclical stocks. Now I have a number of entertainment and, to some degree, financial services stocks."

Williams recently got a new boss, now that Charles Schwab & Co. has taken over U.S. Trust. But he doubts there will be little change in how the company operates.

Occupation: Managing Director, U.S. Trust
New York, New York

Birth Date: July 4, 1942

Education: BA, Yale University, 1965
MBA, Harvard University, 1974

Biggest Mistake Investors Make: "Listening to other people and taking hot tips. You have to do your own work and at least some simple research."

Best Investment: SAP (Purchased around 1990 and has made about 100 times on his money.)

Worst Investment: Arm Financial Group (Bought three years ago and has lost 50 percent of his investment.)

Advice: "Investing is a puzzle. Listen to all the people you can before making a decision. Don't rely on the advice of any one person. In other words, listen to no one, but listen to everyone."

Market Outlook: Cautious

UPDATE

of *Wall Street's Picks for 2000*

Those of you who read *Wall Street's Picks for 2000* might be wondering, "What should I do with those stocks and mutual funds now?" Well, wonder no more because the answer to that pressing question can be found on the following pages. In most cases, we went back to each of last year's panelists and asked, "How do you feel about your pick from last year going into the new millennium? Do you now consider it to be a buy, sell, or hold?" You'll find their responses on the following pages.

Just so we're clear on definitions, *buy* means they still recommend their pick for purchase in the year 2001; *hold* indicates they suggest holding on if you already own the investment; and *sell* is a sign to take your profits (or losses) and move on to other opportunities.

STOCK	PANELIST	CURRENT ADVICE
Administradora de Fondos ADS	Vivian Lewis	Buy
Excite@Home	Elizabeth Dater	Buy
ATS Medical	Larry Jeddeloh	Hold
Borders Group	David Dreman	Hold
CNF Transportation	David Williams	Buy
Computer Sciences	Elizabeth Bramwell	Buy
Conseco	Ronald Muhlenkamp	Buy
Dell Computer	Cappy McGarr	Buy
Eaton Corporation	Robert Sanborn	Hold
EMC Corporation	James Collins	Buy
ESG Re Limited	Ed Walczak	Sell
Goodyear	James O'Shaughnessy	Sell
IBM	Art Bonnel	Sell
International Game Technology	John Rogers	Buy
LaSalle Re Holdings	Martin Whitman	Buy
The Limited	Susan Byrne	Hold
Pervasive Software	Kevin Landis	Hold
Rite Aid	Vita Nelson	Buy
Rouge Industries	Al Frank	Hold
Simula	Marcus Robins	Hold
State Street	L. Roy Papp	Buy
Tellabs	Alan Bond	Hold
Uniphase	Joseph Battipaglia	Buy
USG Corporation	Seth Glickenhaus	Buy
VISX	Louis Navellier	Sell

FUND	PANELIST	CURRENT ADVICE
Ameristock	Thurman Smith	Hold
Artisan International	Stephen Savage	Buy
Brazos Micro Cap	Louis Stanasolovich	Buy
Dodge & Cox Stock	Michael Hirsch	Buy
Janus Growth and Income	Janet Brown	Buy
ProFunds Ultra Bull	Paul Merriman	Hold
Royce Special Equity	Don Phillips	Hold
Vanguard International Value	Robert Bingham	Buy
Vanguard Total Stock Market	Sheldon Jacobs	Buy
White Oak Growth	Bob Markman	Buy
Wilshire Large Company Growth	Harold Evensky	Buy

GLOSSARY

of Investment Terms

American depositary receipt (ADR) Receipt for the shares of a foreign-based stock that are held by a U.S. bank and entitle shareholders to all dividends and capital gains. It's a way for Americans to buy shares in foreign-based companies on a U.S. stock exchange.

annual report Yearly statement of a corporation's financial condition. It must be distributed to all shareholders of record.

asked or **offer price** The lowest amount a seller is willing to take for shares of a stock.

asset allocation Act of spreading investment funds across various categories of assets, such as stocks, bonds, and cash.

beta A coefficient measure of a stock's relative volatility in relation to the Standard & Poor's 500 index, which has a beta of 1.

bid price The highest amount a buyer is willing to pay for shares of a stock.

blue chip Common stock of a nationally known company with a long record of profit growth, dividend payments, and a reputation for quality products and services.

bond Any interest-bearing or discounted government or corporate obligation that pays a specified sum of money, usually at regular intervals.

book value What a company would be worth if all assets were sold (assets minus liabilities). Also, the price at which an asset is carried on a balance sheet.

bottom-up investing The search for outstanding individual stocks with little regard for overall economic trends.

broker Person who acts as an intermediary between a buyer and a seller.

buy-and-hold strategy Technique that calls for accumulating and keeping shares in a company over many years regardless of price swings.

cash ratio Ratio of cash and marketable securities to current liabilities. Tells the extent to which liabilities could be immediately liquidated.

chief executive officer (CEO) Individual responsible for the overall operations of a corporation.

contrarian Investor who does the opposite of the majority at any particular time.

convertible bond Security that can be exchanged for other securities of the issuer (under certain conditions), usually from preferred stock or bonds into common stock.

current ratio Current assets divided by current liabilities. Shows a company's ability to pay current debts from current assets.

debt-to-equity ratio Long-term debt divided by shareholders' equity. Indicates how highly leveraged a company is. (A figure greater than 1.5 should raise a red flag.)

diversification Spreading risk by putting assets into several different investment categories, like stocks, bonds, and cash.

dividend Distribution of earnings to shareholders.

dividend yield The cash dividend paid per share each year divided by the current share price.

dollar cost averaging The process of accumulating positions in stocks and mutual funds by investing a set amount of money each month, thus buying more shares when prices are down, less when they are up.

Dow Jones Industrial Average The oldest and most widely quoted stock market indicator. Represents the price direction of 30 blue chip stocks on the New York Stock Exchange. (Doesn't always give an accurate view of what's happening with the market as a whole.)

fair market value Price at which an asset or service is or can be passed on from a willing buyer to a willing seller.

Form 10-K Annual report filed with the Securities and Exchange Commission showing a company's total sales, revenues, and pretax operating income, along with sales figures for each of the firm's different lines or businesses over the past five years.

good-till-canceled order (GTC) A brokerage order to buy or sell shares of a security at a given price that remains in effect until executed or canceled.

growth stock Stock of a corporation that shows greater-than-average gains in earnings.

institutional investor Organization that trades a large volume of securities, like a mutual fund, bank, or insurance company.

intrinsic value Worth of a company; comparable to the prevailing market price.

limit order Order to buy or sell a security at a specific price or better.

market capitalization or **market value** Calculated by multiplying the number of shares outstanding by the per share price of a stock. One can also categorize equities into several different classes, including micro-cap, small-cap, mid-cap, and large-cap. The general guidelines for these classifications are as follows:

- **micro-cap**—market capitalizations of $0 to $300 million
- **small-cap**—market capitalizations of $300 to $1.5 billion
- **mid-cap**—market capitalizations of $1.5 billion to $5 billion
- **large-cap**—market capitalizations of $5 billion or more

market order Order to buy or sell a security at the best available price.

mutual fund An investment company that raises money from shareholders and puts it to work in stocks, options, bonds, or money market securities. Offers investors diversification and professional management.

Nasdaq Composite An index of the National Association of Securities Dealers weighted by market value and representing domestic companies that are sold over the counter.

net current assets Assets calculated by taking current assets minus current liabilities. Also referred to as working capital.

price-earnings ratio (PE) Price of a stock divided by its earnings per share.

price-to-book ratio (PB) Ratio calculated by dividing shareholders' equity by the number of outstanding shares. If under 1, it means a stock is selling for less than the price the company paid for its assets, though this is not necessarily indicative of a good value.

Standard & Poor's Composite Index of 500 Stocks (S&P 500) An index that tracks the performance of 500 stocks, mostly blue chips, and represents almost two-thirds of the U.S. stock market's total value. It is weighted by market value. (As an equity investor, your goal should be to beat the return of the S&P 500. This is not an easy task, and roughly 75 percent of all mutual fund managers fail to do so.)

stock Represents ownership in a corporation. Usually listed in terms of shares.

INDEX